THE PRESBYTERIAN STORY

Origins & Progress of a Reformed Tradition

Second Edition

S. DONALD FORTSON III

WIPF & STOCK · Eugene, Oregon

Wipf and Stock Publishers
199 W 8th Ave, Suite 3
Eugene, OR 97401

The Presbyterian Story
Origins & Progress of a Reformed Tradition
By Fortson, S. Donald, III
Copyright©2013 by Fortson, S. Donald, III
ISBN 13: 978-1-5326-1646-4
Publication date 8/24/2017
Previously published by Presbyterian Lay Committee, 2013

To
Mae Hancock Huie Fortson
who loves a story

TABLE OF CONTENTS

PREFACE

Denominational histories are unpopular with professional historians these days. The author concurs with the spirit behind this sentiment which favors emphasizing the common story that Christians share rather than focusing on sectarian distinctions. On the other hand, since denominations are the primary instrument through which most Christians have organized their common life, it remains pertinent to pass on this account to the next generation. Presbyterianism is a particular embodiment of the "holy catholic church" which includes not only all living followers of Christ but also saints who have proceeded them to glory. Through two millennia the whole church is historically as well as spiritually linked into one body with one head, the Lord Jesus Christ.

Being Presbyterian involves multiple layers of identity and connection. As Christians, Presbyterians are "catholic," sharing the common heritage of ancient Christianity with all believers, of all times, in all places. Presbyterians are Protestant by conviction sharing the rich spiritual heritage of the sixteenth century in reaffirming the primacy of Scripture and the rediscovery of the Gospel. Within the sixteenth-century Protestant Reformation, Presbyterians identify themselves uniquely with one of the church families known as the "Reformed Tradition." In this stream, Presbyterians view themselves in special connection to the reforms of John Calvin, John Knox and the English Puritans. Historically, Presbyterians are also part of the evangelical movement; that is, they have embraced the legacy of the eighteenth-century revivals (awakenings) in America and Britain and thus believe in the necessity of conversion experience, personal holiness and being missional. Each of these historic layers is equally important to Presbyterian identity and this book will seek to underscore that reality.

Approaching an overview of Presbyterianism, the author is keenly aware that the "institutional church," identified with denominations, has fallen on bad times in western culture. How often the disclaimer is heard: "I love Jesus but not the church," suggesting that one can embrace Christ and scorn His body simultaneously. Aversion to church membership or denominational affiliation is symptomatic of American individualism and has little to do with the Biblical picture of authentic Christian community. The contemporary neglect of Biblical teaching on the church has produced a truncated Christianity wherein the distinction between believers and unbelievers is frequently negligible. The American church is in crisis and a partial answer is both serious re-engagement with Scripture and, for many a first time encounter with church history.

The Christian tradition for two thousand years has consistently interpreted Scripture as teaching the absolute necessity of being connectional – that is, committed to a local church fellowship and being in submission to spiritual shepherds who are responsible for one's feeding, care and correction. As members of the invisible Church, believers express this spiritual reality visibly in the earth through membership in a particular congregation as well as connection to the larger body of Christ. The New Testament is full of the connectional element among Christian churches – the church in Palestine sending leaders to Greek churches in order to strengthen them in the faith; Greek churches taking up collections for aiding the poor churches in Palestine; problems in Gentile churches referred to apostles and elders in Jerusalem for resolution; apostolic visitation of mission churches for both encouragement and correction.

Autonomous churches are a modern invention. Living in union and being responsible for one another in the Lord are kingdom relationships central to being God's people during the sojourn upon earth. As believers pursue this common life, they continue to write the Christian story in their own generation, adding another chapter to an old story passed down through the centuries. One small part of the expansive family narrative we call Christian history is the story of a people called Presbyterians.

A unique feature of this book is the Connections section at the end of each chapter. The author realizes that not everyone is hooked on history like he is and thus asking the "so what" question of historical accounts is legitimate. All chapters conclude with suggestions on how particular portions of the story still have relevance to the present and, while these suggestions are not the last word, they should stimulate thinking and application of the historical materials. At the end of the book a Study Guide is provided for individual or group reflection, which includes recommended reading, discussion questions and relevant Scripture texts for those interested in digging deeper into the story.

1

CHURCH HISTORY MATTERS
"Tradition" is not a Four-Letter Word

"So then, brothers, stand firm and hold to the traditions that you were taught by us, either by our spoken word or by our letter."[1]
2 Thessalonians 2:15

"Tradition is the living faith of the dead, traditionalism is the dead faith of the living. ... it is traditionalism that gives tradition such a bad name."[2]
Jaroslav Pelikan, church historian (1923-2006)

There is an old television show called "To Tell the Truth," in which a panel of celebrities tried to determine which contestant was telling the truth. After interviewing three contestants, with two of them lying and one being truthful, the celebrities cast their votes for the one they believed to be telling the truth. After the votes were tallied, the host finally announced, *"Will the real _____ please stand up."* This famous TV line captures the essence of what many outsiders think about Christianity. With so many diverse groups claiming to be "Christian," how is one to know what the real story is – *will the real Christianity please stand up*. Church history helps us answer this crucial question.

The subject of history has fallen on bad times, and confusion about the nature of genuine Christianity is not surprising when one considers the current cultural apathy toward historical awareness. Enlightened persons confidently reject outmoded ways of thinking and living in the past as archaic patterns that are no longer useful. Many moderns appear to have long ago delegated historical sensitivities to the trash heap. The current breath-taking advances in science and technology have exacerbated the situation as the rapid pace of change seems to have made the study of history irrelevant to contemporary life. There are professionals who continue to study and write history but it has no practical purpose in the minds of many.

Alongside the apathy is widespread ignorance of the past in the general population. Cultural watchdogs continue to point out how uninformed the typical American student is about American and world history. Many followers of Christ likewise appear to be rather unaware of their own Christian story. The Christian faith did not begin with a man named Luther nor did the faith cease to develop after St. John passed away on Patmos. Jesus told his disciples that the Father would send the Spirit who will "teach you all things" (John 14:26). The church would continue to go deeper in its understanding of the faith as the Spirit unfolded the truth to her. Christianity is a religion of history, and believers have a rich story that includes not only the bad and the ugly, but also much good to be emulated. Human sinfulness has been all too evident in the Christian past, yet there is a triumphant progress of God's church through history. Jesus promised his disciples that the gates of hell would not overpower his church (Matthew 16:18).

Knowledge of the Christian heritage is essential to every generation of believers. The story of the church through the ages provides us with glimpses of Biblical faith and establishes a pattern whereby we can test the variety of truth claims among "Christian" groups clamoring for recognition. Christianity has two millennia of experience and this history is available for anyone to explore. Certain core values have characterized God's people over these two thousand years; if any of these essential elements are missing a group may not legitimately claim to be Christian. But the problem is that few know the story anymore or know only a few choice lines from one or two of the chapters. Part of the answer to the question of real Christianity is found in the knowledge of what it has meant historically for people to be Christian.

If one listens to the way some evangelicals talk, there seems to be a sense that true believers are the "Bible only" crowd, and it's the Roman Catholics, Orthodox and liberal Protestants who put too much stock in tradition. Some appear to have embraced the idea that tradition is bad while Scripture alone is good. It is almost implied that the Holy Spirit has been on vacation for the last 2,000 years! The paranoia over tradition is cult-like (we alone have "the truth") and can be very dangerous. Given this aversion to tradition, perhaps we should not be so shocked to observe bizarre forms of faith among those claiming to follow the Bible alone. There is a serious misunderstanding of the proper role of tradition among many in the body of Christ. The issue is not Scripture versus tradition, but bad tradition versus positive tradition that is useful to God's people.

Tradition is not something to be avoided. When properly understood it is a priceless treasure of the Church. On the other hand, when tradition becomes an end in itself it can be toxic. The tradition of the Church must always be open to reform under the Word of God. When speaking about tradition one should start with a definition since this is much of the problem. One person may perceive tradition to be the teaching and practices of the church which have no warrant from the Scriptures and have taken God's people down wrong paths. Someone else may think of tradition as those things that churches practice because they have always uncritically done it that way. Another definition is simply the historic interpretation of the Bible – in other words, how have God's people understood the Scripture down through the centuries. Those definitions are very dissimilar and make a huge difference in how one approaches the subject of tradition.

Professor Heiko Oberman has made a useful distinction to help explain the concept of tradition. In his study of late medieval Christianity, he observed that many of the medieval theologians, while highly valuing tradition, understood it to be the history of Biblical interpretation. We may call this view "Tradition I." The writings of the Fathers that interpreted the Bible were recognized as useful tools for the church. While final authority for all teaching in the church is Holy Scripture, a secondary source of insight into God's truth is the faithful interpretation of that Word by the Fathers. In other words, there is a traditional way of interpreting the Bible that must be taken seriously. Each new generation of believers is not free to reinterpret the Bible in an arbitrary way to suit its own purposes. One way the church ensures that she stays within the boundaries of apostolic Christianity is to interpret Scripture in historical continuity with God's people down through the centuries.

Oberman contrasts Tradition I (the historical interpretation of the Bible) with another perspective that understands tradition as a secondary source of revelation from God – that is, equally authoritative with the inspired Scriptures. We may call this view "Tradition II." It is this latter definition that the Protestant mind so often associates with the term "tradition." Tradition II became enshrined at the Roman Catholic Council of Trent (1545-63) which declared: "Following, then, the example of the orthodox fathers, it receives and venerates with a feeling of piety and reverence all the books both of the Old and New Testaments, since one God is the Author of both; also the traditions, whether they relate to faith or to morals, as having been dictated either orally by Christ or by the Holy Ghost, and preserved in the Catholic Church in unbroken succession." (Fourth Session, April 8, 1546). The Protestant Reformers rejected Tradition II as adding to the Word of God, the words of men. Tradition I, on the other hand, was very important to them.[3]

Tradition can be a good thing; the old voices often give us needed perspective. We must listen to the voices from long ago as well as the voices of present day Christian leaders who point us to the teaching of Scripture. The old as well as the new are necessary. G.K. Chesterton put it this way, "Tradition means giving votes to the most obscure of all classes, our ancestors. It is the democracy of the dead. Tradition refuses to submit to that arrogant oligarchy who merely happens to be walking around."[4]

PROTESTANT REFORMERS AND 'TRADITION'

Martin Luther changed all this overemphasis on tradition, right? Didn't Luther reject the writings of the Fathers in favor of the "Bible alone" principle? We know that Luther sometimes wrote the names of medieval theologians upside down in the margins of books in order to show his disdain for their errors in doctrine. He also acknowledged that church councils had erred. On the other hand, Luther viewed ancient creeds, such as the Apostles' Creed, as a "holy possession" of the church and utilized this traditional creed as a teaching guide in his Smaller and Large Catechisms.

Historian Jaroslav Pelikan has offered a most constructive way to understand Martin Luther's reform. According to Pelikan, one observes in Luther a tension between "catholic substance" and "protestant principle." Luther was not inventing a new religion, and he rejected the charges of "novelty" heaped upon him by Roman Catholic critics. The Protestant movement was a return to ancient Christianity (catholic substance), the initial centuries after Christ not to simply apostolic times. In the earlier periods of church history, God's people had faithfully stood upon the teachings of Scripture and formulated many of the accepted doctrines and practices of the church. The heritage of the early church had been perverted in the late medieval period and it was the distortion of the Patristic tradition (the Fathers) that Luther rejected, not tradition itself. Alongside the inherited "catholic substance" was the new "protestant principle" – mid-course corrections of church reform in the light of the gospel.[5]

Luther's insight into justification by faith alone and salvation by grace alone were certainly based upon the *sola scriptura* principle. Yet these doctrines, while in many ways significant theological breakthroughs, were also doctrines consistent with the ancient faith of the church. Salvation solely on the basis of God's prevenient grace had been clearly taught in the ancient and medieval church beginning with St. Augustine in the fourth century. Augustine had written volumes on the utter sinfulness of man and the absolute necessity of God's electing grace in Christ. Justification by faith alone pointed to Christ alone as the object of justifying faith. The Creed of Nicaea (325) had emphasized that the second person of the Trinity became man "for us men and our salvation." Justification by faith alone was not a new doctrine that Luther discovered. It was an old Biblical truth that Luther refined through his study of St. Paul's epistles and it was consistent with the theology of a number of earlier ecclesiastical teachers. The *Augsburg Confession* (1530), one of the earliest Protestant testimonies, after describing salvation by faith and not works, adds this statement: "That no new interpretation is here introduced can be demonstrated from Augustine, who discusses this question thoroughly and teaches the same thing namely, that we obtain grace and are justified before God through faith in Christ and not through works. His whole book *De spiritu et litera,* proves this."[6]

A few radical Protestants carried Luther's *sola scriptura* principle to extremes far beyond anything Luther intended by rejecting any use of tradition whatsoever. Some of the fanatics even jettisoned the doctrine of the Trinity because they did not believe this teaching could be found in the pages of Scripture. Luther was horrified at the crass misinterpretation of the Bible by heretics. Ralph Waldo Emerson would later quip, "Luther would cut his hand off sooner than write theses against the pope if he suspected that he was bringing on with all his might the pale negations of Boston Unitarianism."[7] It was never Luther's plan to divorce the Protestant movement from the great dogmas of church history, but where the church's teaching had strayed from Biblical truth it was rightly to be condemned.

John Calvin also had a deep appreciation for the legacy of the ancient church. In the early years of his ministry, Calvin criticized some of the language in the Nicene Creed, but as the Reformation continued to grow, he came to a greater appreciation of the necessity of creedal statements to protect orthodoxy. The doctrine of the Trinity was part of the tradition of the church that must be safeguarded. Some Protestants objected to using the terms "person" and "Trinity" when referring to God because they were humanly devised and not in the Bible. Calvin answered that the history of the church had proven their usefulness and made them a necessity for articulating the orthodox faith.

Calvin makes notable use of the church fathers in his writings. For example, there are references to St. Augustine hundreds of times in *Calvin's Institutes of the Christian Religion*. Calvin was convinced that his theology was consistent with much of what the Fathers had said previously. He insisted that if many of the beloved Fathers were alive in his day, they would side with the Protestants. In response to Catholic criticism that the Reformers had forsaken the uniform consent of the Christian past, Calvin replied: "... our agreement with antiquity is far closer than yours, but that all we have attempted has been to renew that ancient form of the Church."[8]

Many Protestants today are confused about the role of history in theology and often forget the wisdom of the first Protestant reformers. Luther and Calvin were both opposed to the elevation of individual interpretation over the corporate judgment of the church. Private interpretation is the mother of heresy and the radical Protestants who began to deny the deity of Christ and the Trinity were proof of this very real danger. Biblically-sound Christian theology must have foundations in the interpretation of the Scriptures by the historic Church lest the Bible become a nose of wax that can be molded to suit the whims of each new generation.

PATTERNS OF PRACTICE

There are many things that the Scriptures do not specifically address. Certain ecclesiastical questions arise for which the church must seek insight from general principles of the Scriptures (if there are some that apply) but she also looks to the historic church for light on these matters. Learning from the wisdom of the past is a part of God's design of one generation teaching another. Passing down insights accumulated from years of trial and error are priceless treasures. Why not learn from church history's track record rather than solely relying on one's own limited experience as the only source of illumination.

Several issues could illustrate the kinds of questions the church must address. The details of church government would be one such series of questions. Rule by elders and deacons is clear in the New Testament, however, the particulars of orderly church administration and mutual accountability systems are not described for us in the pages of Scripture. The church must use her sanctified common sense in many instances while always seeking to rely on the general principles of the Bible for guidance. Over the centuries consensus insight has been recorded in books of order and discipline. These manuals provide helpful suggestions for regulating church life in a God-honoring way. Contemporary believers are not left on their own to create new guidelines for ecclesiastical practice but may lean on the learning of earlier saints for aid in the present time.

The proper administration of the sacraments would be another area where the history of Christian practice is important. The New Testament gives us the commands of Christ about the Lord's Supper and Baptism, but not much detail is included about the specific administration of these holy things. From the beginning early church leaders provided regulations for handling the sacraments in local congregations. One example is the uniform practice of having the clergy officiate at the celebration of the sacraments. This unique role of the minister is not specifically mandated in Scripture but it has been the universal practice of the church for centuries. One of the key pastoral tasks is to safeguard the sanctity of Christ's sacraments and to administer them in his name. There may be a few Protestants who reject this "tradition" but they do so at their own peril and risk profaning God's holy things with innovations that devalue the deep meaning of these precious gifts to the body of Christ.

Christian worship has continuously reflected the church's history to every new generation of believers. The early church adopted patterns of Jewish worship that would be familiar to Jewish Christian believers, but in time a number of liturgical traditions would emerge in the different geographical areas and cultures. Alongside this diversity of worship practices was also a continuity with the past. The Holy Scriptures described the essential elements of worship – singing, sacraments, prayer and preaching, but again many particulars would be developed in a variety of people groups and time periods. There has always been a certain degree of flexibility in the historic forms of worship but the common elements have provided a functional stability for the whole church. Ancient patterns of worship may be helpful guides for us lest we be so swayed by the moment that we unwittingly jettison time-tested elements of worship that both glorify God and edify His people.

An example of unwarranted neglect of the past would be the current tendency among some congregations to abandon the use of ancient creeds (i.e., Apostles' Creed, Nicene Creed) in worship because they are deemed irrelevant to people's experience. If one is exclusively following the latest trends in worship styles, without recognizing the ongoing value of historic components of worship, one may find that this neglect leads to a shallow worship deprived of the theological substance that builds up the Lord's people. The old, as well as the new, can edify the people of God, and every generation probably needs a healthy dose of each in order to be both sufficiently grounded and relevant.

An interesting case study of how Christian history influences contemporary church practice is the issue of baptism. The Bible does not provide much detail on the actual administration of baptism other than to command believers to practice it. Given this absence of specific guidelines, the early church had to develop set patterns for baptismal practice and began to codify these practices in ancient books of church order such as the *Didache, Apostolic Tradition, Didascalia Apostolorum,* and *Apostolic Constitutions.* The practices recorded in these works had been handed down by church leaders from one generation to the next.[9] In these books one finds instructions on the proper subjects of baptism as well as details on the proper administration of baptism. Provision is made for the baptism of children and adults along with directions for what modes of baptism (pouring and immersion) are permitted. The early sources indicate that there is to be only one baptism. The fourth-century *Apostolic Constitutions* stated, "Be ye likewise contented with one baptism alone, ... For as there is one God, one Christ, and one Comforter, and one death of the Lord in the body, so let that baptism which is unto Him be but one."[10] This instruction reflected the teaching of the New Testament. The apostle Paul had stated, "There is one body and one Spirit – just as you were called to one hope when you were called – one Lord, one faith, one baptism" (Ephesians 4: 4-5).

Controversy erupted in the early church over the question of rebaptism for those who had "lapsed" during the periods of persecution. A few voices advocated rebaptizing individuals who had denied the faith under persecution because it was believed they had lost their salvation or never had true saving faith to begin with (St. Cyprian). Some of these groups went so far as to separate themselves from the rest of the church which they considered impure for accepting these apostates back into the church (Novationists). The majority of the church rejected these excessive views and held strictly to the apostolic principle that there is one Church and one baptism. This strong stand against rebaptism became universally recognized orthodox teaching through the Nicene Creed which stated: "We believe in *one baptism* for the remission of sins."

St. Augustine also made a valuable contribution to the theology of baptism during the Donatist controversy in North Africa. The Donatists were a puritan group that had separated from the Catholic Church and rebaptized their adherents, declaring themselves to be the "true" church. The Donatists raised questions about the validity of baptism by impious priests, and they believed the Church was comprised of only the faithful. Augustine replied that it was preposterous to suggest that true Christians lived only in North Africa. He countered that the Church will always be made up of the wheat and the tares until Christ returns as Scripture indicated. And on the question of legitimate baptism, Augustine replied:

> ... in the question of baptism we have to consider, not who gives,
> but what he gives; not who receives, but what he receives; ... when
> baptism is given in the words of the gospel, however great be the
> perverseness of understanding on the part either of him through
> whom, or of him to whom it is given, the sacrament is holy in
> itself on account of Him whose sacrament it is.[11]

According to Augustine, the validity of baptism depended on neither the worthiness of the minister, nor the candidate for baptism, but on the merits of Christ Himself who instituted baptism. Augustine's Biblical arguments were so powerful that his theology of baptism became the accepted teaching of the church (including the Protestant Reformers) and eventually Donatism completely collapsed.

The Reformers honored the orthodox teaching of the early church on baptism and repeatedly cited St. Augustine and other church fathers as authorities on the doctrine of baptism. The reformers were opposed to the rebaptism of Roman Catholics based upon the teaching of the New Testament and the uniform practice of the early church. Luther, Zwingli and Calvin never envisioned rebaptism as having any part in the Protestant movement. They viewed the sixteenth-century Anabaptists (rebaptizers) as guilty of old Donatist errors. The church had settled the rebaptism issue long ago.[12] Calvin emphasized that Christians were baptized into God's name and neither ignorance nor impiety invalidated the sacrament. The unrepeatable nature of baptism was seen clearly in the Old Testament parallel of circumcision. Calvin stated:

> Thus it was no hindrance to the Jews to be circumcised by impure
> and apostate priests; nor was the sign therefore void so that it had
> to be repeated, ... For when in ancient times circumcision was
> corrupted by many superstitions, it did not cease nevertheless
> to be regarded as a symbol of grace. And when Josiah and
> Hezekiah called out of all Israel those who had forsaken God [II
> Kings, chp. 22; 23; 18], they did not summon them to a second
> circumcision.[13]

Building upon the solid foundation of the Reformation, the Westminster Divines crafted confessional statements on baptism that were consistent with Scripture and the consensus tradition of the Church. American Presbyterians adopted the *Westminster Confession of Faith* thereby embracing the historic practice which understood rebaptism as unwarranted by any command or adequate example in Scripture. The Confession's chapter "On Baptism" states:

> The effectiveness of baptism is not tied to that moment in time in which it is administered. However, by the correct use of this sacrament the grace promised in it is not only offered but actually embodied and conferred by the Holy Spirit to everyone (adult or infant) to whom that grace is given, according to the purpose of God's own will and in His appointed time. The sacrament of baptism should be administered only once to a person.[14]

One can trace in this case study on baptism a historic linkage from the early church through the Protestant Reformers to the present day practice of Reformed churches in America. Throughout this history there is a consistent Biblical interpretation that is reaffirmed during each period. The Scripture always remains the ultimate standard, but a consensus interpretation of the sacred page adds significant weight to one's confidence in discerning the true meaning of Scripture.

WISDOM OF THE SAINTS

Those who have gone before have a lot to teach us about what it means to be Christian – what to believe, how to live and how to organize our life together in the Lord's household, the church. We are mentored by the saints who have preceded us through their voluminous writings in sermons, theological treatises, church councils, church records, books of order and recorded histories. These works regularly prove themselves trustworthy guides for God's people along treacherous paths in a fallen world. The church is impoverished by her ignorance of this great storehouse of spiritual knowledge.

It has been said, "We are what we read." There is truth in this statement because people are always influenced to some degree by the materials they read. Present-day believers would do well to spend as much time reading the writings of the church fathers as they do contemporary

Christian literature. Too much of the material available in Christian bookstores is fluffy and devoid of substance; these books will pass from popularity in a flash. Contrast this with the weighty books of Christian history that contain time-tested articulations of Biblical insight that have blessed generations of believers in many cultures. Do you want to spend time reading books that have really counted over centuries or limit yourself only to the fleeting paperbacks that are here today and gone tomorrow? Some of the existing shallowness of Christianity in America is attributable to its poor reading habits. Of course, Scripture reading must be paramount but when one chooses to supplement this reading with Christian literature, why not choose substantial books and redeem the precious time to expand one's mind for God's glory.

One genre of literature that has influenced multitudes is Christian biography. The departed saints dwelling in Christ's presence still mentor us through the telling of their stories of courage and determination. Missionaries often relate how they were inspired to dare something great for God by reading the account of other missionaries who made great sacrifices. Thousands of these biographies sit on bookshelves unread by modern believers, who, being caught up in the urgent moments of their lives, have lost the big picture perspective on the kingdom of God. These passive mentors offer a vision of Christian life far greater than the myopic viewpoint that informs how many believers live today. The lives of the saints recount a Christian faithfulness in the world with an other-worldly purpose that is nothing less than an inspiring model to emulate. St. Paul spoke about the benefits of examining the lives of devout believers: "Brothers, join in imitating me, and keep your eyes on those who walk according to the example you have in us." (Philippians 3:17)

In addition to teaching about kingdom living, the saints have left a testimony to the truths of the gospel. In the 1920's J. Gresham Machen, Professor of New Testament at Princeton Theological Seminary, witnessed the inroads of liberal ideas into the American Presbyterian Church when some church leaders began questioning traditional Christian doctrine. Responding to this dilemma, Machen wrote a book entitled *Christianity and Liberalism* (1923). In the book, he made this piercing observation:

> Yet how great is the common heritage which unites the Roman
> Catholic Church, with its maintenance of the authority of Holy
> Scripture and with its acceptance of the great early creeds, to
> devout Protestants today! We would not indeed obscure the
> difference which divides us from Rome. The gulf is indeed
> profound. But profound as it is, it seems almost trifling compared
> to the abyss which stands between us and many ministers of our
> own Church. The Church of Rome may represent a perversion
> of the Christian religion; but naturalistic liberalism is not
> Christianity at all.[15]

Machen realized that those who divorce themselves from established doctrine, held by Catholics and Protestants, are in danger of denying the faith altogether. These words were prophetic as some contemporary versions of liberalism have returned to old Gnostic heresies and outright denial of both Christ's deity and substitutionary atonement for sin on the cross. Abandonment of historic Christian ethics has followed as some "Christians" endorse abortion on demand and accept the homosexual lifestyle as a legitimate Christian option. These perversions of doctrine and ethics flow from a rejection of the historic interpretation of the Bible. The Christian tradition condemns these sub-Christian positions as outside the boundaries of orthodox Christianity.

Revisionist interpretation of the Scripture is an old phenomena and the Church has battled it from the beginning. One significant safeguard of orthodoxy and orthopraxis (right Christian living), in addition to the primacy of legitimate Biblical exegesis, is appeal to interpretation by God's people down through the centuries. A sure sign of false teaching is a new explanation of a particular doctrine when there is no precedent in the church's history for this novel understanding. Historic interpretation may be fallible but a strong consensus witness is strong evidence of a correct understanding of the Holy Scripture. The alternative is each new generation's reinterpretation of the Bible in the light of its own limited frame of reference. As someone has stated, "Wisdom is learning to test truth by the centuries and not by the moments."

Reading about believers in ages past aids our understanding of Christian unity – what it is and what it isn't. Church history levels the playing field among the numerous denominations within the Christian family of churches. There is a common past that unites Christ's followers in certain basic truths of the faith that are non-negotiable. The apostolic tradition of the early centuries was solidified in the great ecumenical councils which declare a faith common for all Christians, of all times, in all cultures. Creeds form a common bond among Christian brethren; we worship the same Lord, share the same faith and receive the same baptism (Ephesians 4: 4-6). We are united in the head of the Church, the Lord Jesus Christ, who, as both God and man, came down from heaven for our salvation, was crucified and raised from the dead in order to bring us forgiveness and life everlasting.

Church history also demonstrates that there has never been absolute unanimity in the body of Christ. Diversity of practice has been a signpost of Christianity, a religious faith which has flourished in countless societies over many centuries. While there are certainly fundamentals of the faith, there are also multitudes of non-essential elements about which the saints have had great differences. History reminds us to beware of our own arrogance in supposing that we alone have comprehended God's ways correctly. Each Christian group has its own baggage along with its own unique contribution to the larger church of Christ throughout the world.

One of the blessed doctrines of the church is the "communion of the saints," a truth considered central to Christian belief and eventually incorporated into the received text of the Apostles' Creed. The doctrine not only points us to the fellowship we have among ourselves as believers, but also the spiritual communion we share with those who are alive in Christ's glorious presence. When living saints gather on the Lord's Day for worship they join with the heavenly assembly of the faithful in singing praise to the Holy Trinity. Together they participate in the love of God the Father, the grace of the Lord Jesus Christ and the fellowship of the Holy Spirit. Our departed brothers and sisters are alive indeed, and in many ways are more alive than those remaining on earth.

CHURCH HISTORY IS ESSENTIAL

Church history should be an essential part of every Christian's thinking and believers neglect it at their own peril. Christian practice will be superficial if the edifying insights of those who have gone before are ignored. Historic Christianity is the solid foundation upon which the church of the future must build if she is to maintain the truth of God in the midst of a godless generation which seeks to create its own truth anew each day. The brother of our Lord exhorted first-century believers to "contend earnestly for the faith which was once for all delivered to the saints" (Jude 3).

The Protestant movement affirmed that the Bible alone is the final source of authority in matters of Christian faith and practice, but attempting to understand Scripture apart from the historical faith of the church is a precarious venture in which one may fall prey to grave deception. Alongside the infallible Word of God is the rich testimony of the saints which adds confidence in rightly dividing the Word of truth. There is safety in numbers. The faithful testimony of the church is a bulwark against innovation in interpretation and the potential distortion of valid Christian teaching that has stood the test of time. Authentic Christian belief is discerned through the study of Holy Scripture in conversation with the historic witness of the catholic (universal) church. Out of this conversation with the Fathers and Mothers of the church, believers receive godly counsel to guide contemporary pilgrims through the mass of religious confusion in the twenty-first century.

The existence of the New Testament itself is a call for us to study the history of the church. The church did not create the canon of Scripture, but it was the church that received it. It was God's design for his people, through the witness of the Holy Spirit, to be his instrument that would recognize, collect and codify the books of the Bible into established lists of authoritative books. The Bible is self-authenticating – God needs no man to give his imprimatur in order for the Word of God to be legitimate. However, it has been God's sovereign choice to use His church in the formation of the canon. If one takes the Scripture seriously, then one must also take church history seriously.

The church must tell the story of Christianity to her own children. Increasingly, Christian history is excluded from contemporary accounts of both world history and American history. The children of believers will not be exposed to the legacy of the church unless pastors and parents intentionally set aside time to communicate these inspiring accounts of courage and faith.

Young people (and adults) need role models, and none surpass the blessed saints who have preceded us and point to the path of faithfulness.

All human beings are looking for a sense of belonging. Post-modern folks desire to be in authentic community with other human beings. When persons are born again by the Spirit of God they join a new family and become members of the vast body of saints living and deceased who have union together in one Lord, one faith, one baptism. In this fellowship of faith, new believers are introduced to their spiritual relatives and the family stories that have made God's people who they are through two millennia. Knowing the Christian story produces a powerful realization that one is part of something much bigger than ever imagined. It's a story worth retelling to every new follower of Christ and its basic storyline should be committed to memory by the mature.

Rehearsing the remarkable account of church history will bear much fruit as it offers perspective, protection from doctrinal error, and provides the intellectual tools God's people so desperately need for grappling with contemporary issues. One cannot live in the past; it is also true that one can learn from the past – and Christians will remain intellectual and spiritual children if they forget either one of those truths.

THE CONNECTION

Presbyterians have always considered themselves a part of the larger Christian tradition and claim no exclusive corner on the truth. They have tended to have an ecumenical attitude to other Christian bodies and cooperate with them wherever possible in common causes of ministry and outreach. Within this broader Christian context, they are also part of a specific tradition with a unique and long history that we call the "Reformed Tradition." This particular family of churches traces its heritage back to John Calvin and the Protestant Reformation. Because Presbyterians stand within a tradition that is almost five hundred years old, church history has typically been important to them.

In addition to this natural penchant for historical awareness of the sixteenth century, Presbyterians acknowledge their indebtedness to the ancient church fathers that formulated much of the faith and practice that has defined orthodox Christianity for two millennia. The Fathers' and Reformers' meticulous interpretation of sacred Scripture has endured as faithful exposition of God's Word. We stand on the shoulders of Christian giants who have passed down to us the deposit of truth. On the other hand, as good Protestants we must always remember that our ultimate allegiance is to Biblical authority and not to any word of man. As Jaroslav Pelikan stated, when commenting on Martin Luther's appreciation of the church fathers, "Luther knew the difference between gratitude and idolatry."[16] May that important distinction be true for Presbyterians.

2

EARLY CHRISTIANITY
Persecution and Expansion

"And there arose on that day a great persecution against the church in Jerusalem, and they all scattered throughout the regions of Judea and Samaria, except the apostles. ... Now those who were scattered went about preaching the word."

Acts 8:1,4

"The oftener we are mown down by you, the more in number we grow; the blood of Christians is seed."[1]

Tertullian, Christian writer (ca.160-ca. 225)

The New Testament tells us that "in the fullness of time" God sent forth His Son to accomplish the plan of redemption. It was now God's appointed time, for the first-century Greco-Roman world was ripe for its Savior to come. The Romans had achieved political stability through their pervasive influence in the Mediterranean world, but it was an age of spiritual hunger and confusion. Neither the old gods, Greek philosophy nor the new eastern mystery cults had met the deepest needs of the human spirit. In God's providential timing there was a common language, culture and Rome was at peace – the way had been paved for the spread of the gospel. And the Jews were looking for their promised Messiah to bring deliverance from Roman oppressors. Jesus of Nazareth arrived on the scene at the Father's appointed time to bring salvation for the Jew and the Greek.

For the disciples who had followed Jesus, his death was the cruelest tragedy but it was not the end; Jesus Christ rose from the dead and appeared again to his disciples. The resurrection was the beginning of something new, and the risen Christ promised the disciples that He would always be with them, "even to the end of the age." The promise of the Spirit became a reality on the day of Pentecost when "they were all filled with the Holy Spirit." The Spirit was given for a specific purpose as Christ had informed his disciples: "You will receive power when the Holy Spirit has come upon you, and you will be my witnesses" (Acts 1:8). The mission was to go into all the world and preach the Gospel. Pentecost was the birthday of the church – the Father gave the Son; the Son died and rose from the dead; the Spirit was poured out on the believers. The fullness of the Trinity was now revealed in power to the infant church.

Peter initiated his gospel ministry by preaching to his Jewish brethren in Jerusalem, but as persecution arose the disciples scattered to other regions. Wherever they traveled the disciples spread the message in the Jewish synagogues and the marketplaces. Christ called into his service Paul of Tarsus, a former persecutor of the believers who would become the great apostle to the Gentiles. From his base in Antioch, St. Paul established churches in major cities throughout the eastern part of the Roman Empire from among the new Gentile converts. Gradually, as more and more Gentiles became followers of "The Way," tension built among the Jewish believers. Should the uncircumcised Gentiles be required to keep the Jewish ceremonial law? The "Gentile problem" was solved, at least officially, by the Jerusalem Council in AD 49 (Acts 15) which issued authoritative instruction to the whole church concerning what should be required of the Gentiles. While at first Christians were considered a sect of the Jews, gradually they became distinct from Judaism after the Jewish revolts against Rome resulted in the destruction of Jerusalem in AD 70.

It was in Antioch that believers were first called "Christians" (Acts 11:26). Glimpses of early Christian community life appear in the book of Acts which describes believers meeting in homes for prayer, fellowship and sharing meals together. In some cases, followers of Christ pooled their earthly resources for the common good, and consistently they took special care of the needy among them. The primitive Christian community described in the book of Acts is inspiring, but the early church was far from a perfect model. If one looks at the first letter of Paul to the Corinthians, it is clear that some of the earliest Christian congregations had significant problems. The Biblical witness informs us that the Corinthian church experienced division over certain teachers, had incest among members, struggled with questions of marriage and divorce, split on the issue of eating meat offered to idols, misused the Lord's Supper, was confused about speaking in tongues and had received false teaching on the resurrection. This does not sound like a golden age of early Christianity! On the contrary, the first followers of The Way experienced all the sinful behaviors of ecclesiastical life that has plagued Christianity ever since that time. Yet, God used them in spite of themselves just as he has continued to do throughout all of Christian history.

CHRISTIANITY SPREADS

The New Testament church was the seed of a vast fellowship of faith that would eventually spread throughout the whole Roman Empire. With a common mission, commitment to one another and the promise of the Spirit's presence, early generations of Christians pressed on faithfully and sometimes less faithfully. Jesus had declared that "the gates of Hades shall not over power" (Matt. 16:18) his church. The Christian church experienced phenomenal growth during the times of the apostles and afterward by the witness of common believers. By the middle of the second century the faith had spread to all the provinces between Syria and Rome, to Alexandria and Carthage in North Africa and as far as Gaul (France) on the western edges of the Roman world. Church tradition adds that some of the disciples may have taken the Good News as far as India and Ethiopia during the first century. All Christians were involved in the Great Commission given by Christ to his disciples. There was no organized missionary effort; believers spread the word wherever they lived and traveled. Christ had said that gospel witness would spread "to the end of the earth" (Acts 1:8).

One well-known conversion story of a church father, Justin Martyr, illustrates how the faith spread. Justin was born to pagan parents in Flavia Neapolis (Samaria). From his youth he had studied the philosophies of Stoics, Aristotle, Pythagoras and Plato, searching for truth. One day a Christian approached him and explained the way of Christ. Justin discovered that Christianity was the "one sure worthy philosophy" and he was converted around 132. Not only was there verbal witness, but the transformed lives of the first Christians were an open book for all to read. Through deeds of mercy they impressed the pagan world with the reality of the faith they professed. Christ had said: "By this all men will know that you are my disciples, if you have love for one another" (Jn.13:35). The pagan emperor Julian observed: "It is matters like this which have contributed most to the spread of Christianity: mercy to strangers, care for burying the dead, and the obvious honorableness of their conduct."[2]

PERSECUTION OF THE CHURCH

To be a Christian in the earliest centuries was a very dangerous venture. Followers of Christ were singled out for persecution beginning with the emperor Nero in AD 64, and tradition says that it was during this time that both Peter and Paul were martyred in Rome. The Apostle Paul had urged support of the Roman government and had been protected as a Roman citizen (Acts 18, 25); however, the Roman government persecuted the church intermittently for the next 250 years.

The letters to the seven churches of Revelation reflect the second persecution under the emperor Domitian in the last decade of the first century. Altogether there were ten waves of persecution; sometimes persecution was local and occasional with general toleration, at other times, it was an organized state attack upon the Christians. A number of eyewitness accounts survive of heroic martyrdoms such as the aged bishop of Smyrna, Polycarp, a personal acquaintance of St. John, and the young nursing mother Perpetua and her slave Felicitas. Many of the saints faced beasts, the sword, the cross and burning.

The *Martyrium Polycarpi* is the first Martyrology left from the ancient church. This document is a record of Bishop Polycarp's last days as he stood fast for the faith. When persecution began in Smyrna, Polycarp left the city in response to appeals from the Christian population. Outside of the city he continued in prayer for those suffering, and it was revealed to him that he would be burned alive. When his captors arrived he fed them and then willingly accompanied them back into the city where he was taken to the arena. Once in the arena, the proconsul tried to persuade the old man to swear by Caesar and curse Christ. Polycarp replied: "Fourscore and six years have I been His servant, and He hath done me no wrong. How then can I blaspheme my King who saved me?"[3] After he had prayed the fire was lit. Polycarp's death, and many others like him, inspired the early followers of Christ to remain steadfast under severe persecution.

There were many reasons for the persecution of Christians. One of the primary causes was the refusal of believers to participate in the cult of emperor worship. Christians refused to burn incense to Caesar as a god which was treason to Romans, who viewed this rite as an act of state allegiance. Christians were also accused falsely of various immoral activities. Rumors circulated that the Christian "love feasts" were drunken orgies and that Christians were cannibals who drank blood. It was said that followers of Christ were atheists because they did not worship the gods who brought prosperity to the empire. They were slandered as "haters of humanity," that is, anti-social because they withdrew from many civil activities such as gladiator fights and banquets where sacrifices were made to idols.

During the periods of persecution, Christians were attacked not only physically but also intellectually. The church was blessed with "apologists" like Justin Martyr and Tertullian who defended the faith with counterarguments that Christians in fact were good citizens of the empire, even praying for the emperor. Answering pagan accusations of "novelty," the apologists pointed out that Christianity in reality was an ancient faith rooted in Judaism. The apologists' writings also went on the offensive, arguing for the reasonableness of Christian belief in contrast to foolish Greek myths about gods and goddesses.

As far as the Roman government was concerned, Christians were a nuisance. An early picture of how government officials dealt with Christians is seen in the correspondence between Pliny, governor of Bithynia, and the emperor Trajan in 112. Pliny writes:

> ... this is the course that I have adopted in the case of those
> brought before me as Christians. I ask them if they are Christians.
> If they admit it, I repeat the question a second and third time,
> threatening capital punishment; if they persist I sentence them to
> death. For I do not doubt that, whatever kind of crime it may be

to which they confessed, their pertinacity and inflexible obstinacy should certainly be punished.

The emperor Trajan replied:

> ... no hard and fast rule can be laid down, of universal application. They are not to be sought out; if they are informed against and the charge is proved, they are to be punished, with this reservation – that if anyone denies that he is a Christian, and actually proves it, that is by worshiping our gods, he shall be pardoned as a result of his recantation, however suspect he may have been with respect to the past.[4]

Eusebius of Caesarea (ca. 260 – ca. 340), known as "the father of church history," wrote about the suffering of Christians in Lyons, Gaul (France) at the hands of pagan mobs in 177: "They nobly sustained all the evils that were heaped upon them by the populace, clamours and blows, plundering and robberies, stonings and imprisonments, and what so ever a savage people delight to inflict upon enemies."[5] Many of these Christians were brought before the governor to be tortured and killed.

In 250, an empire-wide persecution began when the emperor Decius published an imperial edict that commanded every citizen to offer sacrifices to the Roman gods. Those who sacrificed were given a "libellus" or certificate of sacrifice indicating they had met the necessary requirement. Many Christians were arrested and persecuted for refusing to participate in this civic ritual. Some, however, chose to make the sacrifice or purchased a "libellus" from corrupt officials when they in fact had not made the sacrifice. Still others chose to go into hiding until persecution subsided. These varied responses to persecution would raise new questions for the church when the persecution was over.

The final and fiercest persecution broke out in 303 under Diocletian and Galerius and in some parts of the empire lasted for ten years. It was during this period that the "Thundering Legion" was martyred in Armenia. Forty Christian soldiers were left naked on the ice of a frozen pond with baths of hot water on the bank as a temptation to deny Christ. Only one of the forty gave way, and his place was immediately taken by a member of the on-looking guard who had been converted by the constancy of the rest. The killing during this era was so severe that even the pagans sickened of the slaughter.

Throughout the Roman persecution the church had continued to grow as the faith of the martyrs inspired believers and drew new converts. The apologists were breaking ground for Christianity's appeal to intellectuals in Roman society. By the time of Constantine, it is estimated that there were as many as ten million converts to Christianity. At the close of the second century, Tertullian had boasted: "We are but of yesterday and we have filled every place among you – cities, islands, fortresses, towns, market-places, the very camps, tribes, companies, palace, Senate, and Forum. We have left you only the temples."[6]

The state persecution of Christians raised a number of issues for the church. One problem was how to deal with individuals who had denied the faith or fled during persecution. When a particular wave of persecution was over, how was the church to deal with the "lapsed?" If they repented, should they be readmitted to the church or had they committed an unpardonable sin? Christians were split on this issue. A group known as the Novatianists believed that the lapsed were unworthy and refused to receive them back. This strict group cited Hebrews 6:4-6 to justify their position, claiming that after baptism a major sin such as apostasy was unpardonable. The majority of the church, however, favored a more lenient approach to the lapsed and formulated set patterns of church discipline or "penance." They based their argument on Peter's denial of Christ and subsequent restoration (John18, 21), as well as Christ's command to forgive seventy times seven (Matt. 18:22). Therefore, those having once renounced Christ can be restored upon repentance. Eventually, the issue came to a head and a major schism occurred in 251. Novatian and his party formed a new "true" church and anyone entering their churches had to be rebaptized. They were regarded as heretics by some, but in time, were brought back into the catholic church.

Another issue was the place of martyrdom in the life of the church. There were believers who viewed the "baptism in blood" (martyrdom) as an ideal which Christians should seek in imitation of the Savior. To be truly spiritual was to be a martyr for the faith. The high value placed upon martyrdom birthed a movement to venerate martyrs, and a number of believers began praying to martyrs to intercede on their behalf before God. There were festivals or "birthday" celebrations commemorating these deaths in certain regions, and relics of the martyrs were preserved and honored.

SETTING BOUNDARIES

During the three centuries of Roman oppression, the church also endured many troubles from within. From the very beginning there were false teachers who had gained a hearing in the church. Jesus had said, "Beware of the false prophets who come to you" (Matthew 7:15), and Paul the apostle had warned, "from among your own selves men will arise, speaking perverse things, to draw away the disciples after them" (Acts 20:30).

In the second century, Gnosticism became popular in a few corners of the church. Gnosticism was a dualistic Greek philosophy that interpreted Christianity as a "higher knowledge" (*gnosis*) by which the intellectual elite could arrive at spiritual truth. They viewed all matter as having been created by an evil god; therefore, salvation was to escape the physical body which led to ascetic attitudes towards sex and marriage. Gnosticism was not an organized religious movement as much as it was a way of thinking. There are early hints of Gnostic-like ideas condemned in several New Testament epistles (Colossians 2:18ff; 1 Timothy 1:3-7, 4:1-3; 2 Timothy 2:14-18). One implication of Gnostic thinking was the denial of the incarnation of Christ because the pure spirit God could not be united with the evil flesh of a man. Some Gnostics therefore believed that Jesus Christ was not a real man but simply appeared to be so. This thinking was known as Docetism (Gk: "to appear") because it denied the genuine physicality of Jesus Christ. John's epistles stress the "flesh" and "blood" of Christ in apparent opposition to this Gnostic denial of Christ's humanity. (1 John 4:2; 5:6-8).

In order to gain church approval for their ideas, the Gnostics produced gospels and epistles which they claimed were written by some of the original disciples of Jesus. The church then faced the question of deciding which books were authentically apostolic and thus authoritative for Christians. Should books like the *Gospel According to Thomas*, the *Acts of Peter*, or the *Apocryphon of John* be read in the churches along with Matthew, Acts and Romans? One sectarian teacher named Marcion, who started a rival church (Marcionites), rejected the entire Old Testament, Matthew, Mark, Acts, Hebrews and the Pastoral Epistles. He accepted only a portion of Luke and ten of Paul's epistles as the true canon of Scripture. Marcion believed the god of the Old Testament was an evil god in contrast to the loving Father of Christ in the New Testament, and he denied the infancy of Jesus claiming that he simply appeared on earth as a grown man. Errors like these and worse could not be ignored by church leaders who were compelled to lay down explicit boundaries for the faith that would safeguard the Lord's sheep from heretical ideas.

These challenges compelled church leaders to begin building their own list of accepted writings. The books of the New Testament were in circulation, but an authoritative collection was nonexistent. One of the first lists was known as the "Muratorian Canon" (ca. 200) which names all the present New Testament books except Hebrews, James, 1 and 2 Peter and 3 John, but does add the Wisdom of Solomon and the Apocalypse of Peter. Later canonical lists included a few other books not in the present New Testament. The first known record of the common twenty-seven New Testament books is included in the Easter letter of Athanasius in 367, which the eastern part of the church accepted. In the west, the completed canon list was approved by the Council of Carthage in 397.

Another group that influenced the question of the canon was the Montanists of Asia Minor. Montanus began prophesying ecstatically (ca. 155-175) and claiming to be the human instrument of the Holy Spirit. Two prophetesses soon joined him in proclaiming the time of preparation for the New Jerusalem. The Montanists attracted a significant following, but they were not perceived as orthodox by many because of their emphasis on prophecy, speaking in tongues and visions. Against what standard were these direct revelations to be measured? Some Montanist prophecies proved false and the group refused to submit themselves to the discernment of the bishops. While not heretics, the Montanists were viewed with suspicion and accused of threatening the apostolic tradition.

The books of the New Testament were not selected by a group of leaders in the ancient church nor were the books immediately gathered into a collection when the last apostle died. The "canon" (Gk: rule or standard) came into existence as the result of a dynamic process, but the stage had been set by the existence of a Hebrew canon. The church slowly began to sense the necessity of an established set of apostolic books that were "inspired" and therefore equally authoritative with the Old Testament Scriptures.

There were several tests of canonicity that the early church applied. First was the test of inspiration. Origen (ca. 250) speaks of "... the divine inspiration of holy Scripture, which extends throughout its body," and then he quotes Paul from 2 Corinthians. He adds: "For if our books induced men to believe because they were composed either by rhetorical art or by the wisdom of philosophy, then undoubtedly our faith would be considered to be based on the art of words, and on human wisdom, and not upon the power of God."[7]

A second test was apostolicity – was it written by an apostle or a close associate? Irenaeus had used this criterion as early as 185. Eusebius reported that the Gospel of Mark was authorized by Peter, and concerning Luke, he wrote: "In his own gospel, he delivered the certain account of those things that he himself had fully received from his intimacy and stay with Paul, and also, his intercourse with the other apostles."[8] An authentic canonical book had to have, in some form, the mark of an apostle of Christ which was the standard for exclusion of certain apocryphal writings claiming to be apostolic. In the Muratorian Canon, the writer mentioned spurious books that were "forged under Paul's name to further the heresy of Marcion." Then he added: "And there are many others which cannot be received into the Catholic Church. For it is not fitting for gall to be mixed with honey."[9] A strong indicator of the importance of apostolic authorship was the multiple attempts at forgery.

A third test was the consistency of the internal contents of the books with the accepted apostolic teaching. If a book contradicted the doctrine of the acknowledged apostolic writings it was excluded. In Eusebius's canonical list he also mentions several "spurious" books which are "not embodied in the canon." Concerning these spurious books, he stated: "The character of the style itself is very different from that of the apostles, and the sentiments, and the purport of those things that are advanced in them, deviating as far as possible from the sound orthodoxy, evidently proves they are the fictions of heretical men."[10]

The church applied these tests as a means for recognizing the boundaries of the Holy Scripture which in turn provided uniformity to Christian belief and enhanced the unity of the Church. The Biblical canon was the standard of truth for early Christianity. Augustine (354-430) wrote to his scholar friend Jerome:

> I confess to you that I have learned to respect and honour only those books of the Scriptures now referred to as canonical. I firmly believe that none of the authors of these books has erred in writing, and if I should find fault with anything in them which appears to conflict with the truth, I am sure that the reason must be that there is some textual error or that the translator did not follow what was said or that I do not understand it properly. ... since the Holy Scriptures are founded on the highest summit of divine authority, I will read them convinced and assured of their truth; ...[11]

With heretical and schismatic groups competing for disciples, the early church also had to clarify its understanding of what it meant to be the "true church." The word "catholic" (universal) came to be understood as the original church descended from the apostles in distinction from heretical or schismatic churches. Irenaeus (ca. 130 – ca. 200), wrote *Against the Heresies* in which he gave three tests for the church. The catholic, or "true" church, acknowledges the writings of the apostles, the tradition of the apostles, and the bishops as successors of the apostles.

The earliest groups of believers were organized in a variety of patterns. In Jerusalem, Peter, and then James, was the key leader according to the New Testament. Each congregation had its own leaders, but it is not known whether they were appointed, chosen, or just emerged as the "gifted" ones. By the later part of the New Testament period, there seems to be more organization with fixed offices of elders and deacons (Pastoral Epistles). Elders and deacons served in the first-century church, including deaconesses in some places. In the New Testament the word "elder," (Gk. *presbuteros*) and the word "bishop" (Gk. *episkopos*) were used interchangeably. By the early second century the term "bishop" was no longer synonymous with elder but was a distinct office of chief leader among the elders in a congregation. Ignatius (ca. 35 – ca. 107), bishop of Antioch, wrote to the church at Smyrna: "Do ye all, follow your bishop, as Jesus Christ followed the Father, and the presbytery as the apostles; and to the deacons pay respect, as to God's commandment."[12] In the third century, a bishop was over a group of churches in a city or surrounding area, but by the next century there were metropolitan bishops in capital cities who were responsible for lower bishops. As the bishops' power increased, so did the emphasis on apostolic succession. The notion of bishops as successors to the apostles meant continuity of authority in governing churches and the role of passing on the authentic gospel to the next generation. Clement, bishop of Rome, wrote to the church in Corinth around AD 96: "And our apostles knew through our Lord Jesus that there would be strife over the name of the bishop's office. So for this cause therefore, having received complete foreknowledge, they appointed the aforesaid persons (bishops), and afterwards they provided a continuance, that if these should fall asleep, other approved men should succeed to their ministration."[13]

The office of bishop evolved rather naturally as the church grew because solidarity of leadership became a necessity for survival. In time, however, the bishop was considered to be the vessel of apostolic truth and apart from the bishops, the church does not exist. Cyprian, bishop of Carthage, wrote an epistle on the episcopate (ca. 250) in which he argued that church unity comes through the bishops and it is their responsibility to uphold unity; therefore, the bishops must be one and undivided. Cyprian declared, "The bishop is in the Church and the Church is in the bishop, and that if any one be not with the bishop he is not in the Church."[14]

Creeds also became very important as doctrinal protection for the catholic church. Early creeds, known as the "rule of faith," were recited at baptism and began to set standards for Christian profession. One of the earliest creedal statements was the "Old Roman" interrogatory creed (ca. 215) used at baptism by Bishop Hippolytus of Rome. The Apostles' Creed can be traced back to this Trinitarian baptismal formula and other similar statements collectively known as the "rule of faith." While not written directly by the apostles, the creed does reflect the apostolic Gospel as it was preached in the first century, and therefore the title is appropriate. The Apostles' Creed functioned as a summary of the faith, a standard against false teaching and a tool for catechizing new converts.

By the third century, church authority was founded upon the canon, the bishop and the creed. New errors from false teachers within forced the church to clarify her thinking and solidify her organization. The church established standards of belief and order and so withstood the assaults of heretics. The common element in the canon, creed and office of bishop (church leadership) was its connection to the apostles – the canon of genuine apostolic writings, the bishops as successors of the apostles and the creedal summary of apostolic teaching. The apostolic foundations of historic Christianity were unmistakable.

UNITING WITH THE EMPIRE

The emperor Constantine had some kind of Christian conversion experience in 312 at the Milvian Bridge as he prepared for battle. The next year he issued the Edict of Milan legalizing Christianity, and by 323 he was the sole ruler of the great Roman Empire. As official persecution came to an end, Eusebius wrote about the Christian response: "With choirs and hymns, in the cities and villages, ... they celebrated and extolled first of all God the universal King ... then they also celebrated the praises of the pious emperor ... There was a perfect oblivion of past wickedness that was buried in forgetfulness. There was nothing but enjoyment of the present blessings, and expectation of those yet to come."[15] When Constantine became emperor, a new era for the church was inaugurated – violence against Christians ceased, and the faith gradually became the favored religion of the empire. The relationship of church and state had entered a new phase which would last for centuries.

Constantine, followed by his three sons, paved the way for Christianity to become the new state religion. The Roman Empire, as most ancient societies, was held together by the social bond of a priest-king or semi-divine ruler. Constantine, desiring to secure the unity of the empire, united his empire's religious and social life through the church. Increasingly, Roman emperors would claim authority in the church, and in many instances this was welcomed by the empire's Christian population. Constantine and later emperors would intervene to settle church disputes over doctrine and punish or exile heretics. Emperor Theodosius I (r. 379-395), made this decree against those who denied the orthodox view of the Trinity:

> According to the apostolic teaching and the doctrine of the
> Gospel, let us believe the one deity of the Father, the Son and
> the Holy Spirit, in equal majesty and in a holy Trinity. We
> authorize the followers of this law to assume the title of Catholic
> Christians; but as for the others, since, in our judgment, they are
> foolish madmen, we decree that they shall be branded with the
> ignominious name of heretics, and shall not presume to give to
> their conventicles the name of churches. They will suffer in the
> first place the chastisement of the divine condemnation, and in
> the second the punishment which our authority, in accordance
> with the will of Heaven, shall decide to inflict.[16]

The emperors began with more or less severity at different times
to restrict pagan worship and practices. Old pagan temples were
closed or destroyed, and sacrifices to the gods were prohibited. The
repression also included: abolishing privileges given to pagan priests,
forbidding admission to the army, withholding public office, exile
and confiscation of goods. The emperor Julian (r. 361-363), known as
the "Apostate," made one last attempt to return the empire to pagan
worship but was unsuccessful. By 378, the rest of the emperors were
Catholic Christians.

One problem the church faced as a result of favored status was the
struggle among church leaders for power and position. The holding
of church office became of great advantage socially and politically
and the emperors installed bishops favorable to their imperial
policies. By the fifth century, the church could boast the majority
of the empire's citizens but many were nominally Christian. The
church was becoming wordlier as persecution had ceased, but due to
the protection granted by the state, the church became stronger in
political influence and ecclesiastical structure. Had Christians been
more faithful as a persecuted minority? It is an interesting question
to consider but a simple answer is not forthcoming. While there were
certainly negative consequences to this new union of church and state,
it also provided the environment for strengthening the body of Christ
doctrinally (the ecumenical creeds) in ways that forever changed the
face of Christianity.

CHRISTIAN WORSHIP

During the first centuries, styles of worship evolved gradually just like most other areas of the Church's faith and practice. Early foretastes of Christian worship were evident in the New Testament and our knowledge of worship in the Jewish synagogue. The churches of the first three centuries patterned their worship after the various parts of Jewish worship including prayers, scripture reading, and singing. Christians worshiped on the first day of the week in memory of Christ's resurrection (1 Corinthians 16:1,2; Acts 20:7). Ignatius (d.ca. 107), bishop of Antioch, wrote: "Those, then, who lived by ancient practices arrived at a new hope. They ceased to keep the Sabbath and lived by the Lord's Day, on which our life as well as theirs shone forth, thanks to Him and his death ..."[17] Sunday did not become a day of "rest" however until the time of Constantine.

Sunday worship was highlighted by the celebration of the Lord's Supper. At first, the Lord's Supper was incorporated into a full meal as part of an "agape" feast but later was separated. Participation in the "Eucharist" (thanksgiving) was only for the baptized. The second-century *Didache*, a Greek handbook on morals and church order, states: "Let none eat or drink of your Eucharist, save such are baptized into the name of the Lord."[18] By the middle of the third century the worship service had been divided into two parts with the second part being the Lord's Supper when unbelievers and catechumens (candidates for baptism) were escorted out by the deacons. Initially, the Lord's Supper was a commemoration of Christ's death, but it slowly became a rite wherein it was believed Christ was really present in some sense. The language of sacrifice was used in the liturgy, but this was not the fully-developed medieval theory of transubstantiation. In the mid-third century St. Cyprian wrote:

> If Christ Jesus our Lord and God is Himself the high priest of God the Father and first offered Himself as a sacrifice to the Father, and commanded this to be done in remembrance of Himself, then assuredly the priest acts truly in Christ's room, when he imitates what Christ did, and he offers then a true and complete sacrifice to God the Father, if he so begin to offer as he sees Christ Himself has offered.[19]

Fixed liturgies eventually appeared in church practice, particularly related to the service of the Eucharist. There was considerable variation based on ethnic differences, but fixed written forms of service were more and more the trend. Certain rites, in time, gained prominence and their basic form became the accepted practice of the church. Service books were available to clergy including forms of services and lectionaries (set Bible readings for various occasions). By the end of the sixth century Christian worship had taken the forms they have retained in Roman Catholic and Eastern Orthodox churches.

Another important feature of developing Christian worship was baptismal practice. The New Testament does not describe in detail exactly how persons were baptized but mentions profession of faith and baptism with water. The *Didache* prescribed these directions for baptism:

> Concerning baptism, baptize in this way. Having first rehearsed
> all these things, baptize in the name of the Father and of the Son
> and of the Holy Ghost, in living water. But if you have not living
> water, baptize in to other water; and, if thou canst not in cold, in
> warm. If you have neither, pour water thrice on the head ...[20]

Candidates for baptism had to go through a lengthy time of preparation, sometimes as much as three years in certain corners of the church. In the *Apostolic Tradition* (ca. 225), the immediate preparation before the actual day of baptism included: exorcisms, the Thursday bath, more exorcisms and the Saturday night vigil, Scripture readings and final instruction. Baptism was not to be received rashly for it was a sacred rite which some of the Fathers called a "mystery."

Who was baptized? Was it only for believers, or were their children included? There is no explicit mention of infant baptism in the New Testament other than possible implicit references in "household baptisms" (Acts 10:48; 16:15, 33; 1 Corinthians 1:16; 16:15). Irenaeus of Lyon, in the late second century, is the first church father to mention the practice of infant baptism. Origen of Alexandria (ca. 185-ca. 254), declared that "the Church received from the apostles the tradition of baptizing infants too." Cyprian, bishop of Carthage, writing in mid-third century addressed the parallel of baptism and circumcision and added: "Moreover, belief in divine Scripture declares to us that among all – whether infants or those who are older – there is the same equality of the divine gift. ... whereas the Holy Spirit is not given with measure, but by the love and mercy of the Father alike to all. ... – and nobody is hindered from baptism and from grace – how much rather ought we to shrink from hindering an infant."[21]

Early books of order stipulated procedures for baptism that also included instructions for baptizing little ones. The *Apostolic Tradition*, attributed to Hippolytus of Rome (ca. 170-236), mentions the baptism of children: "And first baptize the small children. And each one who is able to speak for themselves [*sic*], let them speak. But those not able to speak for themselves, let their parents or another one belonging to their family speak for them. Afterward, baptize the grown men, and, finally the women. ..." The *Apostolic Constitutions* (ca. 375) gave these directions about infant baptism: "Baptize your infants also and bring them up in the nurture and admonition of God. For He says, 'Allow the little children to come unto me and do not forbid them.'"[22]

In the New Testament baptism was a symbol of the forgiveness of sins, union with Christ and the baptism of the Holy Spirit. In the second century and beyond, baptism became for some a rite that conveys actual forgiveness. It was therefore delayed until later in life to be sure past sins were wiped out. By the third and fourth century, both believer's and infant baptism were commonplace, but church leaders did not view the two approaches as mutually exclusive, rather they recognized both as legitimate Christian baptism.

As the number of Christians grew, there was demand for larger worship spaces. The earliest known church building at Dura-Europos (modern Syria) dates from the 230s and held about one hundred people. After the time of Constantine, there was a great influx of people into the church, and large church buildings were constructed to address the new situation. The "Christian Year" became more formalized as the church celebrated Easter, Christmas, Lent, Holy Week, Advent, Epiphany and Pentecost in more elaborate ways. The veneration of the saints and Mary grew, and special days were set to honor them. Now that Christianity was the favored religion of the empire, the church's worship and festivals became a focal point of community life.

THE CONNECTION

The early centuries of Christian growth and development are the common heritage of all modern-day believers, including Presbyterians. Christian witness was normative for the ancient Church as was persecution. Any survey of contemporary global Christianity makes it clear that things have not changed. Some versions of the Presbyterian Book of Order would capture the early church legacy of witness in this statement: "Evangelism is the primary and urgent task of the Church."[23]

This period of our Presbyterian story reminds us of the necessity of discipline for sustaining the health of the church. Those who profess Christian faith may deny that faith publicly by "lapses" into Christ-denying behavior. The church has no option but to deal both graciously and firmly with the fallen in order to reclaim them for the kingdom. Reformed churches have traditionally spoken of three marks of the "true church" – preaching of the Word, proper administration of the sacraments and the exercise of church discipline.

The ancient boundaries for faith (canon, creed, bishop) are still fundamental components of what it means to be genuinely Christian. Church government provides the necessary structure and lines of authority that life in community requires. The canon of Scripture remains our final court of appeal in all matters of faith and practice, and the essential truths of the Apostles' Creed continue to stir the believer's heart as one recites this ancient testimony to the gospel of Christ. Roman Catholics, the Eastern Orthodox churches and Protestants have tended to emphasize different parts of these ancient boundaries (Protestants, the canon; Roman Catholics, the bishop; Orthodox, the creeds), but each of the three boundaries has played a significant historic role in maintaining vitality and orthodoxy in the church.

Presbyterians maintain the tradition of baptizing believers' children that has been handed down from the ancient church. In addition to infant baptism's Biblical roots in the covenant concept, it was consistently encouraged by the church fathers which points to the likelihood of the practice coming directly from the apostles themselves. Presbyterians have typically been charitable toward other Protestants who favor exclusive believer's baptism and thus allow Christian parents to delay baptism of their children if they so choose.

3

CHURCH FATHERS
The Legacy of Ancient Christianity

*"In the beginning was the Word, and the Word was with God, and
the Word was God. ... And the Word became flesh and dwelt among
us, and we have seen His glory, glory as of the only Son from the
Father, full of grace and truth. ... No one has ever seen God; the only
God, who is at the Father's side, He has made Him known."*
John 1:1,14,18

*"For surely if the Son of God by nature became son of man by
mercy for the sake of the sons of men ... the sons of men by nature
can become the sons of God by grace and dwell in God; ... it was to
persuade of this that the Son of God came to share in our mortality."*[1]
Augustine, Bishop of Hippo (354-430)

The emperors' involvement with the affairs of the church, beginning in
the fourth century, had a long-term impact on theological development.
Doctrinal uniformity was very important if an emperor desired
harmony among his many subjects that filled the churches. While
the mingling of church and state brought with it inherent difficulties,
the new political situation providentially provided an opportunity for
the church to corporately deliberate on theological issues in ways that
had not been possible during persecution. Beginning with the time of
Constantine, the orthodox doctrine of the Trinity would be discussed
in council meetings with bishops from all over the empire, but the final

doctrinal formula would emerge only after prolonged ecclesiastical and political battles.

The early church of the first three centuries did not possess a fully developed Trinitarian theology. From New Testament times Jesus Christ had been worshipped as God, but all the implications of Christ's deity had not been conceptualized. One of the earliest questions the church had to ask was "Who is Jesus Christ?" Jewish Christians who believed "the Lord our God is one Lord" began to refer to Jesus Christ as "Lord" also. The apostle John speaks of Christ as the "Son of God" and the "Word" in his gospel, but the disciples had also known him as a human being. Who was this person? The answer ultimately took the form of ecumenical (universally recognized) creeds.

Some of the early thinking on the Trinity arose in reaction to a heresy called "Monarchianism," which had emphasized the oneness of God. The most popular form of this idea was taught by a man named Sabellius (ca. 215), thus the heresy has sometimes been called "Sabellianism." Sabellius believed that God was a single divine person who had appeared at different times in different modes or forms. Jesus Christ and the Holy Spirit are therefore temporary manifestations of God the Father; God the Father became God the Son, and there is no personal distinction between them. Tertullian, a theologian in Carthage, in answer to these views, stated: "... the Father is God and the Son is God, and the Holy Spirit is God, and each is God ... the title of God and Lord is suitable both to the Father, and to the Son and to the Holy Ghost. ..."[2] Tertullian was the first Christian teacher to use the Latin word *trinitas*. He gave the Western church some of its early terminology about God when he spoke of God as one substance and three persons.

In the Eastern church, a North African Father named Origen fought the Monarchian doctrines. Origen asserted that the Father, Son and Holy Spirit were three distinct persons (Gk. *hypostases*) or personal subsistences. He was the first to speak of the "eternal generation" of the Son, which implied a relationship between Father and Son that is without beginning, and therefore different from a human father/son relationship. However, in Origen there was a subordination of the Son and Spirit to the Father (the Father is the "source" of divinity) which the church ultimately rejected. Clarity on the doctrine of the Trinity was emerging but a theological crisis in the fourth century would bring the

Trinitarian issue before the whole church. This produced a definitive consensus statement on this fundamental affirmation of Christianity.

NICAEA AND CHALCEDON

The great Trinitarian battle arose in the fourth century when Arius (318), a presbyter of Alexandria, began to publicly articulate his anti-Trinitarian views. Arius started with the basic premise of the Monarchians – there is only one uncreated, all-powerful being of God, therefore, the Son was a created being and not eternal like God the Father. The Son is a secondary deity and does not share the Father's essence. The Holy Spirit is an even lesser deity who is subordinate to the Son.

The views of Arius spread throughout the eastern part of the empire, and tension became so great that the emperor Constantine called for a general council of bishops to settle the dispute. In 325, over two hundred bishops met in Nicaea, with the emperor himself presiding at this first assembly of all the Christian bishops, to discuss theological matters. The bishops rejected the views of Arius, but there was considerable debate over the language that would be incorporated into the creedal testimony to the truth about the triune God.

The bishops decided that a word meaning "one substance" (Gk. *homoousios*) made clear that the Son was of the same essence with the Father, that is, equal in deity. After much discussion, the Creed of Nicaea (which later served as the basis of the Nicene Creed) was written, and anathemas were pronounced against Arius. The original Creed of Nicaea (325) described the Son as "God of God, Light of Light, true God of True God, begotten not made, of one substance with the Father."[3] The council's decision, however, did not settle the controversy. The ongoing ecclesiastical struggle was as much political as it was theological. The church gradually became Arian or semi-Arian in numerous places, and the emperors over the next fifty years usually sided with the majority. Semi-Arianism which taught that Christ was of a "like substance" (Gk. *homoiousios*) with the Father prevailed for a season in the Eastern church, while the Western church was predominantly loyal to the Council of Nicaea. The East had been strongly influenced by the subordinationism of Origen and still struggled with the full equality of the Father and Son. One of the key factors in the continuing debate was the language barrier between the Latin West and the Greek-speaking East. Part of the diversity was simply a failure to understand what each side intended by the various Greek and Latin terms utilized in the Trinitarian debates.

During the years of controversy over the Trinitarian definitions of Nicaea, the chief opponent of Arian views was Athanasius (ca. 296-373), the bishop of Alexandria. Five times he was exiled, but each time he became more determined to defend what he believed was the orthodox faith. Athanasius' motivation for combating Arianism was his belief that Christ could not be less than God and be Savior of the world. In Athanasius' *On the Incarnation*, he wrote:

> For being the Word of the Father, and above all, He alone of
> natural fitness was both able to re-create everything, and worthy
> to suffer on behalf of all and to be ambassador for all with the
> Father. ... And thus taking from our bodies one of like nature,
> because all were under penalty of the corruption of death He gave
> it over to death in the stead of all, and offered it to the Father.[4]

In 381, the emperor Theodosius summoned the general Council of Constantinople, which declared its approval of Nicaea and added several statements affirming the deity of the Holy Spirit. This second ecumenical Council of Constantinople produced what became known as the "Nicene Creed," which adds this declaration about the Spirit: "Who proceeds from the Father; who with the Father and Son together is worshiped and glorified." In the following centuries, the Western Church inserted the controversial *filioque* (Lt. "and the Son") clause which adjusted the creed to say that the Spirit "proceeds from the Father *and the Son.*"[5] The Eastern church never favored this amendment because it was added later and therefore not part of the original Nicene Creed of 381. This significant modification became a divisive issue in East/West tensions in the centuries that followed.

The Trinitarian definitions of Nicaea and Constantinople set the standard of orthodoxy for the future of Christianity. Athanasius referred to the Nicene Creed as a "signpost against all heresies." The orthodox view of the Trinity included three basic assertions: there is only one true God; the Father, Son and Spirit each is fully divine; the three divine persons are distinct from one another. The ancient church did not ultimately "explain" the Trinity, which is a spiritual mystery of faith, but it did set some parameters for talking Biblically about the doctrine of God in order to protect the church from heresy.

A related question to the Trinitarian discussion concerned the relationship of the human and divine natures in Jesus Christ. The ancients struggled with the full humanity of Christ as well as his deity. The ecclesiastical debates, known as the "Christological controversies," pressed the church to delineate an explicit statement on the person of Christ. What does it mean that the second person of the Trinity was "born of the virgin Mary?"

In the latter part of the fourth century, Apollinarius, the bishop of Laodicea, attempted to explain the problem by denying the full manhood of Christ. Jesus had a human body and soul (life principle), but the "Logos" took the place of the human spirit (mind and will). The church rejected the views of Apollinarius as destroying the full humanity of Christ. Nestorius, who became bishop of Constantinople in 428, suggested another idea, which he argued would do justice to the true humanity of Christ. He believed that Christ had two distinct human and divine natures that were held together by a moral unity. Nestorius could not conceive of the divine nature being involved in human suffering or change, hence he wanted to hold the natures apart. The bishop was accused of teaching that Jesus Christ was two persons; consequently, his views were rejected by the Church. A third solution was offered by Eutyches (d. 454) who proposed a scheme in which Christ possessed only one nature after the incarnation because the human nature was absorbed into the divine nature. Again, church leaders condemned these ideas as a denial of Christ's full humanity as taught by the apostles.

In the process of defining the parameters of orthodox Christology, the bishops had rejected these aberrant views about the person of Christ:

Docetism: Jesus wholly divine, His manhood an illusion

Arianism: Jesus less than God, more than a man

Sabellianism: One God at different times as Father, Son, Spirit

Apollinarianism: Jesus fully God, only partially man

Nestorianism: Jesus fully God, fully man, two persons

Eutychianism: Jesus' manhood absorbed into His divine nature

The consensus truth about Christ was recognized by the bishops at the Council of Chalcedon in 451. The Chalcedonian Creed included careful language that excluded each of these heresies and clearly articulated the Biblical boundaries of orthodox Christology. The Definition of Chalcedon, in part, stated:

> We, then, following the holy Fathers, all with one consent, teach
> men to confess one and the same Son, our Lord Jesus Christ,
> the same perfect in Godhead and also perfect in manhood, truly
> God and truly man, ... acknowledged in two natures, *inconfusedly,*
> *unchangeably, indivisibly, inseparably*; the distinction of natures
> being by no means taken away by the union, but rather the
> property of each nature being preserved, and concurring in one
> Person. ...[6]

How important was a creed such as Chalcedon? Why could the church not just answer heretical views with "The Scriptures say ..."? The problem was that the heretics used the Bible too, therefore the issue became whose interpretation of Scripture was correct. The "Vincentian Canon" (400s) described the situation this way:

> ... some one will ask, since the canon of Scripture is complete,
> and is in itself abundantly sufficient, what need is there to join
> to it the interpretation of the Church? The answer is that because
> of the very depth of Scripture all men do not place one identical
> interpretation upon it ... Therefore because of the intricacies of
> error, which is so multiform, there is great need for the laying
> down of a rule for the exposition of Prophets and Apostles in
> accordance with the standard of the interpretation of the
> Church Catholic.[7]

The church, of necessity, had to produce creeds that expressed the accepted interpretation of the Bible on matters essential to the faith. The creedal formulations were built upon the faith of the ancient church but clarified the particulars of those beliefs to distinguish them from heretical views. Presbyterian theologian John Leith made this observation:

> The attempt to dispense with dogma and to minimize creeds
> has never been successful ... there has never been a non-theological
> period in the history of the Church. Even when the Church
> has been held together only by a common life in the spirit, a
> creed has always been implicit. The endeavor to have no creed
> but the Bible is successful only so long as there is common
> agreement as to what the Bible teaches. In the long run,
> organizational necessities demonstrate the need for creeds, and
> organizational integrity requires some kind of
> creedal subscription.[8]

The creeds were "catholic" in that they intended to state what was believed by the whole church not just a part of it. The Council of Chalcedon, for example, was very catholic as it drew together the differing theological perspectives from Antioch, Alexandria and Rome in crafting an affirmation of faith they all agreed upon. These doctrinal statements grew out of specific historical circumstances and bear the marks of this history by the use of the language and concepts of their era. They have stood the test of time as authentic expressions of Christian belief. The ecumenical creeds were not esoteric theological puzzles, rather they were directed at the heart of the Gospel. The second person of the Holy Trinity became man and offered up his life for the sins of the world. The Nicene Creed described the work of Christ, "... who, for us men and *for our salvation, came down from heaven*, and was incarnate by the Holy Ghost of the Virgin Mary, and was made man; and was *crucified also for us* under Pontius Pilate; he suffered and was buried; and the third day he rose again, ..."[9]

During the discussions concerning the person of Christ, some of the Fathers began to speak more about the Virgin Mary's role. If Christ was indeed fully human as Chalcedon and Nicaea declared, the place of the Blessed Virgin Mary as the human mother of the Christ child was of vital significance. An apocryphal book, the *Protevangelium of*

James (second century), described a miraculous birth of Mary to an elderly couple, Anne and Joachim. The perpetual virginity of Mary was taught by a number of the church fathers including Athanasius and Augustine, who considered her a role model for Christians. In the Christological debates, Mary was given the title *theotokos* (Gk. "God-bearer"), often translated as "Mother of God," a term which had been used in the Creed of Chalcedon. The phrase Mother of God though later popularly abused, was originally intended to underscore both the human and divine reality of the God-man that issued forth from Mary's body. The Roman Catholic doctrines of the Immaculate Conception (Mary's supernatural birth) and the Assumption of Mary to heaven after death were much later concepts which did not become official Roman Catholic dogmas until 1854 and 1950 respectively.

The veneration of Mary increased over the centuries as she was honored by feasts and churches dedicated to her. Gradually, Mary's name was inserted into the liturgy and prayers were offered to her as an intercessor for believers. Roman Catholic beliefs strayed beyond explicit Biblical teaching, and the Protestant Reformers corrected the wrongful elevation of Mary. Even so, they continued to respect her esteemed place in the plan of redemption. Some modern Protestants have overreacted to Roman Catholic excesses and neglect the proper honor due the blessed woman the Father chose as His instrument for the eternal Son's incarnation.

THE BISHOP OF ROME

During the fourth through the fifth centuries, the Western Empire experienced repeated invasions by Germanic tribes, and by the end of the fifth century the imperial power of Rome was gone forever. The only institution that survived and preserved parts of Roman culture was the church. One of the early signs of the demise of Rome was the Battle of Adrianople in 378, when the Visigoths defeated the Roman Army. The city of Rome was captured by the Visigoth King Alaric in 410 and later the Huns and Vandals also sacked Rome. The last Roman Emperor in the West was deposed by 476 and thus the old Roman empire disappeared.

The Visigoths settled in southern Gaul and Spain; the Vandals moved into North Africa and the Franks conquered northern Gaul. The Anglo-Saxons invaded the British Isles, and in Italy the Ostrogoths and Lombards gained control. There was no longer an effective Roman government in the West. In the Eastern Empire, the emperors in Constantinople remained in contact with the independent German tribal kings, some of whom swore allegiance to the Byzantine emperor. The Byzantine Empire of the East lasted a thousand years after Rome had fallen.

Most of the Germanic invaders were Arians not catholic Christians. The Visigoths in the fourth century had converted to the Arian faith during their occupation of the empire, and Arianism had spread to other tribes as well. Some of the Germanic tribes were tolerant of the catholic church, while others, like the Arian Vandals in North Africa, persecuted the church for almost a hundred years. In time, however, the barbarians converted to the catholic faith through the labors of Christian missionaries.

Christianity not only survived the fall of the Western Empire, but the church was the only remaining institution that could provide unity and stability in the midst of the chaos. The Western church had developed models of organization and administration that gave a sense of continuity to a culture splitting at the seams. She owned vast tracts of land and wealth that were used to help meet the basic needs of society. Christians served the poor and sick through the establishment of hospitals, orphanages, poor houses and homes for the aged. Even the pagans were amazed at how well the believers cared not only for their own needy but also hurting pagans who had nowhere to turn.

Classical Roman culture continued through the church's art, architecture and use of the Latin language in the literature and liturgy of the church. Ecclesiastical structure was patterned after that of the Roman state in both holy orders and geographical divisions. This pattern of hierarchical church government was passed on to future generations, but ironically, few Christians had served in the imperial government which they now copied. Even with the breakup of the Roman world that had given birth to Christianity, the church maintained her vitality as she spread into new cultures.

From earliest Christian times, the church at Rome had enjoyed a very prominent place in Christendom since it was in Rome that both Peter and Paul had been martyred under Nero's persecution. Located in the capital city of the empire, the Roman church had a very prestigious position, and the "Old Roman Creed" (Apostles' Creed) as well as the formation of the canon was identified with the city of Rome. The bishop of Rome increasingly exercised a unique role in the Western church as the centuries passed.

Irenaeus, in the late second century, spoke of the Roman church as founded by Peter and Paul: "It is a matter of necessity that every Church should agree with this Church, on account of its preeminent authority, ..."[10] For Irenaeus, the apostolic tradition had passed down through this church in the succession of bishops. An early exercise of power by the Roman bishop was Victor's excommunication of congregations (189) who refused the Roman practice of the Easter celebration, which was met with great protest from many church leaders. The authority of the bishop of Rome continued to increase into the third and fourth centuries with Rome becoming one of the five most important sees (bishop's seat, Lt. *sedes*) – Jerusalem, Antioch, Alexandria, Constantinople and Rome. In 343 a council of Western bishops granted significant judicial authority to the Roman bishop, but a claim to universal ecclesiastical supremacy by a bishop of Rome did not come until the fifth century. Innocent I (d. 417), who made more substantial claims for authority in all matters of faith than any of his predecessors, is sometimes called "the first pope."

Leo I "the great" (d. 461) significantly enhanced the popes' position by his emphasis on the primacy of Peter among the apostles and the claim that Peter had passed this authority on to his successors, the bishops of Rome. Leo appealed to Matthew 16:18-19 to substantiate his contention that Rome had predominance over all other bishops. He exercised much power in the Western Empire but not in the east which deferred to the patriarch (head bishop) of Constantinople, the capital of the Eastern Empire. Leo desired to see the church unified under the Roman bishop and made significant gains in bringing uniformity to the Western church. In 445 he procured an edict from the Western Emperor that ordered all to obey the Roman bishop, as having the "primacy of St. Peter." According to tradition, it was Leo who negotiated with Atilla the Hun, convincing him to leave Italy.

There was ongoing contention among the two chief sees of Rome and Constantinople that lasted for centuries. Pope Felix III exercised bold ecclesiastical power when he excommunicated Acacius the

Patriarch of Constantinople in 484 in response to Acacius' backing of a modification of Chalcedon. This caused a schism between the Eastern church and Rome for 35 years but was eventually healed, ending in a papal victory.

One of the most influential early popes was Gregory I "The Great" (590) who filled an important political vacuum in Rome when there was little stability in society. During his fourteen years as pope he combated political corruption, managed the care of the poor, raised an army and made peace with the Lombards on his own authority. Gregory inaugurated mission work among the Arian Lombards and sent monks to England which enhanced Rome's position among the Celtic churches. The papal power of Gregory also reached into France and Spain. Gregory proclaimed: "... by the Lord's voice the care of the whole church was committed to the holy Apostle and prince of all the apostles, Peter."[11]

The political and ecclesiastical clout exercised by Leo and Gregory were high points of prestige for the Bishop of Rome. Both used their power politically to rescue Rome from being overrun by barbarians, and they solidified the organization of the church in ways that enhanced uniformity of practice and heightened the preeminence of the Roman see. As the Roman Empire crumbled, the popes began to fill the function of the old Western emperors. Since society was already accustomed to rule by one person in the imperial government, the rise of papal primacy developed naturally in a context of political instability. Monarchical power would continue in the Western Mediterranean world, even after Rome fell, through the "Roman" Catholic Church.

AUGUSTINE OF HIPPO

Arguably, the preeminent theologian of the ancient church was St. Augustine, bishop of Hippo in North Africa. During his lifetime (354-430) the Roman Empire began to crumble, and the Christian church encountered the theological challenges of the Donatists and Pelagians. From the pen of Augustine we have thorough and persuasive responses to these crises that faced the church during the closing years of antiquity. Even though early North African Christianity would eventually be almost destroyed by the Muslims, the writings of Augustine have survived and been cherished by every generation of Christians since his time.

The inspiring record of Augustine's *Confessions* (397) allows one to get a glimpse of the heart of the great Christian thinker as he recounts his spiritual autobiography. Augustine had lived a pagan life as a young man and sought answers in Manichaeanism (similar to Gnosticism) and Greek philosophy. At thirty-three he was dramatically converted by the Spirit, and his heart was turned permanently to the love of his Creator. His gratitude to God is expressed in the *Confessions*:

> Thou hast loosed my bonds. I will offer to thee the sacrifice of
> thanksgiving. Let my heart and my tongue praise thee, and let
> all my bones say, Lord, who is like thee? ... And what at one time
> I feared to lose it was now a joy to put away ... Now was my
> soul free from the gnawing cares of seeking and getting, and of
> wallowing and exciting the itch of lust. And I babbled unto thee,
> my brightness, my riches, and my health, the Lord my God.[12]

The fall of Rome deeply affected Augustine and, indeed, all Christians in the west. Pagans charged that Roman misfortune was attributable to the favored status of Christianity and the forsaking of the ancient gods. Augustine set out to answer these questions in his classic work, *The City of God*, written between 413-426 and containing twenty-two books. In this immense treatise, he left for the church a Christian worldview and philosophy of history that has had a widespread influence on Christian faith through the ages.

In *The City of God*, Augustine traces the history of the world, particularly the human perversity that had existed in the Roman Empire long before Christianity had arrived, thus demonstrating the fallacy of blaming Christians for Rome's demise. Human life since the fall has always been tragic, and he attempted to show that supposed pagan virtues were really vices. Augustine charged the citizens of Rome with having a self-absorbed lifestyle: "... the injuries you suffer, you impute to Christianity. Depraved by good fortune, and not chastened by adversity, what you desire, the restoration of a peaceful and secure state, is not the tranquility of the commonwealth, but the impunity of your own vicious luxury."[13]

Augustine presents his analysis of history with the imagery of two cities, the City of God and the opposing earthly city or city of the devil. History is the story of the inhabitants of these two cities which he described in this way:

> ... two cities have been formed by two loves: the earthly by the love of self, even to the contempt of God; the heavenly by the love of God, even to the contempt of self. The former, in a word, glories in itself, the latter in the Lord. For the one seeks glory from men; but the greatest glory of the other is God ... In the one, the princes and the nations it subdues are ruled by the love of ruling; in the other, the princes and the subjects serve one another in love ... The wise men of the one city, living according to man, have sought for profit to their own bodies or souls ... But in the other city there is no human wisdom, but only godliness, which offers due worship to the true God, and looks for its reward in the society of the saints ...[14]

Augustine did not identify the City of God with the visible church on earth because she contained both elect and non-elect; only the judgment day will ultimately separate the two. In heaven, true citizens of the city of God will fully enjoy the benefits of God's eternal city that they merely tasted as pilgrims upon the earth.

DONATISTS AND PELAGIANS

Donatists were an autonomous Christian group in North Africa who believed that they alone were the true church. Named for their second leader, Donatus, they traced their origins to the last great persecution before Constantine became emperor. Donatists refused fellowship with any Christian who had yielded to imperial orders mandating sacrifice to pagan gods or had handed over copies of the Scriptures for burning. By Augustine's time the Donatist churches contained half of the Christian population of North Africa, and a few of them had turned to violence. Augustine viewed these separatists as undermining the catholicity of the church and considered it his pastoral duty as bishop to reunify the African church under his care.

Donatists insisted that the church be holy, declaring that the impure have no place in the body of Christ. Claiming that only Donatist sacraments were valid, they were advocates of rebaptism for one who had been baptized by a "traditores" (a bishop who had handed over the Scriptures). Augustine accused the schismatic Donatists of being self-centered, narrow and forsakers of brotherly love in their blurring of the distinction between the visible and invisible church. The church has and always will contain wheat and tares until the end, and the true church's existence is not dependent on the personal holiness of every visible church member.

He argued against their doctrine of rebaptism by pointing out that the moral quality of the priest has nothing to do with the efficacy of the sacraments. Augustine repudiated the breaking off of a group from the catholic church as disruptive of Christian unity. He considered the Donatists as having cut themselves off from the body of Christ. He confronted the Donatists: "... if thou art not in the body, thou art not under the Head. ... He loves His body. If thou hast cut thyself off from His body, the Head hath not cut itself off from its body."[15] The Donatists were eventually repressed by the government, which Augustine defended as loving discipline. Over time the schism was healed, and the Donatists were reincorporated into the catholic church of North Africa.

One of the lasting imprints of Augustine's theology comes from his lengthy theological battle with Pelagianism. Pelagius was an ascetic Briton who had been teaching in Rome and moved to North Africa where he encountered Augustine's teachings. Pelagius and his disciple Coelestius were committed to ideas of the freedom of the human will to live a virtuous life. One day Pelagius was reading a passage from Augustine's *Confessions*, "Give what you command and command what you will," and is said to have burst into a fit of anger over these words. He attacked Augustine's views as undermining human ability to pursue a holy life. Augustine responded with some of his most significant works: *On the Spirit and the Letter, On Nature and Grace*, and *On Original Sin*.

Pelagius believed that Adam was created morally neutral with a capacity for both good and evil. Adam's mortality was not dependent on his choice; he was created mortal. The fall injured no one but Adam himself, therefore, there is no transmission of a fallen nature or guilt to future generations. It would be absurd and unjust to condemn all for the sin of one person. All human beings are born in the same condition as Adam before the fall. As a result, no one is of necessity inclined by human nature to sin. In fact, everyone has perfect freedom of the will and can choose to do the good if he/she so desires. According to Pelagius, the very fact that God commands humanity to do what is good is proof positive that human beings have the innate ability to obey. The Old Testament indicated that there were people before the time of Christ who lived lives of perfect holiness, and this was possible for anyone if the person only willed it to be. Grace, for Pelagius, was not an inward work of the Holy Spirit but external gifts that aid the free human will.

Based upon his study of Scripture, Augustine's views on sin and grace were quite different from those of Pelagius. Augustine believed humankind was created by God in perfect holiness and was, therefore, created immortal. Through disobedience to God, Adam and Eve lost the ability not to sin and became mortal. As a result of this original sin, humanity was totally unable to do any spiritual good. What is good in God's sight is only that which springs from the motive of love to God. Augustine says of Adam's sin:

> ... by his sin the whole race of which he was the root was corrupted in him, and thereby subjected to the penalty of death ... The whole mass of the human race was under condemnation, was lying steeped and wallowing in misery, and was being tossed from one form of evil to another ... paying the well-merited penalty of that impious rebellion.[16]

Given Augustine's pessimistic view of fallen human nature, salvation was completely out of man's grasp, because his will was in bondage to sin. The human will must be renewed by a work of God's Spirit. With a renewed will, imparted as a gracious gift, one can then freely choose to do the good. Augustine stated: "Now it is freely that he is justified thereby – that is, on account of no antecedent merits of his own works; 'otherwise grace is no more grace,' since it is bestowed on us, not because we have done good works, but that we may be able to do them – in other words, not because we have fulfilled the law, but in order that we may be able to fulfill the law."[17] Faith is a gift of the Holy Spirit, and the Spirit's work of grace includes the entire renewal of the person. Salvation from start to finish is exclusively a work of divine grace. However, the renewed will of a person does cooperate with God's grace in the life-long work of sanctification.

Augustine's perspective on grace led to his acceptance of predestination. What God does at a given moment to renew the human will, He willed to do in His eternal plan – predestination is salvation from the viewpoint of eternity. God gives His grace to the elect and passes over others who perish because of their own sin; why God saves some and not others is hidden in the judgments of God. It is important to note that for Augustine predestination was not mere speculation but the teaching of St. Paul firmly establishing human salvation as the unmerited result of God's love and grace to fallen humanity.

The positions of Pelagius were condemned by the Council of Ephesus in 431, which also condemned Nestorius. Augustine's views of sin and grace were generally accepted by the church, but there were some who did not completely embrace Augustine's teaching. Instead they believed that man's will cooperated with divine grace in salvation, a view that would become known as "semi-Pelagianism." Human nature was not dead but only weakened by the Fall and therefore possessed a certain ability to turn towards God on its own. Predestination from this viewpoint was God's foreknowledge of future events and thus his knowledge of who would have faith. Semi-Pelagianism was condemned at the Council of Orange (529). The Council declared:

> We must, under the blessing of God, preach and believe as
> follows. The sin of the first man has so impaired and weakened
> free will that no one there after can either love God as he ought
> or believe in God or do good for God's sake, unless the grace of
> divine mercy has preceded him.[18]

Though condemned as contrary to the orthodox faith, semi-Pelagian ideas would show up again in the medieval church within a theological system called the *via moderna*, or late medieval Nominalism. Luther was taught this theology as a monk and scholar but eventually rejected it and returned to the Augustinian understanding of grace.

Augustine has been called the "Doctor of Grace" because of his consuming passion to glorify God alone in the work of salvation. As man is humbled, God is exalted. Augustine said: "Let human merits, which perished through Adam, here keep silence, and let God's grace reign through Jesus Christ."[19] Augustine's thought would influence not only medieval Roman Catholic theology but also the doctrines of the Protestant Reformation. No other theologian, with the exception of St. Paul, has had such a long-lasting impact in shaping Christian doctrine.

THE CONNECTION

Responding to serious theological error, the church fathers defended traditional belief against multiple attacks. The gathered bishops solidified Christian teaching about Christ and his relationship to God the Father in the great ecumenical councils. These ancient consensus declarations have set the standard for accepted Christian doctrine ever since, and Presbyterians have incorporated these truths into their own confessional documents. To be Christian is to be Trinitarian. The historic testimony about Christ remains as a bulwark against critics in modern times. The Nicene Creed has achieved universal recognition because of its faithful summary of what Scripture teaches. This creed continues to unify believers around the globe through its affirmations of essential Christian theology.

The development of the papacy raises questions for Christians regarding the issues of church government. Is there one "Biblical" form of church order or are there varieties of possibilities? What role should historical church practices play in shaping contemporary polity? Given the necessity of structure and organization for the church, which form of church government functions best? How should secular government structure influence the church's pattern of government? Historically, Christians have offered different answers to these questions, but as we shall see later, Presbyterians believe that Scripture does give us a clear pattern for church leadership.

St. Augustine is loved by Roman Catholics and Protestants alike – Catholics are drawn to his teaching on the unity of the church; Protestants are particularly attracted to his powerful statements about sin, grace and predestination. From his own conversion experience and the study of Scripture, Augustine convincingly argued for the sovereignty of God in salvation from beginning to end. Presbyterians understand themselves to be "Augustinian" in the sense of our historic connection to his teachings on grace. Augustine's vision of an undivided church persists as a challenge to the fractured body of Christ in the modern world. Presbyterian theologian B.B. Warfield summarized Augustine's lasting influence this way: "... it is Augustine who gave us the Reformation. For the Reformation, inwardly considered, was just the ultimate triumph of Augustine's doctrine of grace over Augustine's doctrine of the Church."[20]

4

THE MIDDLE YEARS
Light in the Midst of Darkness

*"For in Him all the fullness of God was pleased to dwell, and through
Him to reconcile to Himself all things, whether on earth or in heaven,
making peace by the blood of His cross. And you ... He has now
reconciled in His body of flesh by His death, in order to present you
holy and blameless and above reproach before Him, ..."*

Colossians 1:19-22

*"... the city on high is to be completed from among men, and that
this can be accomplished only through the remission of sins, which a
man can gain only through the Man who is Himself God and who
reconciles sinful men to God through His death. Clearly, then, we
have found Christ, who we confess as God and Man who died for us."*[1]

Anselm, Archbishop of Canterbury, (ca.1033-1109)

The period from roughly five hundred to fifteen hundred is known as
the "middle ages." With the breakup of the Roman Empire, Europe
became increasingly separated into many small kingdoms with local
rulers, many of whom were pagans. Culture and learning declined to
such an extent that the early Middle Ages were sometimes referred to
as the "Dark Ages" by Renaissance scholars. In this context of social
and political upheaval, the church was at times the only institution that
preserved the knowledge of antiquity. In addition to keeping learning
alive in its era, the medieval church has passed on to posterity the

witness and writing of many pious souls who served Christ faithfully during the often difficult middle years.

THE DESCENT OF DARKNESS

Clovis, King of the Franks, was converted to Christianity around the year five hundred. He and his successors exercised dominion over the churches within their borders, appointing laymen as bishops and selling church offices ("simony"). Pope Gregory the Great tried to reform these practices but with little success under the Frank Merovingian rulers. With the continuing theological and political distance from the Greek-speaking church in the east, the papacy now turned to the powerful Germanic kings for protection. An official alliance between the papacy and the Frank Carolingian kings was established when Pepin the Short appealed to the pope to sanction his kingship and in 754 was crowned "protector of the Romans" by the pope. Pepin defeated the invading Lombards in Italy and gave both civil authority and the conquered lands to the pope. This was the first phase of what would later become the Italian Papal States.

The new church-state alliance was solidified under Pepin's son, Charlemagne, who was the greatest of the Frankish rulers. Charlemagne extended the boundaries of his kingdom to include France, Italy, Spain, the Low Countries and much of Germany. On Christmas day in eight hundred, he was crowned as "Holy Roman Emperor" by the pope. For many in Europe this signaled a rebirth of the old Roman Empire under Christian emperors in late antiquity. The crowning of Charlemagne foreshadowed the endless contest between royal power and papal authority for domination in medieval society.

Charlemagne took aggressive leadership in church life within his vast empire. He called thirty-three councils, nominated candidates for bishop and reformed monasteries, clerical dress, the church's music and liturgy. He was instrumental in the "Carolingian Renaissance," which emphasized the study of classical literature and the copying/preserving of these older texts.

After his death, Charlemagne's empire began to disintegrate through civil wars and the destruction resulting from invasions of Magyars from the east and the Vikings from the north. By nine hundred there were no strong kings, and anarchy prevailed, resulting in feudalism that would persist in parts of Europe for centuries. In this decentralized feudal form of government, local petty lords who owned land became the sovereigns of all who dwelled on their property. Peasants were vassals of the noble who might live in a castle, and for their service, the noble promised protection. The local lord was in turn the vassal of a greater lord up to the king. Many nobles, however, were known to resist their sovereigns in the extension of their own power.

In the midst of this civil disorder, church property was either plundered by invaders or taken over by nobles. Often the local lords built their own churches and appointed clergy and bishops to serve in them. Sometimes church office was given to relatives or sold to the highest bidder. The popes became pawns of the Italian nobility and several popes were corrupt men who abused their office for personal advantage. Church life sunk to new depths as society collapsed into anarchy.

Another contributing factor to this "descent of darkness" was the birth of Islam in the year 622. Muhammad's proclamation of Islam ("submission to God") was not accepted in Mecca, so he retreated with his followers to Medina in 622 (the *Hegira*) and established headquarters. Mohammad announced the impending judgment of the world where everyone would receive reward or punishment based upon one's deeds. Allah is the great judge who has revealed the divine will in the Koran. There were five "pillars" of Islam: the confession, "There is no god but Allah, and Muhammad is his prophet," prayer five times daily, charitable gifts, fasting in the holy month of Ramadan and pilgrimage to Mecca. Mohammad returned to Mecca, purified the city and spread his message throughout all of Arabia by the time of his death in 632.

The followers of Mohammed extended their power by the sword as the Koran directed: "Let them therefore fight for the religion of God, who part with the present life in exchange for that which is to come; for whosoever fighteth for the religion of God, whether he be slain, or be victorious, we will surely give him a great reward."[2] The Mohammedan Empire by 715 had taken over Syria, Jerusalem, much of North Africa, and parts of Spain. The church in these places was allowed liberty for a season but was increasingly swallowed up by Islam. The areas of Western Europe which were lost to the Muslims would later be liberated but this was not the case in the East. By the middle of the tenth century Christianity in the West had sunk to a new low; but despite the darkness, there were rays of light, and the fires of faith kept burning.

MONASTICISM

The omnipresent monasteries of medieval society had deep roots in the earliest centuries of the church. The first generations of believers saw the life of Christ (simplicity, prayer, fasting, celibacy) as a model for true spiritual life; to follow Christ was to reject the world. For some, this meant a physical separation from worldly temptation to a solitary place for contemplation. The first monks were hermits who left society for the wilderness areas where they could practice extreme measures of self-denial. History records that some of the ascetics: abstained from marriage, ate no meat, denounced possessions, slept while standing, wore no clothing, would not cut their hair, or refused to speak. One well known "pillar hermit," named Simeon Stylites (400s), lived on top of a column sixty feet high for thirty-six years. While his disciples attended to his needs, Simeon would exhort the crowds who came seeking his counsel.

The most famous of the hermits was St. Anthony of Egypt (d.ca. 350) who sold all his possessions and entered the desert to live a life of complete devotion to Christ. Anthony practiced rigorous renunciation becoming a great spiritual hero in the church. Athanasius, the famous defender of Nicene orthodoxy, wrote a popular biography, *The Life of Anthony*, which helped further the influence of the ascetic lifestyle in the Western church. Evagrius of Pontus recorded the sayings of the "Desert Fathers" in the *Praktikos* ("on Practice"), and John Cassian translated Evagrius' writings into Latin so that the West would have access to the desert monks' wisdom.

It was not long before ascetics organized themselves into communities, producing recognized "rules" for each group which gave uniformity to their particular practice of the spiritual disciplines. The early monastic communities ate and worshiped together daily, and monks were required to work so that the community could be self-supporting. Monasteries often provided assistance for travelers, the poor, orphans and the sick.

In the Western church, the most important development in monasticism was the "rule" written by Benedict of Nursia at the monastery of Monte Cassino in Italy. The *Benedictine Rule* (529) included specific directions for worship, which was four hours daily, distributed through seven periods, some solitary and some communal. The rule also provided guidelines for required labor and study. Someone desiring to be admitted to the monastery went through a one-year probationary period before taking a threefold vow of obedience, poverty and chastity. This was a lifelong commitment from which one could be released only by the abbot's permission. The *Benedictine Rule* became the model rule and official form of monasticism in much of the West. It was the universal form of monasticism throughout all of Charlemagne's empire.

One of the great contributions of monasticism was the missionary efforts of the monks who evangelized Europe and spread the *Benedictine Rule* in new monasteries established among converts. Gregory the Great sent Benedictine monks to England under the leadership of St. Augustine of Canterbury who preached to the Anglo-Saxons. By 650, most of England had become Christian, and missionaries from England were sent back to the European continent. These missionaries from England were either Irish Celtic monks, whose spiritual ancestor had been St. Patrick in the fifth century, or Benedictine monks. Missions from the British Isles carried the Gospel message to France, Switzerland, Italy, Holland and Germany.

The story of St. Patrick (ca. 390-ca. 460) was illustrative of the brave missionary monks who risked their lives in spreading the gospel among pagan peoples. Patrick had been raised in a Christian family in old Roman Britain where Christianity had arrived in the earliest centuries after apostolic times. Kidnapped by invading Irish warriors as a teenager, Patrick was taken to Ireland as a slave and labored as a shepherd for six years. While in Ireland, Patrick had much time for prayer as he tended sheep. Eventually, he escaped and was able to make his way back to England, but God stirred Patrick's heart to return to the land of his idol-worshipping captors. God blessed his evangelistic efforts, protecting him from Druids and giving him a great harvest of Irish souls. Patrick organized the Irish church around monasteries, which he built in every community where Christianity took root.

Another noteworthy medieval missionary was a Benedictine monk named Boniface who labored among the barbarian Germanic tribes. With the support of the pope, Boniface began his ministry among the Franks in 718, destroying pagan idols, building churches and monasteries and reforming existing churches that had become semi-pagan. As an old man in his seventies, he continued his missionary labors and traveled to Frisia (Holland) preaching to pagans. He was killed there with fifty other Christians by a violent mob.

Monks were instrumental in the preservation of learning and ancient manuscripts during the middle ages, often serving as teachers of both classical education and the Christian faith. Some of the monasteries had great libraries and copying rooms where ancient literature and writings of the church fathers were preserved for later generations. Monasteries also served as the training centers for clergy during a time when European civilization was preoccupied with other matters. Monasticism and ascetic principles are easy to criticize because of their excesses, spiritual elitism and seclusion from the world. Nonetheless, it was the monks who evangelized, handed down the faith and gave the church its leaders for a thousand years.

THE EASTERN CHURCH

A massive branch of the worldwide body of Christ is the Eastern Orthodox family of churches (Greek, Russian, Bulgarian, Romanian, etc.) which have deep roots in ancient Christianity. A distinctive practice of Christianity developed in the East over many centuries. Differences with the West were primarily in the areas of liturgy and polity, although there were some variations in points of doctrine. There were also unique languages and cultures in the East which augmented an ever-widening chasm between the Greek East and the Latin West. The ecclesiastical bond eroded over time as certain historical events exacerbated the already strained relationship. Formal separation finally took place during the middle ages, and sadly the schism would prove to be permanent.

The Churches of the East shared with the West a common catholic faith that is, a universally recognized orthodoxy on fundamental elements of the faith. The doctrinal consensus displayed in the ecumenical creeds of the first five centuries was embraced by both East and West. Eastern Orthodox patterns of observing the sacraments and monasticism all shared the common heritage of earliest Christian practice. The greatest preacher of the early church was from the East, St. John Chrysostom ("the golden mouth") bishop of Constantinople (d.407) who was known for his powerful expository sermons. Over a thousand years later, John Calvin would be a student of Chrysostom, copiously citing the famous fourth-century preacher in his own writings.

At certain times Orthodox churches recognized the primacy of the Roman see, but the competition for power between the patriarch of Constantinople and the pope increasingly became an obstacle to unity. In the East, ecclesiastical authority ultimately resided in collegial church councils with the bishops representing the whole church and not in one Roman bishop. When Constantine and his successors made their primary residence in the East, the see of Constantinople (modern Istanbul) became more prominent for Eastern churches.

Eastern Orthodox Christianity stressed "other-worldliness" with more focus on ascetic withdrawal from the world and contemplation rather than scholarship or service. Mysticism was more pronounced among the Eastern monks. From an Eastern perspective, the "Divine Liturgy" (true worship) was the context for theology – God is an incomprehensible mystery who cannot be described in human language. Orthodox worship was known for its incense, bells, icons, chanting and priestly vestments – sometimes described as theology in color. "Holy Tradition" was an inclusive Orthodox term that referred to ecumenical councils, writings of the Fathers, the liturgy, canon law, icons and Holy Scripture. Orthodox converts take this vow: "I accept and understand Holy Scripture in accordance with the interpretation which was and is held by the Holy Orthodox Catholic Church of the East, our Mother."

Specific points of divergence from the Roman church included: the date of Easter, celibacy of clergy, clergy hairstyle, use of unleavened bread in the Eucharist, purgatory, primacy of the pope and the "filioque" addition to the Nicene Creed. Several attempts to reconcile the conflicting beliefs were made but were ultimately unsatisfactory. It was a growing distrust and competing claims to ecclesiastical authority that finally consummated the split. One episode accentuates the conflict between Constantinople and Rome – known as the "Photian Schism" (858-880). Photius had been appointed Patriarch (bishop) of Constantinople when the Patriarch Ignatius was deposed by the emperor. Meanwhile, the Roman pope, Nicolas I, inserted his own authority into the affair by declaring Ignatius the true patriarch and deposing Photius who responded by denouncing the Latin Church, particularly stating his objections to the *filioque* clause in the Creed. An Eastern council meeting in Constantinople pronounced a sentence of deposition against the pope, but a new Byzantine Emperor reinstated Ignatius. When the emperor died, Photius was restored by a council with the consent of the pope, thus the twenty-year breach between the Latin and Greek Church was healed but only temporarily.

The schism of 1054 is the traditional date for the final rift between Roman and Orthodox churches. A clash occurred between Pope Leo IX and the Patriarch Michael Cerularius of Constantinople over authority in the churches of Sicily. Representatives of the pope laid on the altar of St. Sophia, the great church in Constantinople, a sentence of excommunication and denunciation of Michael when he refused to receive the papal delegation. In part the denunciation stated: "Let them be anathema ... with all heretics: yea with the devil and his angels. Amen, Amen, Amen."[3] The patriarch consequently condemned the pope and his legates. There were later negotiations attempting to mend the breach but the church in East and West had at last gone their separate ways.

One of the greatest challenges to Eastern Christendom was the Islamic invasion into the Byzantine Empire which experienced great losses of territory including Palestine; even Constantinople itself was at times in danger. Under these desperate circumstances the Emperor Alexius appealed to Pope Urban II for help to fight the Seljuk Turks in the late eleventh century. Urban responded with a summons of the European nobility to undertake a crusade to rescue the Holy Land from infidels. The victorious First Crusade captured Jerusalem in 1099, and the crusaders established four independent Latin kingdoms rather than return the territory to the Byzantine Emperor, which led to conflicting claims of jurisdiction by Rome and Constantinople. Succeeding crusades were not as successful as the first one, as parts of the Holy Land were lost and recaptured several times. The tragic Fourth Crusade in 1204 was diverted from its original purpose and ended up pillaging

Constantinople where Western rule was imposed for fifty years until control was regained by Eastern authorities. This Western occupation of the capital of Byzantium exacerbated the bitter feelings between East and West. By 1291 all the Crusader states in the east had fallen back into Muslim hands. From a Christian point of view, the Crusades were not wars of aggression but "a belated military response of Christian Europe to over three centuries of Muslim aggression against Christian lands, the systematic mistreatment of the indigenous Christian population of those lands, and harassment of Christian pilgrims."[4]

Despite the turmoil with Muslims and Roman Catholics, the Orthodox church made significant gains through its mission work among the Slavs, Avars, Bulgars and Magyars who had settled in parts of the northern section of the Byzantine empire and by the tenth century had adopted Byzantine culture and Christianity. The most famous of the early missionaries to the Slavs were two Greek brothers named Cyril and Methodius who visited the Slavs in 860 at the request of the prince of Moravia. Out of the brothers' mission endeavors, the Gospel was spread to Bulgarians, Serbia and Romania. The Russians also accepted Christianity in 988 when, according to tradition, Prince Vladimir of Kiev embraced the witness of his emissaries to Constantinople who reported to him the awesome wonders of Orthodox worship at the St. Sophia Church. Vladimir adopted the Orthodox faith as Russia's official religion and ordered the mass baptism of his subjects. The Orthodox churches became ethnic state churches that utilized national languages rather than pressing for uniformity like the Latin West. The Eastern church continued to expand north and east even after Constantinople finally fell to the Turks in 1453.

In the Eastern church there was more willing subordination to the state than in the West where church/state relations were a perpetual power struggle between popes and kings. For centuries the Byzantine emperors practiced "caesaropapism" – the supreme authority of a secular ruler over the church so that even doctrine is subject to state control. Constantine was the initiator of imperial church management, and successive Eastern emperors maintained ecclesiastical uniformity through government enforcement. Unity of the empire demanded that divisions and quarrels be settled among the Christian population. Emperors summoned bishops to "ecumenical councils" where the head of state presided; he guaranteed that council decisions became official law and "heretics" were deprived of church office and exiled. Orthodox emperors issued decrees on church matters and nominated the patriarch of Constantinople who could not hold office without imperial consent.

An example of the emperors' dominance over the church was the Iconoclastic Controversy (726-787). Icons – images of Christ, Mary, angels and saints, had become popular in many churches, but some bishops preached against icon veneration as idolatry. The Emperor Leo III launched an attack on icons ordering that all religious icons in churches or public places had to be destroyed. There was popular rebellion against this edict, and Leo reacted by having the icon supporters excommunicated and exiled. Other emperors were not so energetic in opposing icons, but finally the Empress Irene, in order to restore peace to her realm, called into session the Second Council of Nicea (787) which endorsed the use of images in worship. The council declared:

> ... the venerable and holy images, as well in painting and mosaic
> as of other fit materials, should be set forth in the holy Churches
> of God ... For by so much more frequently as they are seen in
> artistic representation, by so much more readily are men lifted
> up to the memory of their prototypes, and to a longing after
> them; and to these should be given due salutation and honorable
> reverence, not indeed that true worship of faith which pertains
> alone to the divine nature; ... For the honor which is paid to the
> image passes on to that which the image represents, and he who
> reveres the image, reveres in it the subject represented ...[5]

Iconoclasm (destruction of icons) did not cease with the council decree as later emperors would again be sympathetic to iconoclasm. In 843 the iconoclasts were ultimately condemned and the controversy ended, but throughout the conflict, it was the emperor who determined church practice and punished dissenters to imperial policy.

While most Eastern Christians willingly submitted to government authorities, there was resistance to enforced theological uniformity among eastern Monophysite churches who were therefore persecuted. The Monophysites had rejected the fifth-century Chalcedonian definition of the person of Christ and believed instead that Jesus Christ had only one nature. Monophysitism had its greatest support in parts of the Eastern empire that had been conquered by Muslims. There independent Monophysite churches existed among Egyptian Copts, Syrian Jacobites, and the national church of Armenia. There were also independent African churches in Nubia (Sudan) and Ethiopia which depended on the Coptic Church for support. Another autonomous eastern group was the ancient Nestorian Church ("Church of the East") whose missionary settlements reached as far as Arabia, India and east Asia and still survive today as a small group of "Assyrian Christians" in Kurdistan.

WESTERN MEDIEVAL CHRISTIANITY

In the medieval Holy Roman Empire of the West, beginning with the tenth-century ruler Otto I, the church was dominated by German kings. The kings controlled the appointment of bishops, abbots and the pope, a practice called "lay investiture" (laymen appointing to church office), which remained a contested issue between church and state for many years. A reforming monastic movement at Cluny in central France (910) had as one of its major goals independence from control of local lords and the king. The Cluniac reform of monasteries and church life spread through much of Western Europe.

A series of reforming popes elevated the papacy to new heights during the second half of the middle years, beginning with Leo IX who brought reform by instituting a college of cardinals responsible for electing the pope thus attempting to secure independence from state interference. Hildebrand (Gregory VII), who became pope in 1073, claimed absolute supremacy over all kings as testified by the document *Dictatus Papae* (usually associated with Gregory's views). It boldly proclaimed: "The Roman bishop alone is properly called universal ... he alone has the power to depose bishops and reinstate them ... the Pope is the only person whose feet are kissed by all princes ... he has the power to depose emperors ... he can be judged by no man ... The Roman Church has never erred, nor ever, by the testimony of Scripture, shall err, to all eternity."[6] Gregory's reforms included enforced clerical celibacy which was met with much opposition at the time but ultimately triumphed in the Roman Catholic Church.

Gregory won several significant victories over the lay investiture question, the most glaring example being his victory over Henry IV. The Emperor Henry IV had defied Gregory's claims to authority and appointed his own bishops, compelling them to renounce the pope. Gregory retaliated by excommunicating Henry and by issuing a papal decree that stated: "I withdraw the government of the whole kingdom of the Germans and of Italy from Henry the King ... For he has risen up against the Church with unheard of arrogance ... And I forbid anyone to serve Him as king."[7] The German nobles used the decree as an opportunity to revolt, and Henry, now in a politically precarious position, humbly submitted to the pope. After making Henry wait three days, barefooted in the snow outside the castle of Canossa, Gregory finally forgave the emperor. A compromise on the lay investiture question was reached at the Concordat of Worms in 1122 – the church could elect its own bishops, but the king should be present to receive homage and confer temporal rights.

The papacy reached the peak of its power under Innocent III (r. 1198-1216) who forced his will on the German Emperor as well as the kings of England and France. Using the method of interdict (prohibiting the administration of sacraments), he compelled secular rulers to follow his wishes. Innocent's authority was also recognized in Spain, Norway, Sweden, Prussia and Poland; by this period Scandinavia had been evangelized by the German church, and Eastern Europe had been introduced to Western Christianity by the English. In 1215, Innocent summoned to Rome representatives from all of Christendom, including the Eastern Christians, to the Fourth Lateran Council, an ecclesiastical gathering of almost five hundred bishops. The pope presented, and the council approved, decrees and canons affirming such doctrines as transubstantiation, papal primacy and the necessity of annual confession to a priest. Never again would papal prestige wield such widespread influence in affairs of both church and state.

With the papal reform came an increase in study and education. During the dark times of Europe, learning had survived only in the monasteries and cathedral schools in the large cities where bishops resided. The best teachers in the cathedral schools began to attract more students, and new schools were established which gradually led to the founding of the universities. The medieval universities began under the auspices of the church, obtained their charters from the pope and drew most of the professors from monasteries. Instruction in the arts and sciences were offered along with the "queen of sciences" – theology. The first universities were started in Paris and Oxford by 1150, and it was the university faculties, "the Schoolmen," who developed and articulated the medieval theology of the Roman Catholic Church. The academic work of these scholars became known as "Scholasticism" which referred to theological subject matter as well as a particular method of instruction. The universities set the standard for theological inquiry in Western Christendom for centuries.

The medieval Schoolmen attempted to blend philosophy and theology into one system using Aristotle's logic as a means for expressing Christian doctrine. Natural reason was viewed as a complement to faith and should be utilized to understand God's revelation. Theological truth can be rationally demonstrated and, therefore, aids the church in understanding and explaining its beliefs. For the Scholastics, faith and reason were harmonious, but certain church leaders were not so enthusiastic about the new learning. Bernard of Clairvaux and Hugo of St. Victor were skeptical about the usefulness of reason and philosophy believing instead that mystical union with Christ provided certainty to faith. True understanding comes through mystical knowledge of Christ and the sacraments of the church apart from reason.

A remarkable theologian of this period was Anselm who was appointed the Archbishop of Canterbury in 1093. Anselm is best known for his ontological argument (argument from the nature of being) for God's existence and his famous words: "I believe so that I may understand." It was his discussion of the atonement, however, that had the most far-reaching influence in the Western Church. In *Cur Deus Homo* (Why the God Man) he expressed the classic satisfaction theory of the atonement, explaining that humanity had dishonored God by sin, therefore God must demand satisfaction. God cannot simply forgive for that would upset the moral order of the universe and destroy God's integrity. Since humankind sinned, a human being must offer satisfaction to God, but no person can offer more than is already owed. The God-Man, Jesus Christ, was God's solution – as a human being and infinite (as God), Christ died on the cross, satisfying God's honor and, therefore, making salvation possible.

Peter Abelard (d. 1142), master of the school at Notre Dame in Paris, challenged the "satisfaction theory" of Anselm, offering his own ideas about Christ's death. Abelard believed God the Father could take no pleasure in the death of His Son as the ground of forgiveness – God is love and ready to forgive without satisfaction, only requiring that men be penitent. Christ revealed His love by sharing our nature and persevering even unto death. This love awakens a responsive love in the sinner which liberates from the power of sin. Abelard's concept has been called the "moral influence theory" of the atonement, a precursor of modern liberal views that would emerge much later. Church leaders like Bernard of Clairvaux opposed Abelard who was eventually condemned for his heretical views and excommunicated.

Abelard's legacy continued through one of his pupils, Peter Lombard (d. 1160), who wrote the *Sentences*, the standard theological textbook of the middle ages. Lombard's *Sentences* was a system of Christian doctrine that combined citations from the Fathers and creeds on particular topics and then attempted to resolve conflicting statements by the use of reason. Even in the sixteenth-century Reformation era, university students like Martin Luther were still writing commentaries on the *Sentences* of Lombard.

The high water mark of Scholasticism was the writing of Thomas Aquinas in the thirteenth century. Aquinas became famous as a philosopher for "the five ways" or proofs for the existence of God and his use of analogy for language about God. His greatest achievement was the massive *Summa Theologica*, in which he employed Aristotelian logic to help explain the major themes of Christian faith. Aquinas believed that revelation and reason were non-contradictory since both come from God. However, many Christian truths, though not contrary to reason, could not be rationally demonstrated. Reason lays the foundation that was completed by faith. Roman Catholic scholastic theology solidified in Aquinas whose theology would receive official sanction at the sixteenth-century Council of Trent, the Roman church's response to the Protestant Reformation.

Aquinas' understanding of how grace worked and salvation was applied to sinners became a bulwark against sixteenth-century Protestant ideas. While acknowledging the necessity of the atonement, Aquinas taught that salvation also included works. By the grace won through

Christ's satisfaction, the Christian is then able to perform works that gain merit with God. If such merits outweigh the sins committed then the individual may avoid purgatory and go directly to heaven; but this is rarely accomplished. If one's sins are greater than one's merit then he must do penance which includes contrition (sorrow for sin), confession (to the priest), absolution (by the priest), and satisfaction (by the sinner). Even the forgiven sinner must pay certain "temporal penalties" which was often satisfaction offered through forms of spiritual discipline such as giving alms and fasting.

There was another alternative, according to Aquinas, because the church had the authority to transfer to the sinner merits earned by Christ and the saints. From this "Treasury of Merits" the pope could withdraw and bestow merit on the Christian in need. This transfer usually came through acts of service such as going on a crusade or visiting a shrine. Later the transfer of merit (indulgences) was sold by popes to raise money for the church. A crucial part of this system was the seven sacraments: baptism, confirmation, penance, Eucharist, extreme unction, marriage, and ordination, each of which conveyed grace to the recipient. The faith of the person receiving the sacrament was not necessary to receive grace but only the proper performance of the sacrament by the priest.

Baptism was ordinarily administered to infants, and those not baptized went to "limbo" (rather than heaven) where they are excluded from full blessedness. A child or adult baptized by a priest received cleansing from original sin, and in an emergency baptism could be administered by a layperson. Confirmation by the bishop's laying on of hands was typically received in adolescence and was understood as conferring additional grace thus enabling the young person to avoid temptation. After baptism and confirmation one might still commit "venial" or "mortal" sins for which the sacrament of penance will be necessary. The Lord's Supper was observed in two forms, the Mass and Communion – in the Mass, only the priest partakes of the elements, in Communion the worshiper partakes of the bread only. The reason for the lay exclusion from the cup was due to the doctrine of "transubstantiation" which assumed that the bread and wine were transformed into the actual body and blood of Christ at the moment of consecration. Aquinas' *Summa* provided a philosophical definition of transubstantiation using Aristotelian categories that distinguished "substance" (the essence of something) and "accidents" (outward characteristics). According to this teaching, the whole substance of the bread and wine become the whole substance of Christ's body and blood, but the outward appearance remains bread and wine.

Extreme unction ("last rites"), or the anointing of the sick, became a sacrament performed only for those in danger of death, providing forgiveness of sin and possible restoration of health. The first five sacraments covered a person from cradle to grave and were intended for all, but marriage and ordination were not for everyone. Marriage is for life and can be annulled only by the church for specific causes. Ordination is by the bishops' laying on of hands so that through apostolic succession the clergyman was enabled to bestow grace through the church's sacraments. The medieval church taught that the sinner was dependent on the "one, holy, catholic and apostolic church" for salvation for only here was grace dispensed through the seven sacraments. All Christians must embrace these teachings of the church and be in subjection to the papacy.

REFORM MOVEMENTS

In the late Middle Ages new nation states emerged in Europe as kings strengthened their control of the nobility. Monarchs began to establish centralized government over national affairs while the papacy was seeking to exercise its own power among the states. Conflict between kings and popes was inevitable and the struggle was particularly significant between the papacy and the French kings. Pope Boniface VIII and Philip IV of France first came into conflict over the question of church taxation when Boniface forbade the payment of any taxes on church properties, although he eventually allowed voluntary payments. It was the arrest of a bishop by Philip that elicited the infamous papal bull, (Lt. *bulla*, "seal") *Unam Sanctam* (1302), in which Boniface declared that the state had no authority to try clerics and insisted on papal supremacy. The bull stated: "… we declare, state, and define and pronounce that it is altogether necessary to salvation for every human creature to be subject to the Roman pontiff."[8]

Philip responded to the papal assertion by having French bishops condemn Boniface as a heretic and sending soldiers to rough up

Boniface, who died shortly thereafter. The king's victory over the pope signaled the end of papal power that could force its will on secular rulers. Following the humiliation of Boniface, the next generation of popes were controlled by French monarchs during the period 1309-1377, called the "Babylonian Captivity of the Papacy," when the papal residence moved to Avignon in southern France. The Avignon papacy was a time of expanding church bureaucracy and wealth – the pope's income now far exceeded that of any European sovereign.

When the papacy finally moved back to Rome, a rival French pope was elected and thus began the "Great Schism" (1378-1417) when there were two or more rival popes, each supported by various nations of Europe. The solution to the Great Schism was sought in the Conciliar Movement, an attempt to assert as the Eastern church had always avowed that a general council was superior in authority over a pope. The bishops at the Council of Constance (1414-1418) were adamant: "This holy Council of Constance ... has its authority immediately from Christ; and that all men, of every rank and condition, including the Pope himself, is bound to obey it in matters concerning the faith, the abolition of the schism, and the reformation of the Church of God in its head and its members."[9] The Council of Constance ended the Great Schism by not recognizing any of the competing claimants to the see of St. Peter and replaced them with a new pope, Martin V, in 1417. The victory of the Conciliar Movement was short lived as Martin V and future popes reasserted their supremacy over the church.

There were various reform movements that reacted to the worldliness of the papacy and the general decline within the Medieval Church. Following in the footsteps of the Cluniac reform, Cistercian monasteries held before the church the ideals of poverty and spiritual devotion, adhering strictly to the Rule of St. Benedict. Under Bernard of Clairvaux's (1090-1153) able leadership, the Cisterians had a profound impact on the spiritual life of the church. Bernard preached and practiced a humility that challenged the affluent church of his day. He criticized papal abuses and called for the church to return to a more vital spirituality. Divine grace was emphasized by Bernard, whom the Protestant Reformers would honor as a medieval saint for his devotion to Christ in a corrupt age.

Bernard's disciples influenced the church from within the monasteries, but two new thirteenth-century orders, the Franciscans

and Dominicans, left monastic seclusion and commenced teaching and
ministry to the populace in the countryside and cities. The Franciscans,
begun by Francis of Assisi who renounced his wealth in 1208 to live a
life of simplicity and service, drew many followers who renounced all
property and begged for food. Once, while being confronted by the
bishop over the impracticality of poverty, Francis replied: "If we have
any possessions we should need weapons and laws to defend them.
This would sometimes prevent us from loving God and our neighbors."
Many legends grew up around this holy man known for his love of
Christ, his fellow man and God's creation. In his latter days, tradition
said Francis bore in his body the "stigmata" – the wound prints that
Christ had borne in His hands, feet, and side – but how he had received
them was unknown. The Franciscans, known for their mission work,
sent missionaries among the Muslims, and Francis himself traveled to
Egypt during the Fifth Crusade (1217-1221) where he unsuccessfully
attempted to convert the Muslim sultan. Franciscans preached the
gospel in Persia, India and even to the Mongol Khan in China.

Dominic of Castile organized the second Mendicant (or begging)
order, the Dominicans, also known as the "Black Friars" in England
or "Jacobins" in France. The Dominican friars ("brothers") decried
the rich lifestyle of some clergy, stressing instead simplicity, morality
and devotion to study. Dominic was convinced that in order for
men to preach well they must be trained. From the Dominicans and
Franciscans would come most of the teachers, scholars and missionaries
of the middle ages. By the 1200s medieval monasticism had lost some
of its appeal, and the new orders of friars were moving about in society
preaching spiritual renewal.

One of the tragic chapters of Christian history is the story of
medieval Christendom's persecution of dissenters who disparaged and
withdrew from the Roman Catholic church. One of the larger heretical
sects were the Cathari (or "Albigensians,") who appeared in Albi, in
southern France, during the twelfth century and spread rapidly among
the common people of France and Italy. Cathari doctrines, which were
similar to those of Gnostics and Manichaeans, asserted that the world
was an evil creation by the devil, and in order to escape evil matter one
must seek liberation of the soul by ascetic living and meditation. The
way of salvation was revealed by the life-giving spirit called Christ,
whose physical body only appeared real. In 1208, Pope Innocent III

proclaimed a crusade against the Albigensians which almost totally destroyed the movement. Dominican friars were sent into Cathari regions to convert them back to the Catholic faith. The French kings also undertook efforts to wipe out the Cathari by passing laws that permitted the state to punish and execute heretics.

As a part of the Cathari campaign, the popes established Inquisitions, using Dominican friars to search out and bring the heretics to trial. The Inquisition became a powerful tool in the hands of the church to suppress dissent through its extreme methods, including the use of torture to attain a confession. The accused frequently were assumed to be guilty, therefore, the safest route was to confess, since persistently insisting on innocence, the accused ran the risk of being judged an impudent heretic for whom the punishment would be death. When a person was found guilty, he was handed over to the secular authority for burning, because the church could not officially participate in the shedding of blood. Milder punishments included imprisonment, confiscation of property, wearing a yellow cross, prayer, fasting, alms giving, flagellation and pilgrimage. While the Inquisition is abhorrent to modern minds, it is important to remember the mood of the times and the church's concern to protect faithful souls from heretical contamination. Thomas Aquinas, in the *Summa Theologica*, justified the Inquisition in this way: "... there is mercy, with a view to the conversion of them that are in error; and therefore the church does not straight way condemn, but after a first and second admonition, as the apostle teaches [Titus iii:10]. After that, if he be found still stubborn, the church gives us hope of his conversion and takes thought for the safety of others, by separating him from the church by sentence of excommunication; and, further, leaves him to the secular court, to be exterminated from the world by death ..."[10]

The Inquisition was used not only against genuine heretics, but other groups who held primitive Protestant-like ideas also suffered. Peter Waldo and his followers, called Waldensians, believed that the Bible was the supreme authority in the church and rejected the Catholic sacraments, use of images and doctrine of purgatory. They were excommunicated for unauthorized preaching in 1184, and once separated from the established church, the Waldensians formed their own churches. They became more radical in their criticism of the Roman church, which they considered the "Whore of Babylon." They were harshly persecuted by the Inquisition and a fifteenth-century crusade. Nonetheless, Waldensian beliefs were later adopted by the Protestant movement.

There were two key proto-Protestant leaders, sometimes called the "forerunners of the Reformation," who questioned Catholic dogma during the century and a half preceding the Protestant Reformation. The first was scholar John Wycliffe (1330-1384), a popular professor in the University of Oxford who challenged the Roman church's power in England. Wycliffe taught that the Holy Scriptures were the highest authority for Christians, and all doctrine should be tested by the Word of God. Following Augustine, Wycliffe believed the church was the body of the elect and cannot be identified with formal membership in the papal church. He criticized the sacramental system of the church, repudiating the doctrine of transubstantiation and advocated a return to the poverty of the early church. Later in life, Wycliffe denounced the pope as anti-Christ and was forced out of his university position but the English king protected him from further persecution. He was posthumously declared a heretic, and his body was exhumed and burned. One of Wycliffe's lasting contributions was the translation of the Bible from Latin into English after his expulsion from Oxford. Wycliffe trained a number of "poor preachers," called Lollards, to evangelize the English people, and although suppressed by church authorities, they continued to thrive and organized themselves into groups with their own ministers.

Wycliffe's ideas were given further circulation by John Huss, a professor in the University of Prague, who mimicked Wycliffe's views on Scripture and the church. He called for reforming church abuses and gained a large following in Bohemia through his preaching at Bethlehem Chapel in Prague. Papal pressure was applied against Huss' followers by the imposition of an interdict forcing Huss to appear before the Council of Constance in 1415. Although he had been promised safe conduct by the emperor, the preacher from Prague was tried and condemned without being allowed to speak in his own defense. When he refused to recant, the Council ordered that Huss be burned at the stake. This is what happened next:

The ritual of degradation followed. Huss's priestly robe was taken
from him. His hair was cut off, and a paper cap like a dunce cap
was placed on his head. Then he was turned over to the emperor,
who commanded a member of his court to burn Huss as a heretic.
Huss was taken to a meadow outside the city of Constance. His
outer garments were removed. His hands were tied behind him.
Then his body was bound to a stake. Bundles of wood and straw
were place about his body up to his chin. The straw was lit, and
Huss began to sing a hymn. Soon he succumbed to the smoke and
heat. His ashes were placed in a wheel barrow and thrown into the
Rhine River.[11]

The horrible image of Huss' death would inspire the Czech people
who formed the Hussite Church of Bohemia. Within a hundred
years, a student named Martin Luther would study Huss' sermons
and referred to him as a holy martyr. Despite the violent persecution
of those whom the Church deemed "heretics," the reforming ideas of
men like Wycliffe and Huss would help set the stage for the sixteenth-
century Protestant Reformation.

THE CONNECTION

Puritanism, which is the English ancestry of Presbyterianism, has been
called "Reformed monasticism." While many Protestants distance
themselves from perceived monastic abuses, monastic piety, with
its stress on personal holiness, continues to remind us about what it
means to live as a Christian. There are certain monastic personalities
like Bernard and Francis who have been models of piety for the church
throughout the centuries. Bernard of Clairvaux is cited in the writings
of John Calvin more than any other medieval man. Francis of Assisi
remains one of those unique Christian disciples whose life story is for
the ages. St. Francis had the audacity to take the ethical teaching of
Christ seriously and practiced a self-denial that has inspired generations
of believers. The call for serious Christian piety has been a hallmark of
the Reformed faith since the time of Calvin who emphasized self denial
as an essential element of the Christian life.

Eastern Orthodoxy is typically unknown territory for Protestants who are much more familiar with Roman Catholicism, yet, Protestants have more affinity to Orthodoxy than is often recognized. Luther had a favorable attitude towards the "Greek Church," because he shared with them a rejection of Roman Catholic teaching on papal supremacy, purgatory, indulgences, celibacy for clergy and other issues. The Greek church remains today an authentic witness to ancient Christian practice and a reminder to Protestants, who tend to be enamored with all things new, that older forms for worship can still edify God's people in the modern world.

From a Presbyterian perspective, theological development in the middle ages went in unhealthy directions, but there were positive steps forward that furthered Christian understanding of Scripture. One of the crucial contributions of medieval theology was the deepening comprehension of Christ's atonement. Christians from earliest times understood that Jesus Christ came to earth and died for human salvation, but explaining the full meaning of that suffering would develop over time. Anselm helped the church of his day grasp that Christ had satisfied the Father by paying the debt that humanity owed for its sin. The "satisfaction theory" of Anselm would be foundational for the Protestant understanding of Christ's substitutionary atonement which is the consensus teaching of evangelical Christians today.

5

THE PROTESTANT MOVEMENTS
Recovering the Gospel

*"Therefore, since we have been justified by faith, we have peace with
God through our Lord Jesus Christ, ... but God shows His own love
for us in that while we were still sinners, Christ died for us. Since,
therefore, we have now been justified by His blood, much more shall
we be saved by Him from the wrath of God."*

Romans 5:1,8,9

*"... justified by faith is he who, excluded from the righteousness of
works, grasps the righteousness of Christ through faith, and clothed
in it, appears in God's sight not as a sinner but as a righteous man.
Therefore, we explain justification simply as the acceptance with
which God receives us into His favor as righteous men. And we say
that it consists in the remission of sins and the imputation of Christ's
righteousness."[1]*

John Calvin, French-Swiss Reformer (1509-1564)

On the eve of the Protestant Reformation, the late medieval church
was tolerating numerous forms of corruption that undermined the
spiritual vitality of the faith. Church office was for sale ("simony") or
given as a political favor, and although the church officially condemned
such practices, they were still widespread. Bishops were notorious for
"absenteeism" – collecting the financial benefits of their office but not
fulfilling their responsibilities. The clergy abused the people by charging

fees for annulments of marriage, baptism, confession, extreme unction, burial, viewing relics, pilgrimages to shrines and masses for the dead.

The papacy of the early sixteenth century, with its selling of indulgences (purchasing release from penance and purgatory), heavy taxation of churches and clergy, and opulent lifestyle bred popular resentment of the church hierarchy. The bishops had tried to retake control of the church in the Conciliar Movement, which was an attempt to reassert the corporate authority of bishops through councils rather than lone papal authority, but these efforts were short-lived. In addition to political corruption, a number of popes, bishops and priests had concubines and ignored their vows of celibacy. Clerical immorality became so prevalent in a few areas that common-law marriage was accepted, and the church merely collected fines for priests' wives and illegitimate children.

There were multiple groups that had pursued church reform such as the Waldensians, Lollards and Hussites which were still active as the Protestant movement unfolded. A late fourteenth-century spiritual renewal movement in Holland, called the "Devotio Moderna" (the modern way of serving God), would play a unique role in spiritual preparation for the Protestant Reformation. Geert Groote and his followers gathered in communities that held all things in common and took the name, "Brethren of the Common Life." The Brethren focused on monastic virtues of simplicity, industry, love for God and neighbor, and meditation on the life and passion of Christ. Their practice of Christian faith was popularized in the book *The Imitation of Christ* by Thomas a' Kempis (first printed in 1471) which became the most widely read book of its time. The book exhorted Christians to seek perfection by imitation of Christ's earthly life. The Brethrens' influence proliferated through schools they established, out of which came some of the early Reformation leaders.

A few medieval theologians and philosophers supplied a fertile intellectual environment for Protestant ideas through their fresh grappling with old questions. Scholasticism had been questioned by the able minds of the Augustinian-Franciscans Duns Scotus (d. 1308) and William of Occam (d.1347) who both taught that reason cannot be the foundation of faith nor provide faith with certainty. Faith has priority over reason, therefore, theology and philosophy should be kept distinct because they deal with different questions. Occam's theology, which emphasized faith and revelation, became known later as the *via moderna*, as opposed to the older *via antiqua* of the scholastic theologians. His influence passed down to Luther, who referred to William of Occam as "his master," through the philosopher Gabriel Biel (d. 1494), a member of the Brethren of the Common Life.

Other intellectual challenges to the church came from the late medieval movement known as the Renaissance. This cultural rebirth that began in Italy and spread throughout Western Europe was an attempt to recapture the values of ancient times. Renewed interest in Greek and Roman art, architecture, literature, law and politics also included fresh attention to classical Christian texts. This period produced not only talented artists like Da Vinci, Raphael and Michelangelo but also gifted scholars that edited new editions of the great works of antiquity. Through the efforts of men such as Petrarch and Lorenzo Valla, study of the Greek text of Scripture and the church fathers led to more critical examination of authoritarian church dogma and tradition.

The scholars who revived classical learning were known as "humanists," a term which referred to one who studied Latin and Greek texts and fashioned his life in conformity with the virtues extolled in this literature. Humanists were committed to liberal arts education including the study of classics and ancient languages. Many of the humanists were Christian scholars who also immersed themselves in the writings of the early church fathers. The obvious incongruity of the historic faith with current church practice compelled Christian humanists to seek ecclesiastical reform. The reforming cry of the humanist was *ad fontes* (Lt. "to the sources") which was a call to revisit original sources (texts) as the road to transformation. Many of the Reformation leaders like John Calvin, who received a humanist education in France, were experts in Biblical languages and the writings of the Fathers.

One of the most influential of the Christian humanists was Erasmus of Rotterdam (d. 1536) who ridiculed the superstitious beliefs of the church, calling for a return to the study of Scripture and the non-scholastic theology of early Christianity. He produced several editions of various church fathers with notes and a new annotated edition of the Greek New Testament (1516) that would become the foundation of Biblical scholarship for the next 300 years. It was Erasmus' hope that the Bible would be translated from the original into the languages of all peoples. Luther would use the second edition of Erasmus' Greek New

Testament (1519) as the basis of his translation of the German Bible. When the Reformation burst forth, it was said that Erasmus laid the egg that Luther hatched. Erasmus replied, "I laid a hen's egg, Luther hatched a game cock!"

LUTHER'S REFORM OF THE CHURCH

In order to understand Luther's story, one must grasp the unique political context in which his work began. Germany was under seven regional German princes who exercised significant autonomous power but depended upon the Holy Roman emperor, Charles V, for peace and defense. The Hapsburg ruler Charles V was a devout Roman Catholic sovereign over an empire that stretched from Spain in the west to Hungary and Bohemia in the east. He became distressed about a troublemaker named Luther who was unsettling his German subjects, but he was preoccupied with the Ottoman Turks threatening the empire and a war over disputed territory with Francis I, the French king. The German princes' military and political support of Charles V was crucial, so when some of the princes decided to side with the Protestant cause, Charles V faced the political necessity of compromise. Germany would eventually be divided into Protestant and Catholic sectors depending on the particular inclination of the territorial prince. For Luther it meant the ability to proceed with his reforming ideas under the protection of his prince, Fredrick the Wise of Saxony.

In 1505, Luther entered the Black Cloister of Observant Augustinians in Erfurt and began his regimen of prayers, fasts and other ascetic practices. Luther was a "good monk" by his own admission, but his soul was in turmoil because of the spiritual uncertainty he felt as he struggled with his own sense of inadequacy before a holy God. As his fears and anxieties intensified, he sought the Lord's peace, but he was increasingly terrified by the wrath of God. Luther was directed by his mentor, Johann Staupitz, to obtain his doctorate in theology at the University of Wittenberg where he later became a Bible professor. At Wittenberg Luther gave himself fully to the study of Scripture, and he began to question some of the theology he had been taught. Through his study of the book of Romans, the peace of God finally came as the words "He who through faith is righteous shall live" (Romans 1:17) gripped his heart. Luther says: "There I began to understand that the righteousness of God is that by which the righteous lives by a gift of God, namely by faith ... Here I felt that I was altogether born again and had entered paradise itself through open gates."[2] It was this rediscovery of God's grace, in justifying the sinner by faith, which would transform the face of the sixteenth-century church. Luther had no original intent of leaving the Roman Catholic church but future events forced him into inescapable circumstances where his departure became inevitable.

The context of Luther's initial protest against the church was the selling of indulgences to finance the rebuilding of St. Peter's basilica in Rome. The papal emissary Johannes Tetzel was traveling throughout Germany preaching plenary indulgences on behalf of Pope Leo X. An indulgence, the church claimed, would release a person from any future time in purgatory and could even be purchased on behalf of dead loved ones currently suffering in purgatory. Tetzel declared to his audiences, "As soon as the coin in the coffer rings, the soul from purgatory springs." Luther was furious over this abuse of the people. He began preaching against indulgences and on October 31, 1517, he posted the "Ninety-Five Theses," which attacked the sale of indulgences, on the door of the castle church in Wittenberg. The Latin theses were intended for academic debate; however, certain printers quickly translated them into German, printed them and they were circulated throughout Germany within two weeks. The printing press had been developed by Guttenberg only seventy years earlier, and the new medium for communication was revolutionary.

> The spirit of Luther's protest against indulgences is captured in these two theses:
>
> # 32. All those who believe themselves certain of their own salvation by means of letters of indulgence, will be eternally damned with their teachers.
>
> # 86. Since the pope's income to-day is larger than that of the wealthiest of wealthy men, why does he not build this one church of St. Peter with his own money, rather than with the money of indigent believers.[3]

As Luther's views became widespread, the sale of indulgences dropped despite attempts by the pope to silence him. The ecclesiastical situation unraveled rapidly as Luther participated in debates with Catholic scholars and church officials over the next two years. By 1520, Luther put his new ideas into print in three short treatises which attacked churchly errors. In the first work, *An Appeal to the Ruling Class of the German Nationality as to the Amelioration of the State of Christendom*, Luther called on the German princes to reform the church since the Roman church would not reform itself.

The Second Treatise, *The Pagan Servitude of the Church* (or called "The Babylonian Captivity of the Church"), was an attack on the sacramental system of the Church. Luther early argued for three sacraments – baptism, Lord's Supper and penance but later said penance was useful but less than a sacrament. The treatise was a pointed attack on the current Eucharist practice of denying the cup to laity, claims of transubstantiation and treating the Mass as a sacrifice. The third document, *The Freedom of a Christian*, described the Christian life as one of both a freedom from slavery to the law and a freedom for loving obedience to Christ. In this treatise, one finds the famous words, "A Christian is a perfectly free lord of all, subject to none. A Christian is a perfectly dutiful servant of all, subject to all."[4]

During the same year (1520), Luther received a papal bull threatening excommunication unless he recanted and ordered that his books be burned. Luther boldly burned the bull of excommunication from Pope Leo X in public. In 1521, against the wishes of his friends, he appeared at the Diet of Worms before the Holy Roman Emperor Charles V and the German princes. He was given no opportunity to speak but only ordered to recant his errors. Given a day to consider his response, the next morning he was asked: "Do you or do you not repudiate your books and the errors which they contain?" Luther answered:

> Since your majesty and your lordships desire a simple reply, I will
> answer without horns and without teeth. Unless I am convicted
> by Scripture and plain reason – I do not accept the authority of
> popes and councils for they have contradicted each other – my
> conscience is captive to the Word of God, I cannot and I will not

recant anything, for to go against conscience is neither right nor safe. God help me. Amen.[5]

Luther was in physical danger since he was now placed under the ban of the empire. Returning to Wittenberg, he was kidnapped by horsemen from Prince Frederick, who hid Luther in Wartburg Castle for his protection. While in seclusion for ten months, Luther wrote profusely and began translating the New Testament into German from Erasmus' edition of the Greek text. Luther finished his own translation of the New Testament in eleven weeks, and five thousand copies were sold within two months of its first printing. A translation team helped him complete the Old Testament. Luther's popular vernacular Bible ultimately made a significant impact upon the German language and Bible versions translated into other languages.

During Luther's stay at Wartburg castle, his followers in Wittenberg began to give more practical expression to the reforming ideas as the new *evangelische kirke* (evangelical church) developed. The term "evangelical" was adapted by Luther from the Greek word for "gospel," but soon after the word "Protestant" became the popular designation when Lutheran princes at the Diet of Speyer (1529) declared that they must "protest" any legislation that would restrict their reforming movement. A tragic event occurred in 1525 when the peasants who had embraced Luther's teaching rebelled against the nobility. Luther asked the princes to put down the revolt. Thousands of peasants were slaughtered costing Luther the sympathy of the peasants and some of the princes. After the Peasants Revolt of 1525 the divide between German Catholics and Protestants grew. The princes who followed Luther governed the new evangelical churches under their domain with Luther's approval.

Luther's reform spread to Scandinavia, where in the 1520s a national Lutheran church was created in newly independent Sweden. Lutheran churches were also established in Finland, Norway, Denmark and the eastern Baltic states. Not since the New Testament era has one individual had such a dramatic effect on the body of Christ in his own lifetime as Martin Luther. Countless volumes have been written on his life and theological insights that gave birth to a renewal of Christian faith. Luther's reform was an attempt to return to the New Testament ideals and ancient Christianity where it had been faithful to Scripture.

He tried to interpret the plain sense of Scripture as the sole guide for Protestant faith and practice.

Luther's theology was the bedrock upon which Protestantism would build. In his writing Luther articulated the fundamental principles of Protestant faith – "scripture alone," "grace alone," "faith alone," and the "priesthood of all believers." On these primary doctrines, all of the evangelical churches agreed even though differences would arise over other matters of faith. Luther's emphasis on the primacy of Scripture is evidenced early on in his debate with theologian Johann Eck at Leipzig (1519) and his refusal to recant at the Diet of Worms (1520). His convictions were based upon the Word of God and not the word of popes and councils. Luther said: "But everyone, indeed, knows that at times they [the fathers] have erred, as men will; therefore, I am ready to trust them only when they give me evidence for their opinions from Scripture, which has never erred."[6] Luther's followers desired to base their doctrines on the Scriptures, as the *Augsburg Confession* (1530), prepared by Philip Melanchthon and approved by Luther, stated: "... it is manifest that nothing is taught in our churches concerning articles of faith that is contrary to the Holy Scriptures or what is common to the Christian church."[7]

The foundational doctrine for Luther was salvation by faith alone through God's grace alone. Semi-Pelagianism had a fresh impetus in the late medieval Roman Church through certain theologians who argued that humanity must make initial steps of moral effort which God will reward with his grace. The Protestant Reformers rejected this merit-based theology. They returned to an Augustinian view of grace which rejected the notion that human beings could in any way prepare themselves for God's gift of grace. In his treatise *Bondage of the Will* (1525), Luther responded to Erasmus' *Diatribe on Free Will* by insisting that all humanity was in complete bondage to sin and the devil; therefore, "the will cannot change itself." Salvation from this bondage was only possible through a sovereign act of God's grace to change the will. Agreeing with Augustine that sovereign grace implied predestination, Luther said it was "blasphemous for men to praise God for saving the undeserving yet accuse God of iniquity when He damns the undeserving."[8]

Closely related to the doctrine of grace was the Protestant affirmation of justification by faith alone. The medieval church since Aquinas had taught salvation by grace but then added that this grace enabled one to do good works which merited even more grace, enabling an increase of more works and final salvation. These good deeds are added to the work of Christ therefore making justification a process leading to eternal life. The Reformers by contrast excluded even the works of faith as playing any part in man's justification before God. Good works only attest to a justification that has already taken place as Luther forcefully stated: "Now the article of justification, which is our sole defense, not only against all the force and craft of man, but also against the gates of hell, is this: that by faith only in Christ, and without works, we are pronounced righteous and saved."[9]

The fourth hallmark of Luther's reform was his teaching on the priesthood of all believers. While Luther was in favor of the special office of the clergy for maintaining church order, he emphasized that all believers are priests. Every Christian is worthy to stand before God and pray because there are not two classes of believers. Luther said, "Since He (Christ) is a priest and we are His brethren, all Christians have the power and must fulfill the commandments to preach and to come before God with our intercessions for one another and to sacrifice ourselves to God."[10]

There were many additional articles of faith that Luther and other Reformers debated during the sixteenth century, but none were as crucial as these four which struck at the root of the Roman Catholic hierarchical and sacramental system. Reclaiming the Biblical gospel of grace called for some serious surgery in the body of Christ. Luther did not want to divide the church but the Reformers' medicine was too much for Catholicism to swallow. Luther did not desire to heap attention on himself and asked his followers not to call themselves "Lutherans." He knew it was not his own power to persuade that had brought about the massive upheaval of the Protestant reform movement, rather it was the power of God's Word that was breaking up the Roman church's spiritual monopoly in Western society. Luther once quipped,

> I opposed indulgences and all the papists, but never with force. I simply taught, preached and wrote God's Word; otherwise I did nothing. And while I slept ... or drank Wittenberg beer with my friends Philip and Amsdorf, the Word so greatly weakened the

papacy that no prince or emperor ever inflicted such loses upon it.
I did nothing. The Word did everything.[11]

ZWINGLI AND THE ANABAPTISTS

Luther's break with the Roman church signaled the beginning of what
would be a mass exodus from Catholicism. The new Protestant groups,
however, had many differences among themselves over matters of
doctrine and practice. Just how far should the reforming effort go in
distancing itself from the traditions of the medieval church? There was
no uniform answer to this question. Not only was there separation
from the Roman Catholic church, but also continued fragmentation
among the various Protestant groups. One of the first places where
inter-Protestant debate surfaced was in Zurich, Switzerland under the
Reformer Ulrich Zwingli.

While Luther had been busy reforming the German church, a
young priest named Zwingli was called to pastor the central church in
Zurich in 1519. He began preaching through Matthew and speaking
out against Catholic errors. Zwingli convinced the town council at a
public disputation that his reforming ideas were not new but were a
return to the purity of the ancient church. By 1525, the city council
had ordered an end to the celebration of Mass in Zurich churches, and
a new simple form of worship was introduced. Images and paintings
were removed, the choir was eliminated and the Lord's Supper was
celebrated with each worshiper sharing in the bread and the cup.

Zwingli's "reformed" church was more extreme than Luther's in
its rejection of Roman Catholic liturgical practices – Luther believed
many of these practices were indifferent, whereas Zwingli desired to
rid the church of ceremonies unwarranted by Scripture. The two men
also differed in their understanding of the Lord's Supper, particularly
the nature of Christ's presence in Communion. This division between
the German-Swiss and Lutherans was becoming significant politically
because Charles V, having been freed from his wars with the French and
Turks, was beginning to turn his attention to the Protestant heretics.
If a theological consensus could be reached, it might provide the basis
for a political-military alliance among the German-speaking Protestant
groups.

In October of 1529, Philip of Hesse called for a joint meeting at Marburg Castle for Luther, Zwingli and other German-speaking church leaders to discuss Protestant beliefs. Those gathered at the "Marburg Colloquy" agreed on fourteen of fifteen points of doctrine, but they could not reach full accord on the Eucharist. All concurred that both bread and wine should be given the laity, and they all denied the sacrificial nature of the Roman Mass. Luther, however, was unbending in his conviction that the words, *hoc est corpus meum* (Lt. "this is my body") meant that Christ's body and blood were truly present with the bread and wine. Zwingli, on the other hand, believed the Lord's Supper was a memorial with Christ only present symbolically. The two men heatedly sparred over the issues, and unable to compromise, the two German groups remained separated.

Open division with Luther in 1529 was not the first time Zwingli had experienced dissatisfaction with his teaching. Believing Zwingli's reform was inadequate, four years previously a Zurich group had split off from the reformed church over infant baptism. This radical group, preferring a swifter reform in Zurich, began meeting in homes and studying the New Testament. Felix Manz questioned the legitimacy of infant baptism in a 1524 letter to the Zurich city council, and Zwingi was asked to publicly address the issue. Zwingli argued for the covenantal continuity of Israel and the church, and thus the analogy of circumcision with baptism. Since the children of Christians obviously belong to God, how can one refuse the sign? Zwingli believed that infant baptism was implicit in the New Testament, as evidenced in the household baptisms of Acts and Christ's embrace of the little children. The faith of the parents who have the child baptized was important and the faith of the whole church. The Zurich Council accepted Zwingli's Biblical defense for continuing infant baptism, ordered that all parents baptize their children on the eighth day and forbade the radical group from meeting any longer. The group disregarded the order and a few days later, baptized one another, and thus received the label "Anabaptists" (rebaptizers). They were severely persecuted in Zurich – some imprisoned, others drowned to mock their views on baptism. Anabaptists experienced widespread persecution from both Catholics and Protestants in the years that followed, with few finding toleration until late in the sixteenth century.

A number of Anabaptist groups (together called "the Radical Reformation") emerged independently throughout Europe. These groups were very diverse, some being heterodox such as the mystics and anti-Trinitarians. Others were highly educated and more orthodox, like Balthasar Hubmaier who was burned at the stake in 1528 for his Anabaptist views. One of the tragic events that marred the reputation of Anabaptists was the 1535 Munster Rebellion. Extremist leaders instituted polygamy in the "New Jerusalem" in Munster, Germany, with Jan van Leyden as "King David." People were forced to receive baptism or leave the city. Fearing violence, the bishop and prince sealed off the city and thousands were slaughtered. The situation was a disaster for the Anabaptist movement because it appeared to confirm Protestant and Catholic critics' fears that all of them were anarchists.

One group was able to salvage a non-violent vision: the Mennonites in the Netherlands. Their leader Menno Simons, a pious man notorious for his rigid application of church discipline, helped reorganize Anabaptists after Munster. Menno held unique beliefs such as rejecting justification by faith alone and teaching a strange view about the "celestial flesh" of Christ which undermined the reality of his human body. While the theology and practice of Anabaptists varied from group to group, there were some common tenets of faith and practice. An early Anabaptist statement of faith, the *Schleitheim Confession* (1527), listed seven principles:

1. believer's baptism – infant baptism being the "first abomination of the pope"
2. the "ban" – church discipline
3. the "breaking of bread" – communion as a remembrance
4. separation from the world
5. shepherds – ethical requirements for church leaders
6. the "sword" – separation of church and state, pacifism
7. oaths – all swearing forbidden

Modern-day Anabaptists include groups like the Mennonites and other small sects that connect their spiritual ancestry back to the Reformation. Most contemporary Baptists do not trace their heritage to the Anabaptists but rather are theological heirs of the seventeenth-century English Baptist movement rooted in Puritanism.

Back to Zurich – Zwingli died in battle alongside the Swiss Protestants who defended themselves against an invading Catholic army in 1531. Chronologically, Zwingli is the father of the "Reformed" (as distinct from Lutheran) branch of Protestantism, but his untimely death undoubtedly cut short his lasting influence. The Reformed church movement continued in Zurich under Zwingli's able successor Heinrich Bullinger and spread in Switzerland and south Germany under the German reformer, Martin Bucer. The most influential leader for the Reformed churches was the Frenchman, John Calvin, whose name is most often associated with the origins of the Reformed Tradition.

CALVIN AND GENEVA

The "poor timid scholar," as John Calvin described himself, provided unparalleled intellectual leadership to the Protestant Reformation. Through his extensive writing and his pastoral work in Geneva, Calvin developed more fully the implications of Luther's Biblical theology. J. I. Packer put it this way, "Calvin orchestrated Protestant theology ... Martin Luther wrote nearly all the tunes."[12] His writings not only directed the Reformed churches but also had an important long-term impact on the social, economic and political life of modern Western society. Who was this Frenchman and what were his unique contributions?

Calvin was born in Noyon, France in 1509 and received clerical training under his father who worked for the local bishop. His formal studies began at age fourteen in Paris and included education in both law and literature at several universities. Part of a group of young humanist scholars in Paris, he was introduced to Protestant ideas and experienced a "sudden conversion." Calvin writes: "And first, since I was too obstinately devoted to the superstitions of Popery to be easily extricated from so profound an abyss of mire, God by a sudden conversion subdued and brought my mind to a teachable frame, which was more hardened in such matters than might have been expected from one at my early period of life."[13] In 1534, the French King, Francis I, responded to public "placards" criticizing the Mass by persecuting the Protestants – Calvin's own brother Charles was killed.

Fearing for his own safety, Calvin fled Paris and settled in Basel where, in 1536, he completed the first edition of *The Institutes of the Christian Religion*, which some have called the single most influential book of the Protestant Reformation. He modified the *Institutes* multiple times during his ministry expanding the book from an initial six chapters to eighty chapters in four books by 1559. Calvin left Basel in 1536 intending to go to Strasbourg for study. He was detained at Geneva and persuaded by William Farel to remain and help reform Geneva, whose City Council had just two months earlier adopted the Protestant faith.

Calvin stayed in Geneva and set about the program of reform, preaching at St. Pierre Church and drawing up articles of faith for the new Protestants. His reforms were too much for some citizens. By 1538, Calvin and Farel were expelled from Geneva by the council over a controversy concerning the ministers' right to refuse the Lord's Supper to the unfit. Calvin left for Basel to resume his quiet life of scholarship; meanwhile, Bucer was imploring him to come to Strasbourg and pursue his studies there. Calvin arrived in Strasbourg and embarked on preaching to the French-speaking refugees, giving public lectures and writing commentaries on the Bible. Eventually Calvin would write commentaries on most of the Old Testament books and all of the New Testament books except second and third John and the book of Revelation (which he claimed he did not understand).

Back in Geneva the City Council was struggling to handle the situation and asked Calvin to come back. Calvin resisted these overtures but was pressured by Farel and other Protestant leaders thus he agreed, and there he lived until his death in 1564. Upon his return to Geneva in 1541, Calvin picked up his preaching where he had stopped three years previously without saying a word. With his supporters in control of the city, Calvin embarked on an ambitious agenda. He wrote a constitution for the Reformed Church, the *Ecclesiastical Ordinances*, so that the company of pastors could administer church affairs, create regulations for the exercise of moral discipline, and prepare a catechism and reformed liturgy.

The *Ecclesiastical Ordinances* included four church orders – pastors, doctors (teachers), elders and deacons. Deacons were responsible for the church's ministry of compassion, while ministers and elders were responsible for faith and morals in Geneva. Calvin believed that decision-making in the church was best made not by an individual (bishop) nor by all the people, but by those chosen by the people for their leadership qualities. This form of order was Biblical as Calvin noted in his commentary on the Jerusalem Council in Acts 15:

> It may be, indeed, that the disputation was had in the presence of the people. But lest any man should think that the common people were suffered hand over head to handle the matter, Luke doth plainly make mention of the apostles and elders, as it was more meet that they should hear the matter and to decide it. But let us know, that here is prescribed by God a form and an order in assembling synod, when there ariseth any controversy which cannot otherwise be decided.[14]

Reform of the liturgy was a priority for Calvin who desired to recover ancient Christianity's simplicity through a worship service without the pomp and trifles of the Latin Mass. Edification of the people required that Reformed worship be in the vernacular and accommodated to the conditions and tastes of the people since there was no one liturgy for everyone. Music must be weighty and majestic, not entertainment songs. According to Calvin, Biblical integrity was central. What was not commanded in Scripture was excluded, yet the church may accommodate itself to some ceremonies, like the use of Communion candles that do not affect the substance of faith. Calvin had wished for the Lord's Supper to be an integral part of weekly public worship, but this was not implemented in Geneva.

According to Calvin the presence of Christ in the sacrament was spiritual, a mystery accomplished by the special operation of the Holy Spirit. There is a spiritual union between the outward signs (bread and wine) and the invisible things signified by them; therefore, the soul is nourished by faith through participation in the Lord's Supper. Calvin stated: "... the godly ought by all means to live by this rule: whenever they see symbols appointed by the Lord, to think and be persuaded that the truth of the thing signified is surely present there. For why should the Lord put in your hand the symbol of His body, except to assure you of a true participation in it?"[15] Calvin's view was a mediating position between Luther and Zwingi. One can only wonder about the outcome of the Marburg Colloquy had Calvin been there.

Calvin placed great importance in Geneva upon believers living an obedient life that honored Christ. In his writings Luther had utilized a law/gospel paradigm that tended to highlight the law's opposition to the gospel. Calvin, on the other hand, while recognizing the law's purpose to restrain evil and convict of sin, also spoke of the law's positive use as a moral guide for the Christian. Self-denial was the crucial element in dealing with the root sin of self-love with which all Christians struggle. Calvin wrote,

> We are not our own; therefore let us not propose it as our end, to seek what may be expedient for us according to the flesh. We are not our own; therefore let us, as far as possible, forget ourselves and all things that are ours. On the contrary, we are God's; to Him, therefore, let us live and die. We are God's; therefore let His wisdom and will preside in all our actions.[16]

The Geneva pastors and elders set aside every Thursday evening for interviewing church members concerning potential church discipline. Those guilty of public sin were typically exhorted to be more faithful in attending sermons and asked to memorize the Lord's Prayer and Apostles' Creed. They were expected to return after a specified time for a follow-up interview. Calvin and the pastors set a high standard of moral living, for they believed the Church could not survive without discipline. Calvin said: "As the saving doctrine of Christ is the soul of the Church, so does discipline serve as its sinews, through which the members of the body hold together, each in its own place."[17] One tragic episode from Calvin's Geneva was the trial and execution of Michael Servetus who had denied the deity of Christ and was therefore burned as a heretic. Though Calvin favored the death sentence, he did request the more humane form – beheading. In this, Calvin and Geneva were products of their age, since religious toleration had not yet reached the status it holds in modern society.

In Geneva, Calvin set up a form of church government by laymen and clergy in a series of graduated courts with church and state separated in specific ways. The city council exercised political power, and the church's responsibility was to influence the magistrates to make good laws in conformity with God's Word. The church was independent of the civil authority, but Calvin believed that if a government failed to carry out its responsibility and became tyrannical, armed rebellion led by other government officials may be appropriate. Some have traced back to Calvin early concepts of democracy and the justification for revolution.

Social justice was a priority for Calvin, and he labored to see Geneva reflect the gospel in its community life. He encouraged the development of sewer systems, establishing cloth factories, socializing medicine, setting fair interest rates and regulating wages. Calvin called the paying of unjust wages "blood sucking." He observed, "When, thus, a man has someone in his service, he ought to ask himself: 'If I were in his place, how would I want to be treated? I would want to be supported!' When it is a question of our profit or loss, we are very able judges, but, when it is a question of others, we are blind."[18] Calvin believed that work and commerce were a good gift from God, and regarding one's trade he said: "One must be concerned whether it is good and profitable to the community and if it is able to serve our neighbors."[19] Through commerce, men commune with each other and share God's bounty. An association between Calvin's thought and the rise of capitalism has been noted by several scholars.

Education was provided for all children and adults, and a Geneva Academy (later, University of Geneva) was founded in 1559 to train ministerial students. The city of Geneva became the showplace of Europe attracting Protestant students as well as refugees fleeing persecution for safe haven. During their sojourn in Geneva, visitors were exposed to the theology and reforms of Calvin and were able to witness firsthand the implementation of these ideals. Newly enlightened guests returned to their countries carrying the principles of Calvin with them.

Calvin's passion was to establish a holy commonwealth in Geneva, a place where every sphere of life would honor God. His activist Protestant faith flowed out of his understanding of the sovereignty of God. If God is sovereign, he will accomplish his purposes in the earth, and this optimism was the driving force behind all that Calvin accomplished. Even Calvin's doctrine of election was an energizing force as historian Roland Bainton has observed, "For Calvin the doctrine of election was an unspeakable comfort because it ... freed man from concern about himself in order that he might devote every energy to the unflagging service of the sovereign Lord."[20] This was the soul of Protestantism – a life of service to a gracious God.

One cannot reflect upon the life of John Calvin without encountering his infamous teaching on predestination. Too much concentration on this concept is misguided, for it was not the organizing principle of Calvin's thought nor was he an innovator. His views on the subject were identical to Luther and Zwingli who preceded him, all of whom learned their theology from Augustine as well as from St. Paul. Predestination was important for Calvin simply because the Scriptures teach it, and to ignore the truth is to censure the Holy Spirit. The problem is occasioned by preaching, not scholastic musing – some respond to preaching and others loathe it – why is this? God in his mercy has ordained some to eternal life and in his justice ordained some to eternal death for their sin. All are justly condemned; the astonishing factor was not God's condemnation, but his mercy. One should be humbled at the immense goodness of God in rescuing the perishing and avoid excessive curiosity about this great mystery.

PROTESTANTISM SPREADS AND CATHOLICS RESPOND

When Calvin died in 1564, Swiss Calvinist leadership fell to Frenchman Theodore Beza, a professor at the Geneva Academy. While guiding the Reformed church in Switzerland, Beza also gave proxy leadership to Protestants in France, called Huguenots. Genevan support for the French Protestant cause had been a priority of Calvin who wrote a confession for the Huguenots, the 1559 *Gallican Confession* (French Confession), smuggled books into France and trained French pastors at the Academy, many of whom returned home to their death. Protestant churches in France proliferated, and tensions with Roman Catholics escalated to the point of civil war. An attempt to find a Catholic-Protestant compromise occurred at the Colloquy of Poissy (1561) near Paris. Beza played a prominent role in the futile negotiations between French bishops, the royal family and Protestant ministers. The Huguenots suffered cruel persecution by French Catholics for many years. The most violent incident was the massacre of St. Bartholomew's Day, August 24, 1572, when thousands of Protestants were murdered by unruly mobs in Paris. Protestantism in France was almost wiped out when the Edict of Nantes (1598), which had granted toleration to Huguenots, was revoked by Louis XIV in 1685. Thousands of

Huguenots either renounced their faith or immigrated to other parts of Europe, England and the New World, finding fellowship with other Reformed churches in these places; only a very small Reformed church remained in France.

The Protestant story in France is exceptionally brutal, but similar circumstances were evident all over Europe as Roman Catholics resisted the massive protest of Protestants. In Spain and Italy, the Inquisition was effective in persecuting Protestants and driving them into exile. As thousands were leaving the Roman church, voices within Catholicism called for reforming abuses and addressing the issues that were shaking the foundations. There had been a few failed attempts at reconciliation by means of Protestant/Catholic colloquies (conferences) in the 1540's to discuss theological differences. Catholic leaders began to call for a church-wide council to address the Protestant problem, and finally a council was convened at Trent by Pope Paul III. The first session of Trent opened in 1545, the final session not concluding until 1564. The three major sessions of Trent condemned clergy abuses but took a hard-line approach in preserving Roman Catholic teaching, therefore sealing the breach between Protestants and Catholics. The Council of Trent reaffirmed Catholic teaching on the seven sacraments including transubstantiation and explicitly repudiated Luther's understanding of justification by faith. Scripture and tradition were declared to be of equal authority, and the Latin Vulgate with the Apocrypha was confirmed as the church's official Bible.

Protestantism continued to spread throughout Europe despite Catholic hostility. Reformed churches had strong leaders and a church organization independent of secular government, making it easily transferable to different regions. International contact with the Geneva Academy and the translation of Calvin's writings into various languages also enhanced the spread of his theology. In Germany, Reformed theology gained a foothold through the University of Heidelberg where Ursinus and Olevianus taught Calvinist doctrines, co-authoring the *Heidelberg Catechism* (1563). Parts of Bohemia and Moravia were also influenced by Calvinism. The Bohemian Brethren later gave birth to the Moravians of the eighteenth century that influenced John Wesley, the founder of Methodism.

The Netherlands became a stronghold of Calvinism and, like France, was the scene of bloody conflict with Catholics. Reformed churches expanded rapidly in the Low Countries which were under the control of Catholic Spain. Philip II of Spain executed multitudes of Protestants, and civil war erupted when Dutch Calvinists joined forces against Spanish troops. In the 1579 Union of Utrecht, seven northern provinces declared independence from Spain while the southern provinces remained Roman Catholic. Calvinists in the Netherlands adopted Dutch translations of the *Belgic Confession* (1566) and the *Heidelberg Catechism* (1568) as statements of faith. Reformed theology in Holland was further refined through the Arminian controversy when students of Leiden professor Jacob Arminius (d. 1609) challenged Calvinist thinking in the 1610 Remonstrance, signed by 46 ministers. The doctrinal conflict that ensued was resolved by the Dutch Reformed church at the Synod of Dordt (1618,19). The synod's so-called "Five Points of Calvinism"[21] described the Reformed understanding of atonement, grace and predestination in response to questions raised by Arminius' disciples. Protestantism in Holland remained predominately Calvinist for centuries.

One of the most effective tools for curbing Protestant advance was the labor of the Jesuits. Ignatius of Loyola (d. 1556) initiated a new religious order known as the "Society of Jesus" (Jesuits) in 1540, which became the aggressive arm of the pope to propagate the decrees and canons of Trent. The Jesuits, sometimes called "the storm-troopers of the Counter-Reformation," were preachers, teachers and missionaries establishing schools all over Europe and bringing many Protestants back into the Catholic fold. Some of the historically Roman Catholic lands of Austria, Hungary, Poland and southern Germany, that had been lost during the sixteenth-century Reformation, were reclaimed for Catholicism during the Thirty-Years War (1618-1648) in Central Europe. Armies from the Holy Roman Empire, Germany, Denmark, Sweden, France and Spain fought horrific battles that were devastating for Europe and the future of Christendom. The Peace of Westphalia (1648) brought an end to the bloodshed but the resulting political and religious boundaries merely returned to where they had been in a previous Protestant/Catholic settlement, the Peace of Augsburg (1555).

THE CONNECTION

The Reformation period is full of rich stories of courageous persons who put their lives on the line for truths they held dear. The renovation of the church in the sixteenth century set in motion patterns of Protestant practice that still continue 500 years later. Reformers reaffirmed the primacy of Holy Scripture for the church and reengaged Augustine's theology of grace, making it the central affirmation of Protestant belief. Lutheran and Reformed churches remained within classical Christian boundaries as they reaffirmed the ancient creedal testimonies about Christ and reconnected with early Christianity. All too often modern believers mistakenly assume that the Protestant movement was simply a return to New Testament Christianity – this is only partially true. The Reformers' faith and practice was always tethered to the ancient church's interpretation of the Scriptures and was not an attempt to reinvent Christianity apart from the history of the church. Unfortunately, much of contemporary Christian practice is more a reflection of American democratic individualism than it is historically-informed Protestant faith.

It is sobering to observe how quickly sixteenth-century Protestant groups were pitted against one another and turned to state-sponsored violence in order to silence opponents. Prevailing notions of church/state separation were foreign during this age, and on this very point Anabaptist belief was prophetic. It is difficult for contemporary believers to comprehend Catholics and Protestants killing one another, because this action is so far removed from the modern experience of religious toleration in the West. In the twentieth century, as Christianity became increasingly marginalized in Western culture, Roman Catholics and Protestants have collaborated on social issues as well as opening more dialogue on theological differences. In an unprecedented breakthrough, the Lutheran World Federation and the Roman Catholic church issued a *Joint Declaration on the Doctrine of Justification* in 1999 which affirmed, "... that on the basis of their dialogue the subscribing Lutheran churches and the Roman Catholic Church are now able to articulate a common understanding of our justification by God's grace through faith in Christ."[22]

Presbyterians are deeply indebted to the theological heritage from the great Protestant thinker, John Calvin. Reformed views of salvation, the church, sacraments, discipline and polity all have their roots in the Genevan reformer and the Christian leaders that built upon Calvin's seminal insights in the next generations. Presbyterian emphasis on education, cultural engagement, political involvement and social service all have linkage back to Calvin's comprehensive reform of Geneva. A "Reformed world and life view" is a phrase present-day Calvinists use to describe this all-inclusive vision of bringing every aspect of human life under the Lordship of Jesus Christ.

6

REFORMATION
IN THE BRITISH ISLES
Purifying the Church

"... Christ also loved the church and gave Himself up for her, that He might sanctify her, having cleansed her by the washing of water with the word, so that He might present the church to Himself in splendor, without spot or wrinkle or any such thing, that she might be holy and without blemish."

Ephesians 5:25-27

"The notes of the true Kirk, therefore, we believe, confess, and avow to be: first, the true preaching of the Word of God, in which God has revealed Himself to us, as the writings of the prophets and apostles declare; secondly, the right administration of the sacraments of Christ Jesus, with which must be associated the Word and promise of God to seal and confirm them in our hearts; and lastly, ecclesiastical discipline uprightly ministered, as God's Word prescribes, whereby vice is repressed and virtue nourished."[1]

John Knox, Scottish Reformer (ca.1513-1572)

The Reformation in England had its genesis in the same discontent that had plagued the continent. Anti-clerical sentiment due to ecclesiastical corruption, the tyranny of clerical fees and the general worldliness of the church fed an already anti-Roman bias that had permeated English culture for several centuries. An independent English spirit, coupled with the geographic distance from Rome, had created an adversarial environment with strong resentment of any papal intrusion into English affairs. Christian humanist scholars in fifteenth-century England had advocated change, and reformist ideas circulated in England as they had elsewhere. Wycliffe's disciples, the Lollards, with their emphasis on gospel preaching and reading the English Bible, were still active in the early sixteenth century and ministering to the common laborers and craftsmen.

The writings of Luther made their way into England through merchants from Germany and the Netherlands. Lutheran pamphlets were circulating at English universities, but Cardinal Thomas Wolsey, Lord Chancellor of England, ordered the burning of Lutheran books in 1521. King Henry VIII, indignant at Luther's *Babylonian Captivity of the Church*, wrote an apology for the seven sacraments, dedicating the work to Pope Leo X who consequently awarded Henry the title "Defender of the Faith." By 1530, Henry issued a royal decree against all Lutheran literature in England.

The most effective evangelist for Protestant ideas in early Reformation England was William Tyndale. In 1524, Tyndale published an English translation of the New Testament in Worms, Germany which was smuggled into England. Tyndale was a wanted man in England and stayed on the move in Europe to avoid spies while continuing his Old Testament translation work. He was betrayed and arrested near Brussels where he remained in prison for sixteen months before being tried for heresy. Being found guilty he was strangled and burned at the stake. Witnesses recorded that among his last words Tyndale uttered: "Lord, open the king of England's eyes."

THE CHURCH OF ENGLAND

The story of King Henry's eventual separation from Rome is a familiar tale of the political and personal intrigue surrounding Henry who was obsessed with having a male heir to maintain Tudor succession in England. For eighteen years Henry was married to Catherine of Aragon (mother of Mary Tudor) of Spanish royalty and the aunt of Hapsburg emperor Charles V. When Henry sought annulment of the marriage in order to marry Anne Boleyn, Queen Catherine resisted and appealed directly to Pope Clement VII who refused to grant an annulment. In 1533, Henry secretly married Anne Boleyn, who was already pregnant with Elizabeth, in order to secure the legitimacy of succession to the throne. A new pope, Paul III, excommunicated Henry who formally separated England from Rome through the 1534 Act of Supremacy, which made the king the head of the Church of England. The Act of Supremacy declared: "... be it enacted by authority of this present Parliament, that the King our Sovereign Lord, his heirs and successors, kings of this realm, shall be taken, accepted, and reputed the only Supreme Head on earth of the Church of England, called *Anglicana Ecclesia*, ..."[2] Protestants in England complained that the title "Head of the Church" belonged only to Christ hence Queen Elizabeth later changed the title to "Supreme Governor" to accommodate this concern.

Through the Act of Supremacy, the Church of England emerged as a distinct ecclesiastical entity with Henry orchestrating church affairs to suit his purposes. Henry initiated the suppression of Catholic monasteries through the 1536 Act of Dissolution, confiscating monastic property in order to replenish the royal treasury which now doubled in revenue. Not everyone in England was pleased with these arrangements. Numerous Englishmen preferred to remain Catholic, while Protestant sympathizers wanted far more radical reform. Henry and his Anglican party initially pursued a middle path through a compromise called the *Ten Articles* (1536), which attempted to incorporate Lutheran ideas of justification and the sacraments into an English doctrinal statement. By 1539, a new *Six Articles*, written by Henry, contained more blatant Roman Catholic positions on transubstantiation, celibacy, monastic vows, communion in one kind (bread only for laity), the necessity of private masses and confession. Known as "A Whip with Six Strings," non-compliance with the Six Articles resulted in five hundred Protestant arrests, imprisonments and for a few executions by burning.

Meanwhile, Henry persisted in his serial marital affairs – marrying Jane Seymour (mother of Edward VI), Anne of Cleves, Catherine Howard and lastly Catherine Parr in his old age. Henry VIII died in 1547, and nine year old prince Edward took the throne with a regency council comprised of Protestant advisors. Protestantism gained ascendancy during the short reign of Edward VI (1537-1553) under the leadership of Thomas Cranmer, the Archbishop of Canterbury. The *Six Articles* were repealed, and unrestricted printing of English Bibles was permitted with royal orders for an English Bible in every parish church. With persecution of Protestants rampant on the continent, England became a haven for refugees with Zwinglian or Calvinist convictions. The first edition of Cranmer's *Book of Common Prayer* was published in 1549 providing a uniform English liturgy to replace the old Latin Mass. An Act of Uniformity (1549) required that the *Prayer Book* order of worship be followed, and anyone resisting faced six months in prison. In 1552, a major revision, the *Second Book of Common Prayer*, made the sermon more central to the service of worship. A Protestant statement of faith, the *Forty-Two Articles*, was composed by a clergy/lay commission led by Cranmer – the basis of the more well-known *Thirty-Nine Articles* (1571) of the Church of England.

Cranmer's leadership of the Protestant movement in England was indispensable as English doctrine and worship were progressively transformed according to Protestant perspectives. University professorships were filled by continental scholars such as Martin Bucer (Strasbourg) at Cambridge and Peter Martyr Vermigli (Italy) at Oxford, which enhanced the influence of Reformed theology in England. Cranmer's greatest legacy is the *Book of Common Prayer*, being the primary author, though other Reformers had input into its content. The *Prayer Book's* beauty of liturgical expression has been unsurpassed in the English-speaking world. Cranmer's timeless prayer of confession still humbles the souls of modern worshipers:

> Almighty and most merciful Father, we have erred and strayed from thy ways, like lost sheep. We have followed too much the devices and desires of our own hearts. We have offended against thy holy laws. We have left undone those things which we ought to have done, and we have done those things which we ought not to have done, and there is no health in us.
>
> But thou, O Lord, have mercy on us miserable offenders. Spare thou them, O God, which confess their faults. Restore thou them that be penitent, according to thy promises declared unto mankind, in Christ Jesus our Lord.

And grant, O most merciful Father, for his sake, that we may
hereafter live a godly, righteous, and sober life, to the glory of thy
holy name. Amen.[3]

The *First Prayer Book* (1549) has been described as: "A splendid
piece of studied ambiguity, sufficiently traditional to satisfy the
conservatives and yet so phrased, especially as to the Eucharist, to permit
the more advanced reformed to use it in good conscience."[4] Beyond
Cranmer's desire to satisfy everyone, he genuinely struggled with his
understanding of the Lord's Supper for many years. Early on he had
endorsed transubstantiation but then moved to a less closely defined
"real presence" position. Eventually he arrived at a "spiritual presence"
view which understood the communicant to be truly receiving the
body and blood of Christ while the elements remain unchanged after
consecration. The sacrament must be received worthily through faith to
be efficacious rather than the priest merely saying the correct liturgical
words. Cranmer's Eucharistic theology rejected both the idea of mere
symbolism and the superstition of transubstantiation. Cranmer's
vacillation on the Lord's Supper was an honest man's wrestling with
the mystery of Holy Communion which ultimately defies explanation.

Edward VI died at sixteen of tuberculosis and was succeeded by
his sister, the infamous Mary Tudor ("Bloody Mary") in 1553. Mary,
having been brought up by her Spanish Catholic mother, Catherine
of Aragon, decided to rid her realm of Edwards' Protestant officials,
bishops and ministers. She restored the Latin Mass and put Protestant
leaders in prison while others escaped to the continent. Under her
prodding, Parliament began to undo Edward's reforms and repealed
the Protestant Acts of Uniformity. There was, however, resistance to
Mary in Parliament which did not comply with her wishes to disinherit
Elizabeth, reinstate the Six Articles, restore harsh laws against Lollards
and reestablish the monasteries. In 1555 bloody persecution began as
Cardinal Pole commissioned bishops to begin trying the Protestant
heretics of whom approximately three hundred were killed by the
crown. A few of the well-known Marian martyrs, whose stories were
popularized by *Foxes' Book of Martyrs* (1563), include Hugh Latimer,
Nicolas Ridley and Thomas Cranmer.

Hugh Latimer was a revered Protestant preacher who attacked
Catholicism, social injustice and the use of violence. He became a

bishop and advisor to Henry VIII after the Act of Supremacy (1534) but was openly critical of the *Six Articles* for which he spent six years in prison. During the reign of Edward VI he was again a prominent Protestant leader, but under Mary he was sent back to prison. Nicolas Ridley was a professor at Cambridge, serving as Cranmer's chaplain and later as the Bishop of London. Ridley influenced Cranmer toward a Protestant understanding of the Eucharist, and as bishop had stone altars replaced by wooden tables for Communion. When Mary became queen, Latimer, Ridley and Cranmer were arrested and sent to prison in Oxford. Latimer and Ridley were examined, and refusing to recant, they were condemned as obstinate heretics and together bravely endured public burning in 1555. As the fire was lit under Dr. Ridley's feet, Latimer said to him: "Be of good comfort, Mr. Ridley, and play the man! We shall this day light such a candle, by God's grace, in England, as I trust never shall be put out."[5] Latimer expired quickly but Ridley's death, due to the arrangement of the wood, was slow with excruciating pain – eyewitnesses never forgot the dreadful sight.

Archbishop Cranmer, who had witnessed the burning of Latimer and Ridley, was visited in prison by numerous persons urging him to repudiate his Protestant views. Cranmer waivered and signed recantation documents, but Mary had secretly determined to execute him as a public example whether he recanted or not. In St. Mary's Chapel at Oxford, Cranmer was given a chance to speak, but church officials, expecting confirmation of his retractions, heard these words:

> And now I come to the great thing, that so much troubleth my
> conscience, more than any thing that ever I did or said in my
> whole life; and this is the setting abroad of a writing contrary
> to the Truth; which now here I renounce and refuse, as things
> written with my hand, contrary to the truth which I thought
> in my heart, and written for fear of death, and to save my life,
> if it might be; and that is, all such bills and papers which I have
> written or signed with my hand since my degradation, wherein
> I have written many things untrue. And forasmuch as my hand
> offended, writing contrary to my heart, my hand shall first be
> punished therefore; for, may I come to the fire it shall be
> first burned.[6]

Cranmer was brought to the ditch opposite Balliol College where Latimer and Ridley had been killed. When the flames rose, he stretched out his right hand and held it steadfastly in the fire so that onlookers could see it burn.

ELIZABETHAN PURITANS

When Mary died in 1558, the succession fell to her half sister, twenty-five year old Elizabeth, who would hold the throne for forty-five years. Under Elizabeth, England became thoroughly Protestant, and she spread the boundaries of the English empire worldwide. Known for her moderation and willingness to compromise, she steered a course between Catholic, Puritan and Anglican parties in her *via media* (middle way), orchestrating an Anglican establishment that could keep Catholics and radical Protestants under control. The 1559 Act of Supremacy ended any papal interference in England. That same year the *Second Prayer Book* of Edward VI was reintroduced by an Act of Uniformity requiring submission to the Queen's ecclesiastical laws or face expulsion from clerical office.

During Queen Elizabeth's reign, the Puritan movement began its initial stages as fresh hope for an advanced Protestant reform reemerged. The movement was not monolithic, generating variegated groups who shared a desire to reform Elizabethan England, but differed about how to implement the vision. There were Puritans loyal to the Church of England and Separatists who refused to participate in the Elizabethan Settlement and sought complete independence from Anglicanism. Another Puritan party favored organizing themselves within the established church – a church within a church. When bishops allowed flexibility with the *Book of Common Prayer,* this version of Puritanism flourished, but at other times, bishops enforced conformity, suspending ministers from office and imprisoning dissenters. Debate raged among Puritan factions over whether or not the *Prayer Book,* vestments and episcopacy were indifferent matters or inherently evil, and therefore Christian conscience demanded their removal.

Puritans favored a skilled preaching ministry and only minimal church ceremonies that could be justified by Scripture. The "regulative principle" of worship was a pledge to worship the Almighty only in a manner prescribed in God's Word with no additional ceremonies of human invention. The sermon, Psalm singing and very selective use of the *Prayer Book* were chief marks of Puritan worship. One group of Puritans believed Presbyterian government was required by Scripture, and they yearned for an established Presbyterianism in England. There was a strong Calvinist bent in Elizabethan Puritanism promoted by Reformed Puritan preaching, the popular Geneva Bible (1560) with its Calvinist marginal notes and the printing of Puritan books. The universities became hotbeds of Puritan sentiment as young men destined for the ministry studied under Puritan tutors and lecturers.

A principal Presbyterian Puritan leader in England was Thomas Cartwright (d. 1603), a teacher at Cambridge who was removed from his teaching post in 1570 for opposing the Elizabethan Settlement. The first presbytery was formed in England in 1572, but the next year there was a major repression of Puritans and many were imprisoned for nonconformity. Cartwright did not relent in his criticism of Anglicanism and wrote *Disciplina Ecclesia* (1584) attacking episcopacy. Anglican apologist Richard Hooker offered a rebuttal to Cartwright's Presbyterianism in *Laws of Ecclesiastical Polity*. Hooker argued that Scripture alone is not sufficient, but historical tradition and natural law (reason) must also be considered in questions of church government.

Certain Puritan preachers secretly organized themselves into conferences within episcopacy with a concealed eldership that practiced discipline. These Presbyterian Puritans were convinced that Scripture taught clergy parity, with church courts directing church affairs not bishops and magistrates. Other Puritan leaders tolerated episcopacy or viewed the bishop as a civil magistrate, while preachers with congregational tendencies received re-ordination from fellow Puritans. Criticism of Anglican polity continued unabated in certain corners resulting in further imprisonment of Puritan leaders charged with "clandestine Presbyterian activities." After 1590, attempts to reform the Elizabethan church were mostly abandoned as Puritan leaders learned to accommodate to the political/ecclesiastical realities of English life. Reform for most Puritans became centered on personal piety and the reformation of morals. Independents who were unwilling to tolerate Anglican worship or episcopacy either went underground or fled to the Netherlands.

At the death of Queen Elizabeth, James VI of Scotland, son of Mary Stuart, became James I, King of Great Britain by right of his mother's descent from Henry VII of England. When James embarked for London in 1603, he was met by Puritans bearing a petition with one thousand signatures – "The Millenary Petition." Written by Cartwright, the document listed grievances against Anglican liturgy, vestments, use of the Apocrypha and abuse of the Lord's Day. The Puritan leaders were invited to meet with the bishops in 1604 at the Hampton Court Conference where King James came to the conclusion, "no bishop, no king" and therefore sided with the bishops against the Puritans. The king's pro-Episcopalian stance effectively brought an end to the Elizabethan Puritan movement.

REFORMATION IN SCOTLAND

Elizabethan Puritan Presbyterianism was not ultimately successful, but in Scotland the story was a striking contrast as a national Scottish Presbyterian Church was the outcome. The Reformation of Scotland, in manifold ways, was the by-product of Herculean efforts by John Knox, "the Father of Presbyterianism." Knox was born in 1514 in Haddington, south of Edinburgh, and attended the University of St. Andrews. He was ordained as a Catholic priest but converted to Protestant principles in 1543, joining the circle of a reforming preacher named George Wishart and serving as his bodyguard. Wishart was burned in Scotland as a heretic by Cardinal Beaton, who in turn was killed by Protestants in retaliation. Knox and his cohorts barricaded themselves at St. Andrews castle where they were besieged by the Catholic French fleet which captured Knox and held him as a galley slave for nineteen months. After his release, Knox spent four years in England (1549-1553), becoming a chaplain to King Edward VI and influencing the composition of both the *Forty-Two Articles* and the *Second Prayer Book*. Knox was offered the office of bishop in the English Church but declined. Upon Mary's accession to the throne, he fled England and spent five years in Europe, including time in Calvin's Geneva which notably shaped his own reform program.

Despite his geographic separation from Scotland, Knox began to put in writing his own thoughts about both the situation in England under bloody Mary and the French Catholic ties of the Scottish royal family.

In 1558, Knox wrote *The First Blast Against the Monstrous Regiment of Women* that denigrated Catholic Mary Tutor and advocated rebellion against godless female rulers as a Christian duty. The timing of the work was terrible, for by the time of its publication, Elizabeth had just become Queen, and the work cost Knox her favor and many friends in England. Knox returned to Scotland in 1559 and embarked on his rigorous preaching and reforming ministry among his countrymen. By 1560, the Reformation Parliament of Scotland had adopted a Protestant statement of faith, the *Scots Confession*, written by Knox and several other ministers. Knox also wrote the *First Book of Discipline* and a *Forme of Prayers* for Reformed worship in the Scottish church. With exceptional organizational ability, Knox helped establish a national Presbyterian church based upon his *Book of Discipline* which included not only a form of government but also provided for a complete system of free public education and a plan for national charities for the needy. The Reformed church was officially declared the only church within the realm in 1567.

Presbyterian polity with lay elders and ministers developed in stages in Scotland. At the outset of reform, bishops remained in place, and superintendents were appointed to oversee churches due to the paucity of Protestant ministers. It was not until the 1580s that a network of presbyteries was inaugurated to serve Scotland's parochial system, and Calvin's model of church government was adapted to the Scottish state-church. Eventually, congregations would have the right to call their own minister under the oversight of the other ministers of presbytery as Calvin had advised.

John Knox, "the thundering Scot," was known as a fearless preacher who applied the Word of God against sin wherever it might appear. In 1559, his first year back in Scotland, he preached a sermon in Perth against idolatry that sparked a riot, including the burning of three monasteries. Knox's sermon style was typically subdued for the first thirty minutes while he calmly did exegesis on the Biblical text, then he pounded the pulpit as he moved to application and exhorted listeners to Christian obedience. One eyewitness records, "He made me so to tremble, I could not hold a pen to write." The influence of Knox's preaching threatened Mary Stuart (Mary Queen of Scots) who summoned him for interviews five times and presided at Knox's trial for treason where he was exonerated. The occasion of the queen's second summons was a report to Mary that Knox had publicly criticized her in a sermon. When Mary questioned Knox about this, he replied: "I am called, Madam, to a public function within the Church of God, and am appointed by God to rebuke the sins and vices of all. ... If Your Grace please to frequent the public sermons, then doubt I not but you shall fully understand both what I like and mislike, as well in Your Majesty as in all others."[7]

In 1567, Mary abdicated and fled to England where she was finally placed under arrest and beheaded for conspiracy (1587) by her cousin Queen Elizabeth. Mary's infant son James VI was crowned king when Mary abdicated, and James Stewart, a friend of Knox, became regent. Knox died in 1572. The mantle of Presbyterian leadership in Scotland fell to professor Andrew Melville (d. 1622), who had returned from Geneva in 1574 and began pressing the Presbyterian program through a *Second Book of Discipline* (1578), which followed the Geneva model with local and district elders (presbytery). Tensions continued within the Scottish Parliament that vacillated between approving Presbyterian government and episcopacy. James I reinvigorated episcopacy in Scotland, which he perceived as more loyal to the crown, by persuading the Scottish Church Assembly to endorse his position. Courts of High Commission were established in 1610 by King James in order to punish Presbyterian nonconformity in Scotland. Andrew Melville fell out of favor spending four years in the Tower of London before his exile in France.

PROGRESS OF REFORM

In Ireland, Elizabeth had her hands full with the Irish common people who perceived the Reformation as a foreign English movement. Elizabeth battled Irish chieftains, with their stronghold in Ulster, in four campaigns throughout her reign and only enforced Anglicanism in the Pale, the English sphere within eastern Ireland. The Protestant movement would have very shallow roots in Ireland which remained predominately Roman Catholic. At the end of Elizabeth's reign, English and lowland Scots settlers began moving into the northern province of Ulster and continued immigration under Elizabeth's successor, James I. The Scots-Irish Ulstermen maintained a separate identity from the native Irish population, including their Protestant Presbyterian faith.

James I was anti-Puritan in his policies, thus during his monarchy the Separatist movement in England gained momentum. Separatists were Puritans who did not believe one could reform the Anglican Church from within but chose instead to establish their own congregations. English Baptist beginnings go back to John Smyth and Thomas Helwys who in 1608 led a Gainsborough group in the English Midlands to Holland where they were shown hospitality by Mennonites. In 1609, Smyth came to the conclusion that baptism was only for believers so he baptized himself, Helwys and the rest of the group. This rebaptism was a dividing line that removed them from association with other Separatist groups. By the next year, Smyth and thirty-one others decided they had been wrong to rebaptize themselves and united with the Dutch Mennonites. Helwys and twelve others disagreed with Smyth and returned to England in 1612, establishing the first General Baptist Church at Spitalfields near London. Helwys, a public advocate for religious toleration of the Baptists, was thrown into prison and died in 1616.

In the same year that Helwys died another assembly of English Baptists was founded by Calvinistic London Independents led by Henry Jacob. These "Particular Baptists," so named for their Reformed understanding of particular atonement, determined that not only was believer's baptism required, immersion was the only mode of Scriptural baptism. Though committed to the Independent "gathered church" principle, the London Baptists collaborated on a confession of faith in 1644 (London Confession). They organized themselves for mutual cooperation in church planting, financial assistance and resolution of controversies. A second London Confession by Particular Baptists (1677) was modeled on the *Westminster Confession* (1647).

James I (r.1603-1625) is known to posterity as the monarch who gave Englishmen a new "authorized" version of the English Bible in 1611 which became a masterpiece of Bible translation. Between the time of Tyndale's translation (1525) and the King James Bible there were nine English translations with four versions appearing in the 1530's – Coverdale, Matthew, Taverner and the Great Bible translated by Miles Coverdale with a preface by Thomas Cranmer. The Geneva Bible, published in Geneva (1560), was the first English version to use verse enumeration and included Calvinist notes in the margins. A new translation under the direction of Elizabeth's Archbishop Matthew Parker remained the official English version until James' Authorized Version of 1611, but it was never as popular as the Calvinist Geneva translation. English Catholics produced a translation known as the Douai-Reims Bible with the New Testament published in 1582 and the Old Testament in 1609.

When James I died in 1625, the succession fell to his son Charles I, King of Great Britain and Ireland (k.1625-1649). Charles, a loyal Anglican who shared his father's commitment to the divine right of kings, appointed William Laud, a High Church Arminian, to enforce conformity as the Archbishop of Canterbury. Archbishop Laud repressed Calvinistic Puritans, some of whom, like John Winthrop, migrated to the New World. King Charles further alienated his Protestant subjects by marrying Henrietta Maria, the Roman Catholic daughter of Henry IV, King of France. Charles' policy in Scotland made things worse as he attempted to impose the *Prayer Book* on the Scottish church. In 1637, riots broke out in Scotland in protest of Charles' policies. By 1638, the Scots ("Covenanters") signed the National Covenant at Greyfriars churchyard in Edinburgh, which proclaimed a commitment to the Reformed faith, a refusal to embrace any ecclesiastical changes until Parliament had input and issued a call for national covenanted Presbyterianism.

Back in England, Charles I had refused to call Parliament into session during 1629-1640, choosing to rule without them. The First Bishop's War with Scottish rebels in 1639 compelled Charles to summon the English Parliament for raising funds, but after the Short Parliament started listing grievances, the king promptly dismissed them. The next year a Second Bishop's War erupted with the Scottish army marching into England, and Charles was again compelled to call Parliament into session. Parliament viewed the Scots as allies, because their resistance provided English royal foes an opportunity to consolidate their forces. In 1641, the Parliament issued a Grand Remonstrance to the king, outlining problems in the realm and calling for a national synod. By 1642, the English Civil War had erupted, pitting the king, nobility and traditionalist Anglicans against Parliament, Puritans, Separatists and the middle class. The Scots joined forces with the English Parliament in the 1643 Solemn League and Covenant which pledged to preserve the Reformed religion in England and Scotland by getting rid of popery and prelacy (hierarchical church government). The Parliamentary armies prevailed, and Charles I was beheaded in 1649.

The period of the English Civil War, during which the Long Parliament (1640-1649) called for an Assembly of Divines (clergy) to recommend ecclesiastical reforms, was the high-water mark for English Puritan theology. Only twenty-five years earlier, James I had authorized an English delegation to the Dutch Synod of Dordt (1618,1619) and though the Canons of Dordt were never officially ratified by the Church of England, the principle outcomes of the Synod represented what English Calvinists believed. The Westminster Assembly demonstrated a solid attachment to historic Reformed themes throughout the confessional documents they produced.

The Assembly convened in Westminster Abbey in 1643 and began revising the *Thirty-Nine Articles* but only completed the first fifteen articles because another assignment was presented after the Solemn League and Covenant was signed. The Assembly's new task included the production of a Presbyterian Form of Government, a Directory for Worship to replace the *Book of Common Prayer*, a *Confession of Faith* and Catechisms. The Assembly originally included ten Lords, twenty commoners and one hundred twenty-one divines, with an additional twenty-one clergymen to make up for absences. There were eight Scots in the Assembly who had the right to speak but no vote. Commissioners to the Assembly spent twenty-seven months working on the Confession of Faith, debating each point and searching Scripture. The most intense debate centered on the topic of church government because conflicting views of Presbyterians, Episcopalians, Independents (Congregationalists) and Erastians (state over church in ecclesiastical matters) were present in the Assembly.

The Confession, in thirty-three chapters, was finished with Scripture proofs in 1647. The *Larger and Shorter Catechisms* were completed by 1648. The Westminster Assembly was not an ecclesiastical synod with its own authority but had only served in an advisory capacity for Parliament. The title page of the Confession read: "The Humble Advice of the Assembly of Divines, Now by Authority of Parliament Sitting at Westminster, Concerning a Confession of Faith: With Quotations and Texts of Scripture Annexed. Presented by Them Lately to Both Houses of Parliament." Ironically, the *Confession of Faith*, which was approved by the General Assembly of Scotland, was never formally authorized by the English Parliament.

In the political vacuum that followed the demise of Charles I, the military leader Oliver Cromwell (d. 1658) became "Lord Protector" of England and the Long Parliament was abolished along with the monarchy and the House of Lords. Cromwell, a Puritan Independent, wanted a national church with no bishops or Prayer Book, thus, he moved England toward more religious freedom, tolerating all Protestants except Quakers who were considered religious radicals. After Cromwell's Protectorate and the short rule of his son Thomas, the monarchy was restored with the accession of Charles II (r. 1660-1685), who, though outwardly conformed to the Anglican Church, was personally inclined to Catholicism and hated Protestants. Charles II persecuted Scottish Covenanters ("the killing time") and ejected 2,000 ministers in England for failure to comply with the 1662 Act of Uniformity.

At the death of Charles II in 1685, James II (r. 1685-1688), the second son of Charles I became King of England, appointing Roman Catholics to civil, military and university offices. James had been received into the Roman church in 1670 and three years later married his second wife, Mary Beatrice, a Roman Catholic princess. James II issued two Declarations of Indulgence with the intention of allowing full freedom of worship for dissenters and Catholics, but this caused him deep trouble with the Anglican establishment. These declarations, his Roman Catholic favoritism and the birth of a son all raised the fear of a Catholic succession to the English throne. James II fled England for France when William, the Dutch Prince of Orange who was married to James' daughter Mary, invaded England in 1688.

William and Mary assented to Parliament's Royal Declaration that repudiated the Roman Catholic Church and the "Glorious Revolution" of 1688 was under way. William III (r.1689-1702) was crowned, with his wife Mary II as Queen. A Toleration Act in 1689 suspended all laws against dissenting Protestants, excluding only Roman Catholics and non-Trinitarians. As long as tithes were paid to the established church, dissenting religious meeting houses could be licensed with an oath of allegiance to the crown, but public office was restricted to Anglicans. Thus, the seventeenth century in England concluded with a significant degree of religious freedom compared with its recent past, but non-Anglicans were still prohibited from full participation in

English society. Immigration to America remained an attractive option for Englishmen interested in religious and political liberty as well as economic opportunities.

THE CONNECTION

The story of the English Reformation is enough to make one dizzy as the pendulum swings between Catholicism, Anglicanism and Puritanism. Kings and queens of England believed that the only way to rule their subjects was to preserve uniformity of religious practice and persecute dissenters. The British Isles, like the continent, struggled long and hard to come to terms with the full implications of the Protestant Reformation. English monarchs enforced the established version of Christian faith through imprisonment and killing, methods foreign to contemporary Western society but methods that had been commonplace since Constantine. Rehearsing English history, one can appreciate yet again the American Founding Fathers' zeal for separation of church and state.

For Presbyterians, the story of Scotland and John Knox is an inspiring account of Christian conscience as the Church of Scotland courageously stood up for her convictions. Presbyterianism in Scotland was not for the faint of heart but for Protestants passionate about completing the reform that Luther had begun. Scottish Presbyterianism, with its robust theology, disciplined government by elders and strict morality, remains a signpost for Reformed Christians today. This admirable program of reform was nonetheless imposed on the Scots and it would remain for New World immigrants to practice Presbyterian principles within the context of complete religious liberty.

The Puritan era in England provided the historical context for the monumental Westminster Assembly and its grand *Confession* and *Catechisms*. A prominent feature of the *Larger and Shorter Catechisms* was an exposition of the Ten Commandments which described what was forbidden and required in the Christian life – here was English Puritan piety at its best – submission to the revealed will of God in humble obedience. The well-known opening question and answer of the *Shorter Catechism* declared: "What is the chief end of man? ... Man's chief end is to glorify God and enjoy Him forever." The glory of God remains the hallmark of Reformed faith and practice – it's not about us, it's about Him! The *Shorter Catechism* has historically been popular among Baptists and Congregationalists as well as Presbyterians. The original Puritan vision of an established English Presbyterian church never became a reality but the *Westminster Confession of Faith* would have an enduring worldwide influence as the Presbyterian creed.

7

NEW CHURCH
AND NEW NATION
Colonial Presbyterians

"Of His own will He brought us forth by the word of truth, ... Therefore put away all filthiness and rampant wickedness and receive with meekness the implanted word, which is able to save your souls. But be doers of the word, and not hearers only, deceiving yourselves."
James 1:18, 21, 22

"Piety without literature, is but little profitable; and learning, without piety, is pernicious to others, and ruinous to the possessor. Religion is the grand concern to us all, as we are men; – whatever be our calling and profession, the salvation of our souls is the one thing needful."[1]
President John Witherspoon, College of New Jersey (1723-1794)

While Luther, Calvin and Knox were pursuing church reform in Europe and Britain, explorers were beginning to discover and settle the New World. Spain and Portugal were the first to sponsor explorations in the Americas. Columbus' historic voyage in 1492 initiated a wave of Spanish conquest in North and South America resulting in new settlements, mission stations and churches. Dominicans, Franciscans and Jesuits accompanied settlers to evangelize the Indians who were regularly forced by conquistadors into the *ecomienda* system of slave labor on Spanish estates. The Roman Catholic church attempted to moderate the unjust treatment of the native population. By the

127

end of the sixteenth century, it had appointed five archbishops in Latin America which would become predominately Catholic in subsequent centuries.

French Catholics made inroads into the New World through Canada and along the Mississippi River as far south as New Orleans. French outposts in these areas had small populations, but by 1689 there were ten thousand French settlers in Canada. Franciscans accompanied French settlers to convert the Native American peoples, and later Jesuits arrived to start Indian schools. The English defeated the French in the French and Indian War (1759) but Catholicism maintained a long-term presence among French Canadians. English Catholics like Lord Baltimore were also interested in the New World, establishing an experimental Maryland colony (1634) as a haven for Catholics and offering religious toleration for all settlers. By 1702, the Anglican Church became the established church in Maryland but the colony retained a significant Catholic population. Roman Catholic numbers in America remained small during the colonial era, but this trend was reversed with substantial waves of Catholic European immigration in the nineteenth century.

PURITAN AMERICA

Spain and France declared territorial rights in the Americas, but British Protestants began arriving to stake their own claims in the New World. Protestants made their way to the American coast in order to escape religious persecution, find new economic opportunity and evangelize the indigenous peoples. English settlers had a vision for continuing the reform begun in the Old World and establishing the godly society that had eluded them in the mother country. Initial immigration to Jamestown (1607) was not primarily driven by religious motives, nevertheless a clergyman led a worship service as soon as they arrived on shore. The original Jamestown settlement was a failure as most settlers died in the first two years; however, others were more successful as they moved farther up the James River.

A group of English Separatists seeking freedom of religious practice had relocated to the Netherlands in 1609. This group immigrated to North America in 1620 aboard the Mayflower establishing Plymouth

Plantation as the first permanent English colony. These Englishmen expressed their sentiments in the famous Mayflower compact: "In ye name of God ... We whose names are underwritten, the loyall subjects of our dread soveraigne Lord, King James, ... doe by these presents solemnly & mutually in ye presence of God, and one of another, covenant & combine ourselves together into a civill body politick. ... for ye generall good of ye Colonie unto which we promise all due submission and obedience."[2] These Pilgrim Fathers became national symbols of American liberty.

The Massachusetts Bay Colony near Boston (1630) was comprised of Congregationalists escaping oppression under Charles I and seeking the creation of a holy commonwealth in the New World. The vision of this Reformed Puritan group was expressed by layman John Winthrop in a sermon aboard the ship *Arabella* as they sailed for America. Winthrop, Governor of the colony, exhorted his brethren to fulfill the Puritan goal of a community (church and state) committed first and foremost to God's glory. He concluded his sermon at sea:

> ... we are entered into covenant with him for this work. ... For we must consider that we shall be as a city upon a hill; the eyes of all people are upon us, so that if we shall deal falsely with our God in this work we have undertaken and so cause him to withdraw his present help from us, we shall be made a story and a by-word through the world; ... Therefore let us choose life, that we and our seed may live by obeying his voice and cleaving to him, for he is our life and our prosperity. [3]

Boston Puritans were of the non-separating variety, hence never formally separated from the mother Church of England. The Puritan vision of a Christian society in the colonies meant that full citizenship included church membership. When Roger Williams immigrated to Massachusetts in 1631, he clashed with authorities by refusing to join the Boston church because of its Anglican connection. The General Court banished him from Massachusetts in 1635 so fleeing to Rhode Island he arrived at a place he named "Providence." A Baptist church was organized at Providence in 1639, which is considered the oldest Baptist congregation in America. In 1644, Parliament granted a charter for Rhode Island based upon the principle of complete religious freedom which was a first for the colonies.

The Cambridge Platform of 1648 was a response to English requests for a definitive statement of New England practice and included Biblical justification for their congregational principles. Boston Congregationalism had some remarkable similarities to Presbyterian connectionalism in terms of its corporate understanding of New England church life – it has been called "Presbyterianized Congregationalism." Church membership became problematic for later Puritan generations, since all citizens routinely had their children baptized but not all of them had personally experienced grace as adults. The original Puritan ideal of a pure church began to erode through the "half-way covenant" arrangement which allowed infant baptism of children of parents, who, though baptized themselves as children, had not become full communing members of the church. Later compromises even allowed these persons to come to the Lord's Table without having made a personal profession of faith. These practices further diminished the spiritual vitality of Congregationalism in New England.

Presbyterian influence within Congregationalism made its most tangible contribution in the Saybrook Platform (1708) of Connecticut Congregationalists. The Saybrook Platform established consociations, with clergy and lay representatives, to render binding judgments in church disputes. It formed ministerial associations for clergy oversight and examination of ministerial candidates. These polity revisions were not accepted by all colonial Congregationalists, some of whom rejected Saybrook as *de facto* Presbyterianism which compromised their understanding of local church autonomy.

PRESBYTERIANS IN THE NEW WORLD

In the early seventeenth century, Presbyterians who immigrated to America typically united with New England Congregational churches with whom they shared Calvinist convictions. The Presbyterian colonists included English Puritans, Continental Reformed Groups (such as Huguenots) or those of Scottish descent. Boston minister, Cotton Mather (d. 1728), claimed that over four thousand Presbyterians immigrated to New England before 1640. As Puritans began moving into the middle colonies in the 1640s, those of Presbyterian persuasion organized themselves into distinct Presbyterian congregations, for example, the Southhampton Church on Long Island (1640).

The great American Presbyterian pioneer was Scots-Irish minister Francis Makemie (1657-1708) who was ordained in 1682 by the Irish Presbytery of Laggan and departed the next year for Maryland, responding to pleas for a Presbyterian clergyman. His early American years were spent in evangelistic work in Maryland, Virginia and North Carolina, where he established five congregations. He also devoted three years to mission work in Barbados (1695-1698). Presbyterians were poor so Makemie financed his itinerate ministry through his 500 acre farm in Accomack county, Virginia and the support of a wealthy father-in-law.

Makemie's honorable designation as "the Father of American Presbyterianism" is associated with his instigation of the first Presbytery in America. Seven ministers from Maryland, Delaware and the Philadelphia area – Samuel Davis, George McNish, John Hampton, Nathaniel Taylor, Jedediah Andrews, John Wilson and Makemie – organized themselves into an official body in 1706. Makemie described the purpose of the Presbytery: "Our design is to meet yearly, and oftener, if necessary, to consult the most proper measures for advancing religion and propagating religion in our Various Stations, and to mentain Such a Correspondence as may conduce to the improvement of our Ministeriall ability ..."[4] Makemie was chosen as the moderator of the new grassroots Presbyterian organization launched in Philadelphia.

One of the reasons Presbyterians had organized themselves was a belief that they could strengthen religious toleration through joint effort. Under the rights of the 1689 Toleration Act of William and Mary, Makemie and other ministers had secured dissenter licenses. Makemie's house had been designated as an authorized preaching point in Anglican-established Virginia, but he encountered resistance when he tried to preach in New York. In 1707 Makemie and John Hampton made a trip to Boston and stopped in New York where they each preached at separate locations. When both were arrested and charged with preaching without a license, Makemie presented his Virginia license and Hampton, a Maryland license, nevertheless, they were held in confinement for forty-six days. Charges against Hampton were dropped but Makemie was remanded for trial. Lord Cornbury, Governor of New York required bond and security "to preach no more in my government," to which Makemie replied: "If his Lordship required it, we would give security for our behaviour; but to give bond and security to preach no more in Your Excellency's government, if invited and desired by any people, we neither can, nor dare do." Cornbury sent Makemie to jail.

In June of 1707 Makemie appeared in court with three lawyers who argued that Cornbury's requirement for a preaching license was not stipulated by law. There was no established church for the province, therefore Makemie's preaching could not be a violation of the Toleration Act. Makemie was acquitted but Cornbury forced him to pay court costs to which the New York Assembly responded with a new law making this illegal. Accusations were brought against Cornbury who in due course was removed from office. Makemie's trial made Presbyterians popular with dissenters, and his legal exoneration became a notable milestone in the advancement of religious liberty in America. The next year Makemie died and was buried on his land in Virginia.

Within a decade of Makemie's death, the massive immigration of the Scots-Irish would commence. Beginning in 1717, a steady stream of Ulster Scots populated the Middle Colonies, particularly the frontier in western Pennsylvania. By the time of American Independence, almost 500,000 Scots-Irish had come to America. These immigrants were descended from lowland Scots colonists who had settled in northern Ireland during the reign of James I. The Ulster Scots had maintained their ethnic identity, organizing presbyteries in Ireland within the established Anglican Church. In Ireland, the Presbyterian ministers were dependent on laity for salaries and church buildings since there were no state tithes. This created an environment where clergy and laity worked more closely together for local church support. When these Irish immigrants came to America they were looking for Presbyterian worship and were accustomed to mutual cooperation between ministers and laymen. American Presbyterianism would mirror the Irish situation more than the national church context of Scotland.

THE ADOPTING ACT

Colonial Presbyterians continued church planting, and by 1716 plans were laid for three more presbyteries – Long Island, New Castle and Snow Hill – to join with the original presbytery and form the Synod of Philadelphia. As Presbyterianism in the colonies grew, it was becoming more imperative to think through the particulars of their communion within the Synod. In these early years of organized American Presbyterianism there had not been any official doctrinal confession. All the ministers shared the common heritage of historic Calvinism, but the necessity of a formal creed had not been apparent. Part of the explanation for this situation was tied to the former British context since requiring allegiance to the Westminster Standards had caused deep division among Presbyterians in both England and Ireland.

A ministerial case of discipline for immorality came before the Synod in 1720, and significant differences surfaced over how to handle the situation. The incident raised the larger question about how the young body of Presbyterians would regulate their ecclesiastical life together. By 1724, New Castle Presbytery had begun requiring candidates to subscribe to the *Westminster Confession* with these words, "I do own the Westminster Confession as the confession of my faith." In 1727, John Thompson of New Castle Presbytery brought an overture to the Synod requesting that subscription to the *Confession* be required of all Presbyterian ministers. Thompson claimed it was not his intention to bring "any heat or contention" to the Synod, but he was concerned for the "vindication and defense of the truths we profess, and for preventing the ingress and spreading of error." The infant Presbyterian church, according to Thompson, had no seminary of learning and was therefore defenseless in an era "of so many pernicious and dangerous corruptions in doctrine."[5]

While Thompson's request seemed reasonable to many, there were others who strongly resisted the idea of imposing the *Confession* as a test of orthodoxy. The opposition leader, Jonathan Dickinson of New Jersey, argued that the Synod already had the necessary external bonds of unity, and confessional subscription would not detect hypocrites nor heretics. Dickinson was of English Puritan stock and represented a segment of the church that believed strict subscription after the

Scottish model would inevitably divide the young American church as had occurred in the old country.

During the debate over this contentious issue, three parties surfaced – strict subscriptionists (largest group), anti-subscriptionists and moderates within both parties. The Synod delayed action on the overture for a couple of years but finally brought the issue before the whole body for a vote in 1729. There was great trepidation in the Synod as they convened in the fall of 1729, fearing that schism might be the outcome. The subscription matter was handed over to a committee of eight for a recommendation to the Synod. Dickinson played a prominent role on this committee that produced a middle ground position which satisfied the diverse parties.

The compromise proposal was unanimously adopted by the Synod "after long debating upon it" and exhibited a charitable spirit that honored the concerns of all parties. The Synod affirmed both freedom of conscience and the necessity of a formal creed for the good of the church. The consensus documents made an important distinction between "all the essential and necessary articles," which each minister shall adopt, and liberty on articles "not essential and necessary." The Synod stated that all ministers,

> ... shall declare their agreement in and approbation of the Confession of Faith with the larger and shorter Catechisms of the assembly of Divines at Westminster, as being in *all the essential and necessary Articles*, good Forms of sound words and systems of Christian Doctrine; and do also adopt the said Confession and Catechisms as the Confession of our Faith. And we do also agree, yt all the Presbyteries within our Bounds shall always take Care not to admit any Candidate of the Ministry into the Exercise of the sacred Function, but what declares his Agreement in opinion with *all the Essential and Necessary Articles* of said Confession, either by subscribing the said Confession of Faith and Catechisms, or by a verbal Declaration of their assent thereto, as such Minister or Candidate shall think best.[6]

The Synod also endorsed a method for securing liberty of conscience by means of publicly stating "scruples." The Synod or Presbytery was to make final judgment on scruples and determine whether or not one's exceptions were about "essential and necessary articles of faith." The paragraph on exceptions stated:

> And in Case any Minister of this Synod or any Candidate for the Ministry shall have any Scruple with respect to any Article or Articles of sd. Confession or Catechisms, he shall at the Time of his making sd. Declaration declare his Sentiments to the Presbytery or Synod, who shall notwithstanding admit him to ye Exercise of the Ministry within our Bounds and to Ministerial Communion if the Synod or Presbytery shall judge his scruple or mistake to be only about *articles not Essential and necessary* in Doctrine, Worship or Government. But if the Synod or Presbytery shall judge such Ministers or Candidates erronious in *Essential and necessary Articles* of Faith, the Synod or Presbytery shall declare them uncapable of Communion with them.[7]

Anticipating differences of opinion, the Synod included a statement of brotherly charity toward all, and denounced prejudice between ministers. The Adopting Act concluded with these words: "And the Synod do solemnly agree, that none of us will traduce or use any opprobrious Terms of those yt differ from us in these *extra-essential and not-necessary points of doctrine*, but treat them with the same friendship, kindness and brotherly Love, as if they had not differed from us in such Sentiments."[8]

In the afternoon of the same day, the Synod reconvened to implement among themselves the new subscription principles they had agreed upon in the morning. After reading the minutes of the morning session, each member of the Synod now had to personally adopt the Westminster Standards as the confession of his faith before the Synod. Each presbyter was given the opportunity of "proposing all the Scruples yt any of them had to make against any Articles and Expressions in the Confession of Faith and larger and shorter Catechisms." The afternoon minute stated that after these opinions were presented, the Synod "unanimously agreed in the solution of those Scruples." After individual scruples were "unanimously agreed" to be acceptable, i.e., not about "essential and necessary" doctrines, the whole Synod "unanimously declare" exceptions to two sections of the *Confession* wherein every member had scruples about "some clauses" that granted authority to civil magistrates in church affairs. Since these scruples were held in common by every member present, they were recorded in the minutes. These uniform exceptions having been noted, the Synod declared the "Confession and Catechisms to be the Confession of their faith."[9]

The Synod accomplished two purposes on September 19, 1729 – principles for understanding the meaning of subscription were adopted; and members of Synod executed those principles among themselves in their adoption of the Westminster Standards individually and as an ecclesiastical body. Both individual and common scruples were voiced that day, but none of the scruples were judged to be about "essential and necessary articles." Having openly acknowledged every scruple before one another as the morning minute had outlined, the Synod had completed their work of adopting the Westminster Standards.

GREAT AWAKENING

One of those present for the subscription debates of 1729 was an Ulster immigrant named William Tennent, Sr. (1673-1746). In 1726, Tennent had relocated his family to the Philadelphia area so that he could pastor Neshaminy Presbyterian Church. Tennent was concerned about the shortage of Presbyterian ministers and the difficulty of traveling to New England or Scotland for ministerial training, so he decided to start his own private ministerial academy in the Middle Colonies. In 1735, he built a log structure near his home where he instructed ministerial candidates in Biblical languages, theology and preaching. Tennent emphasized a balance between "experimental orthodoxy" (piety) and learning, stressing that godly character was the heart of ministry. The "Log College," as detractors referred to it, prepared eighteen men for ministry including four sons of Tennent. As early as 1736, two presbyteries had raised concerns about the adequacy of a Log College education, and an "examining act" was passed which called for an examining committee to test privately educated candidates. The newly established New Brunswick Presbytery defiantly licensed a Log College graduate just three months after the new rule was adopted. As the Great Awakening erupted in the colonies, Log College graduates were among the pro-revival Presbyterians who co-labored with George Whitefield.

The origins of the Great Awakening in America are linked to the preaching of Dutch Reformed minister Jacobus Frelinghuysen. In the 1720s, Frelinghuysen was preaching the necessity of genuine conversion in the Raritan Valley of New Jersey with significant results in the Dutch communities. Presbyterian Gilbert Tennent (1703-1764), son of William Tennent, Sr., joined this effort in the Middle Colonies, having close contact with Frelinghuysen and sharing his views on piety and revival. By the 1730s, other pastors began experiencing local revivals. Congregational minister, Jonathan Edwards, witnessed revival taking place in his Northhampton, Massachusetts congregation in 1734-35 and wrote about what he observed in "A Faithful Narrative of the Surprising Work of God in the Conversion of Many Souls in Northhampton" (1737). When church authorities criticized the emotional excesses popularly associated with the revivals, Edwards ably defended the Awakening by pointing to the distinguishing marks of a genuine work of God's Spirit, which he argued were present in abundance. Edwards maintained close ties with Presbyterians over the years, serving a Presbyterian congregation in New York when he was a young minister and finishing his ministry as President of the College of New Jersey.

Revival preacher Gilbert Tennent, concerned about the spiritual decline of Presbyterian congregations, overtured the 1734 Synod urging special care not to admit any into the ministry that have not "a work of sanctifying grace in their hearts." Tennent and his revival colleagues in New Brunswick Presbytery came into further tension with the brethren when they preached outside the bounds of their own presbytery without permission. As a revivalist, Tennent advocated "preaching the terrors" (wrath of God) in order to awaken secure sinners to their plight before a holy God. He was convinced that ministers not preaching the terrors were hindering the work of God. He believed this so strongly that he publicly rebuked anti-revival ministers through his notorious sermon, "The Danger of an Unconverted Ministry" (1740).

By the time of Tennent's divisive sermon, things were coming to a crossroads between the New Side revival party and the Old Side Presbyterians who opposed revivalist excesses, the unwelcome invasion of pulpits and what they perceived as inferior educational standards. The Old Side brought a protest into the 1741 Synod meeting announcing that it was no longer possible to maintain ecclesiastical fellowship with revivalists because of their "unwearied, unscriptural, antipresbyterial, uncharitable divisive practices." The excluded New Side party withdrew and organized themselves into the "Conjunct Presbyteries of New Brunswick and Londonderry." The Presbytery of New York, which had been absent from Synod in 1741, later united with these brethren to form the Synod of New York in 1745. American Presbyterians had now experienced their first major schism.

Jonathan Dickinson (1688-1747) of Elizabeth Town, New Jersey, who unsuccessfully tried to reunite the two groups in the early years after the schism, was chosen as the first moderator of the Synod of New York. Dickinson, a moderate New Side leader in the revival, had written about the nature of genuine conversions, but also called for restraint of revivalist censoriousness and enthusiasm (emotional excess). Dickinson was an intellectual leader among Presbyterians, defending Reformed commitment to infant baptism, Presbyterian government and Calvinism in numerous widely circulated publications. One of his most famous works was *The Reasonableness of Christianity* (1732) in which he presented "some rational evidence of the truth of Christianity."

When the new Synod of New York convened, its first official act was to reaffirm the *Westminster Confession* and the Adopting Act of 1729. The New Side had come under suspicion from the Old Side who tended to favor a more strict interpretation of confessional subscription. When reunion negotiations between the Synod of Philadelphia and Synod of New York were initiated in 1749, one of the New York Synod's concerns was that the two bodies address "that paragraph about essentials," referring to the original subscription principles of 1729. When Dickinson died, a more temperate Gilbert Tennent assumed leadership of the reconciliation discussions on the New York side, having repented of his censorious spirit. After seventeen years apart, the breach was finally healed in 1758, with Gilbert Tennent chosen as moderator of the united Synod of New York and Philadelphia. Old Side minister, Francis Alison, was asked to preach on the occasion of reunion. He exhorted the two groups with these words: "We must maintain union in essentials, forbearance in lesser matters, and charity in all things. ... In a church like ours in America, collected from different churches of Europe, who have followed different modes and ways of obeying the 'great and general command of the gospel,' there is a peculiar call for charity and forbearance."[10]

PRESBYTERIAN EXPANSION

The Virginia and Carolina piedmont areas were unoccupied before 1730, but Scots-Irish settlers coming down the "Great Philadelphia Wagon Road" began to populate the backcountry. By 1750, they had moved into the South Carolina Piedmont and north Georgia. Scots came into South Carolina as early as the 1680s, forming a presbytery in the Charleston area by 1722. Scottish Highlanders settled along the North Carolina seaboard and coastal areas of Georgia, where an Independent Presbyterian Church in Savannah was organized in 1755.

The Synod of New York, which grew twice the size of the Old Side Synod of Philadelphia, sent missionaries into the Southern colonies. New Side evangelist, Samuel Davies (1723-1761), began his Virginia mission in 1747, establishing seven preaching points. Davies experienced harassment from the Virginia Anglican establishment but continued pressing the case for dissenters' religious liberty. As Presbyterian numbers in Virginia grew, more freedom was eventually granted. When settlers on the Virginia frontier suffered from Indian attacks, Davies recruited troops to fight "the heathen savages and French papists" in the French and Indian War (1756-1763). Davies took special interest in African slaves, teaching them to read the Bible, regularly preaching to three hundred and baptizing over one hundred. The famous Virginia patriot, Patrick Henry, whose mother was Presbyterian, said Davies was the greatest orator he had ever heard.

By 1755, Davies and six other ministers had organized Hanover Presbytery in Virginia, which became the mother presbytery of the Southern Presbyterian church. North Carolina was its new mission field, and in 1764 the Synod of New York and Philadelphia sent two ministers to North Carolina to organize churches. The seven churches of Mecklenburg County – Sugaw Creek, Steele Creek, Hopewell, Centre, Poplar Tent, Rocky River and Providence – are among the oldest Presbyterian congregations in North Carolina. One of the elders at Sugaw Creek, Abraham Alexander, and Rev. Hezekiah Balch of Poplar Tent presided at the Charlotte courthouse convention in May 1775 which produced the "Mecklenburg Declaration" declaring independence from Britain.

As Presbyterian churches in the South and Middle Colonies proliferated, the need for ministers made a new theological school imperative. Presbyterian ministers in 1747 received a charter to start the College of New Jersey for college studies and training ministers. The first President was Synod of New York's Jonathan Dickinson who opened the school in his home but died within five months. He was followed by revival preacher Aaron Burr, under whose presidency (1748-1757) the college relocated to Princeton, new buildings were constructed and the student body grew to seventy. Burr was the husband of Jonathan Edwards' daughter Esther and their son, Aaron Burr, Jr. served as Vice-President of the United States under Thomas Jefferson. Jonathan Edwards became the third President of the college in 1758 but died within three months of a smallpox inoculation. Another brief presidency followed as Samuel Davies, who succeeded Edwards the next year, died of pneumonia within eighteen months.

Being president of the College of New Jersey was apparently hazardous for one's health. When the Board of Trustees identified the fifth president, they had a difficult time convincing his wife! The Trustees selected a Presbyterian minister from Scotland, John Witherspoon (1723-1794), to lead the fledgling school. Witherspoon had an impressive background which was respected in the colonies. Many believed he could be a bridge builder between the former Old Side/New Side parties in the Presbyterian church. His wife Elizabeth finally yielded after letters and visits to Scotland from Richard Stockton and Benjamin Rush – both later signatories of the Declaration of Independence. The Witherspoon family boarded ship for a twelve-week voyage to America, arriving on shore in 1768 to the eager anticipation of New Jersey Presbyterians.

As President and Professor of Divinity, Witherspoon lectured on Moral Philosophy which included ethics, political science and law, teaching students about "social contract theory" and the advantages of free markets. He encouraged interest in science and inserted history and French into the college curriculum. Witherspoon introduced his students to Scottish Common-Sense Realism which was a philosophy developed by Thomas Reid of Glasgow. Reid reasoned that humanity had both an accurate knowledge of the real world and possessed an innate knowledge of basic morality. Scottish Realism's opposition to skepticism, which questioned any certitude, resonated with Witherspoon, for he was convinced that Christianity was reasonable and compatible with common sense.

Witherspoon believed that Christian Liberal Arts should foster piety and duty, preparing students for civic affairs, Christian ministry and scholarship. Enlightenment-inspired theological error and Deism were popular in the eighteenth century, but Witherspoon encouraged the church to persevere in its defense of the truth and not compromise orthodoxy. He asserted: "Let no Christian, therefore, give way to desponding thoughts, though infidelity unresisted spread its poison ... though there are few to support the interest of truth and righteousness ... let us not be discouraged. We plead the cause that shall prevail."[11]

The spirit of Colonial America captured Witherspoon who had embraced the vision of representative government. He became involved politically as he witnessed the oppression of the colonists by the British crown, believing their rights as Englishmen were being violated. In 1774, Witherspoon was part of the state convention in New Brunswick and soon was thrust headlong into the War for Independence. His first political sermon, preached at Nassau Hall in Princeton in May of 1776, urged resistance to tyranny as obedience to God and encouraged listeners to trust in God to bring good out of evil. The sermon was published, drawing praise for Witherspoon as a Patriot, but British loyalists hated him, burning him in effigy. A member of Parliament jested, "Cousin America has run off with a Presbyterian parson."

When the Second Continental Congress convened in Philadelphia, Witherspoon served as a delegate and signed the unanimous declaration of the colonies for independence on July 4, 1776 – the only clergyman to sign the Declaration of Independence. Witherspoon also signed the Articles of Confederation (1778), helped ratify the Constitution (1787) as a member of the New Jersey convention and served on the Board of War and Board of Foreign Affairs. The College of New Jersey was a hotbed of patriotism during the war as numbers of students entered the Continental Army. British troops occupied college buildings in winter 1777, turning Nassau Hall into barracks and stables, but with General Washington's victory at the battle of Princeton, classes resumed that summer. The War of Independence cost Witherspoon dearly, losing two of his sons in battle. He was keenly aware of God's providence in the conflict and wrote several proclamations on behalf of Congress, calling on Americans to thank the Almighty for His mercy. In 1782, as a member of Congress, Witherspoon wrote:

... the United States in Congress assembled, taking into their consideration the many instances of divine goodness to these States, ... do hereby recommend it to the inhabitants of these States in general, to observe, ... a day of solemn thanksgiving to God for all His mercies; and they do further recommend to all ranks and testify their gratitude of God for His goodness, by a cheerful obedience to His laws, and by protecting, each in His station, and by His influence, the practice of true and undefiled religion, which is the great foundation of public prosperity and national happiness. [12]

The most enduring influence of Witherspoon was evident in the almost five-hundred students he taught over his twenty-five years at the college. These students were his legacy and included: a President of the United States (James Madison, "Father of the Constitution"), a Vice-President (Aaron Burr, Jr.), twelve members of the Continental Congress, five delegates to the Constitutional Convention, forty-nine U.S. Representatives, twenty-eight Senators and three Supreme Court justices. Added to this impressive list were one hundred and fourteen ministers of the Gospel, nineteen of whom became presidents of institutions of higher learning.

At the same time the United States was ratifying a Constitution, Presbyterians were organizing themselves into a national General Assembly with their own constitution. In 1785, a committee, chaired by John Witherspoon, started work on a new *Plan of Government* and *Book of Discipline*. The Westminster *Directory for Worship* was revised, and the *Westminster Confession* was amended in chapters twenty, twenty-three and thirty-one to remove any references to state interference in church affairs. The constitutional revisions included a new subscription vow for ordination: "Do you sincerely receive and adopt the confession of faith of this church, as containing the system of doctrine in the Holy Scriptures?" The phrase "system of doctrine" pointed back to 1729 and firmly rooted the Presbyterian Constitution in the historic Adopting Act.

The Presbyterian Constitution was adopted in 1788. It included provisions for future alterations or amendments to the *Confession* that required two-thirds of the presbyteries and the General Assembly to concur. The intrinsic fallibility of the constitutional documents was imbedded in the recognition that, in contrast to Holy Scripture, these documents could be modified. The Introduction to the *Plan of Government* declared: "God alone is Lord of the conscience, and hath left it free from the doctrines and commandments of men; which are in anything contrary to His Word, or beside it in matters of faith or worship. ... The Bible is the only rule that is infallible in matters of faith and practice. It is the only authoritative constitution, and no church may make rules binding upon men's consciences."[13]

The first General Assembly met in Philadelphia in 1789, just four blocks away from the U.S. Constitutional Convention that was in session at the same time. George Washington had been inaugurated as the first President of the United States three weeks previously. The 1789 "General Assembly of the Presbyterian Church in the United States of America" consisted of four Synods and sixteen Presbyteries encompassing four hundred churches and one hundred and seventy-seven ministers. At the close of the century, Presbyterians were scattered throughout the breadth of the new nation and continued to expand their mission work as the nation's frontier moved westward.

THE CONNECTION

Colonial Presbyterians entered into solemn covenant with one another in Presbyteries, Synods and eventually a national General Assembly. Accountability to one another and mutual aid undergirded this grassroots ecclesiastical connection directed toward advancing the gospel message in the New World. Modern day Presbyterians still value the polity inherited from the colonial era. Though not perfect, its numerous advantages continue to make it attractive for present-day ministry. Connectional church government underscores the theological principle that earthly citizens of heaven are connected to Christ not only as King of Heaven but also as head of the visible church on earth. One can never say he loves the head but not the body because the two are indivisible.

The Great Awakening forever changed the face of Christianity and Presbyterianism in America. Most scholars view the eighteenth-century awakenings in Britain and America as the birth of the evangelical movement. David Bebbington has characterized the phenomena of

Evangelicalism with four priorities: (1) *conversionism* – transformation of lives by the Gospel, (2) *activism* – spreading the Gospel and works of charity, (3) *Biblicism* – belief that all spiritual truth is found in the Bible and (4) *crucicentrism* – the atoning work of Christ is central to the faith.[14] These emphases profoundly shaped Presbyterianism as revival preachers reminded the church that piety was of equal importantance with orthodoxy. The great revival also produced schism, and colonial Presbyterians learned the hard way that Christian charity is required if God's people are to live in harmony.

The legacy of colonial Presbyterianism for future generations includes the impressive Adopting Act. The generous spirit of the Adopting Act was embodied in the phrase "essential and necessary," which is repeated five times in the Synod's overture. The "essentials" language of the Adopting Act was a compromise. It required that ministerial communion be based on receiving the "essential and necessary" doctrines of the *Confession* and not a wooden acceptance of every article. The original subscription principles of 1729 have stood the test of time as a prudent path for peace among Presbyterians who still take ordination vows "to receive and adopt the system of doctrine" in the *Confession*.

John Witherspoon had a vision for how faith could be a positive influence in national affairs, and his participation in the Continental Congress has been a model of Christian commitment to the public good. American Presbyterians have engaged social/political issues ever since, believing God has called his church to transform the culture. Witherspoon also modeled Presbyterian commitment to excellence in education. Before the Civil War, Presbyterians had started over forty colleges, more than any other denomination in America. Christian education is still a primary concern for contemporary Presbyterians who view intellectual pursuits as always directed to the glory of God.

8

OLD SCHOOL AND NEW SCHOOL

Unity and Diversity in the Church

"Behold, how good and how pleasant it is
For brothers to dwell in unity! ...
It is like the dew of Hermon,
Coming down upon the mountains of Zion;
For there the Lord commanded the blessing – life forever."
                                              Psalm 133:1, 3

"We cannot see, therefore, how any set of men can with a good
conscience, desire to effect the division of the church until they are
called upon to profess what they do not believe, or required to do what
they cannot approve. This, as far as we can see, is the only principle
which can bear the test; which will acquit us in the sight of God
and man, for tearing asunder that portion of the church of Christ
committed to our care."
        Professor Charles Hodge, Princeton Seminary (1797-1878)[1]

As the new century began, Presbyterians shared American optimism for a new democratic nation expanding her borders westward. The 1803 Louisiana Purchase doubled the size of the United States which now included a vast area between the Mississippi and the Rocky Mountains. The 1800s were an era of unparalleled Presbyterian influence in the

United States as the church spread into the western frontier and regional theological seminaries were established to supply the new mission fields with ministers. Presbyterian clergymen of this period offered the nation intellectual leadership through the proliferation of religious periodicals, newspapers, published sermons and books on a vast array of subjects.

America in the nineteenth century again witnessed the visitation of the Spirit through what became known as the "Second Great Awakening." This time the revival was more Arminian in orientation as opposed to the earlier Awakening under the Calvinists, Whitfield, Edwards and Tennent. Given this theological bent, the new revival exacerbated the already divisive nature of revivalism which regularly provoked conservative reaction. Many Old School Presbyterians were skeptical about what they perceived as a man-centered, manipulative approach to evangelizing the masses, and they were suspicious of New School Presbyterian revival preachers who sometimes appeared to have abandoned Reformed theology. Theological debate between the two parties was a constant of Presbyterian ecclesiastical life in the first half of the century.

THE PLAN OF UNION

Presbyterians and Congregationalists in New England had a long history of cordial relations that went back into the colonial era when the first Presbyterian churches had been organized. By 1801 the two groups decided to formalize an agreement to benefit both churches in their missionary efforts on the American frontier. The 1801 Plan of Union set up an ecclesiastical arrangement for Presbyterians and the General Association of Connecticut (Congregationalists) to cooperate in mission by allowing the churches to share ministers and accommodate one another's polity. A Congregational Church could call a Presbyterian minister, or a Presbyterian Church could call a Congregational minister, and in each situation local church polity would remain in force, whether Presbyterian or Congregational. If a congregation was comprised of both Presbyterians and Congregationalists, a standing committee would be chosen to supervise the flock. Members of this standing committee could vote in a presbytery like any Presbyterian elder. With a prevailing ecumenical spirit at the time, the 1801 Presbyterian General Assembly unanimously adopted the Plan of Union. This cooperative arrangement served the churches well for a season, but there were inherent problems that surfaced in the "Presbygational" system. A key stumbling block was the irritating reality that "committee men," who had not taken ordination vows to the *Westminster Confession*, were voting in presbyteries.

On the theological side, a number of the Congregational churches were heirs of "New England Theology" which was a modification of traditional Calvinism by some of Jonathan Edwards' disciples. Edwards had answered Arminian objections to the doctrine of total depravity through his insightful distinction between man's natural ability and moral inability. Man's will was naturally free and morally responsible; however, the will lacked moral ability due to innate depravity of nature as a result of the Fall. Edwards' grandson, Timothy Dwight (President of Yale), and Congregational pastor Samuel Hopkins, who had been personally tutored by Edwards, seemed to take Edwards' teaching a step further by emphasizing actual sin versus original sin from Adam. In addition to these ideas, a more serious error surfaced when several New England theologians began teaching a general atonement grounded in the moral government of God rather than the substitutionary atonement of Christ. According to the governmental theory, the cross was a public demonstration of God's hatred for sin, not a vicarious payment for sin.

New England theology, popularly referred to as "Hopkinsianism" or "New Divinity," was condemned by traditional Congregational Calvinists as well as conservative Presbyterians who believed these novel ideas diminished doctrinal integrity. The growing antagonism was highlighted by Presbyterian minister Ezra Stiles Ely in his 1811 book, *A Contrast Between Calvinism and Hopkinsianism*, where Ely compared Hopkinsian theology to Arminianism and Pelagianism. The issue came before the General Assembly in 1817, but the Assembly was unwilling to outright condemn Hopkinsianism. Instead it cautioned the church to forsake the clamor that was disturbing the peace and harmony among brethren. Regardless of General Assembly inaction, a few vocal detractors still believed that New Divinity teaching violated Presbyterian ordination vows to the Westminster Standards.

Doctrinal strain became more severe through further novelties coming out of Congregational Yale College in the 1820s. Nathaniel Taylor joined the faculty at Yale in 1822 and developed a distinctive "New Haven Theology" that went still further in diluting Calvinism. Taylor was heavily influenced by Scottish Common Sense Philosophy that exalted the use of reason in theological construction. "Taylorism" included a blatant denial of original sin as an irrational belief, and a redefinition of regeneration as the voluntary change of the governing principle of a person's life not the divine creation of a new disposition. Taylor claimed to be an orthodox Calvinist, but there was grave concern that he had moved dangerously close to Pelagianism. The problem was that Yale graduates were serving as ministers in Presbyterian and Plan of Union churches, but the pervasiveness of New Haven theology in the Presbyterian Church was a much debated question. Fears about Taylorism intensified as his theology became identified with revivalism.

REVIVALS, MISSIONS AND EDUCATION

At the turn of the century preaching campaigns in New England by Timothy Dwight and camp meetings on the Kentucky frontier initiated a wave of revival that swept through the United States. In 1796, Presbyterian minister, James McGready, who had taken oversight of three congregations on the Kentucky frontier, began to stir these congregations through his preaching. A Communion season for preaching and the Lord's Supper was arranged for the Red River church in June of 1800, with local ministers invited to participate. The weekend was a calm Presbyterian Communion until Monday when the congregation began to cry and shout, seeking full assurance of their salvation. McGready, convinced this was a work of God's Spirit, planned another Communion at the Gaspar River meeting house, and as word spread, hundreds traveled to the meeting house, overwhelming the host church. The meetings had a dramatic effect as eyewitnesses recorded, "Sinners were lying powerless in every part of the house, praying and crying for mercy."

The revival spread into Kentucky and Tennessee, and by the end of 1800, thousands were attending the "camp meetings." One of the revival preachers was Presbyterian minister Barton W. Stone who had witnessed revival meetings and scheduled an 1801 "sacramental meeting" for his own Cane Ridge congregation in Kentucky. As many as twenty thousand attended the famous, week-long Cane Ridge revival where Presbyterian, Baptist and Methodist preachers exhorted the crowds as the camp erupted into cries, shouts and the "jerks" (bodily movements). By 1804 Stone and a group of revivalists left the Presbyterian Church describing themselves as "Christians only." Stone met Alexander Campbell in 1830 and joined with the Campbellites to form a group which became known as the Christian Church (Disciples of Christ). Another group of revivalist preachers in Transylvania and Cumberland Presbyteries irritated fellow Presbyterians by licensing preachers without educational credentials. As a result, charges of irregular ordination and denying the doctrine of election resulted in the suspension of two ministers, which was confirmed by the General Assembly in 1809. A number of ministers and congregations in due course separated from the Presbyterian Church establishing a new Cumberland Presbytery that by 1829 became the Cumberland Presbyterian Church.

The preeminent evangelist of the Second Great Awakening was Charles G. Finney (1792-1875), who was ordained as a Presbyterian minister in 1824 and began itinerant revival preaching in western New York. Finney experimented with "new measures" in his revival meetings which included theatrical preaching, an "anxious seat" (a front pew for seekers), "particular prayer" (public praying for the lost by name), the "prayer of faith" (unified prayer guaranting results) and women praying and exhorting in public meetings. At a later stage, Finney preached "perfectionism" or "entire sanctification" during his years as President of Oberlin College after he had abandoned the Presbyterian ministry.

Presbyterians responded to Finney in a variety of ways. New School minister, Lyman Beecher, who had been one of Dwight's students at Yale, was at first skeptical of revivalistic techniques but later became a moderate supporter of Finney. Beecher wrote in 1829: "There is such an amount of truth and power in the preaching of Mr. Finney, and so great an amount of good hopefully done, that if he can be so far restrained as that he shall do more good than evil, then it would be dangerous to oppose him, lest at length we might be found to fight against God; for though some revivals may be so badly managed as to be worse than none, there may, to a certain extent, be great imperfections in them and yet they be, on the whole, blessings to the Church."[2] Old

School men like Princeton Professor Samuel Miller were concerned that Finney's techniques were tied to a faulty theology. In 1833, Miller warned:

> ... when this highly exciting system of calling to 'anxious seats,' – calling out into the aisles to be 'prayed for,' &, is connected, as, to my certain knowledge, it often has been with erroneous doctrines; – for example, with the declaration that nothing is easier than conversion; – that the power of the Holy Spirit is not necessary to enable an impenitent sinner to repent and believe; – that if they only resolve to be for God – resolve to be Christians – that itself is regeneration – the work is already done; ... such doctrinal statements as these, it appears to me adapted to destroy souls by wholesale![3]

The association of Finney-like revivals with extreme Arminian theology was a given to many in the Old School. The New School, however, tended to take the moderate approach of Beecher, objecting to obvious errors but looking for the good in revivals which were producing such a harvest of souls. Debate over revivalism continued for decades.

Presbyterians in America were committed to mission work from the beginning of their organized life together as ministers immigrated from Britain to plant churches in the New World. Missions in the colonial period had included evangelistic work among Native Americans and slaves as well as white settlers. Presbyterian congregations supported missions through annual collections, and by 1802 the General Assembly appointed a standing Committee on Missions, later renamed the Board of Domestic Missions (1816). Presbyterians also united with other denominations in joint efforts to reach the ever-expanding American frontier. In 1826, the American Home Mission Society (AHMS) was organized in New York by Presbyterian, Dutch Reformed and Congregational churches, but in 1828 the General Assembly reorganized its own Board of Missions which set off competition for loyalty among Presbyterians – some preferring distinctively Presbyterian-sponsored missions and others favoring catholicity over sectarian missions.

Multi-denominational mission agencies, called "voluntary societies," included the United Foreign Mission Society (UFMS) established in 1816 as a cooperative effort between Dutch Reformed,

Associate Reformed and Presbyterian Churches. A number of Presbyterians supported the American Board of Commissioners for Foreign Missions (ABCFM), organized by Congregationalists in 1810. ABCFM had come out of the 1806 "haystack revival" when Williams College students in Massachusetts made a pact to serve overseas. By 1826, the ABCFM and the UFMS were united as one organization which was approved by the Presbyterian General Assembly. This troubled certain Presbyterians who worried about accountability and the presence of New England theology in the ABCFM. The 1829 General Assembly steered a middle course, declaring: "... the churches should be left entirely to their own unbiased and deliberate choice of the medium through which their charities shall flow to bless the perishing."[4]

In order to sustain this escalating mission work at home and abroad, it was crucial that the church provide a steady stream of ministers for the task. Presbyterians had always made education obligatory for clergy, but it was a daunting task to provide sufficient opportunity for ministerial training. The Log College and College of New Jersey had met basic needs admirably but many believed more was necessary. Archibald Alexander, addressing the General Assembly in 1808, stated, "We shall not have a regular and sufficient supply of well-qualified ministers of the Gospel until every Presbytery, or at least every Synod, shall have under its direction a seminary." At first, Alexander's idea of geographic seminaries was rebuffed and efforts were focused on establishing one Presbyterian seminary to serve the church as a whole. However, in the following decades the idea was embraced as Presbyterians founded regional schools.

The mother Presbyterian seminary, Princeton, opened its doors in 1812 with Ashbel Green as president (1812-1848) and Archibald Alexander (1812-1851) as the first professor. The Princeton pledge, taken by all professors at the seminary, included this vow: "... I do solemnly promise and engage, not to inculcate, teach, or insinuate anything which shall appear to me to contradict or contravene, either directly or impliedly, anything taught in said Confession of Faith or Catechism; ..."[5] The Princeton pledge was clearly Old School in its strict allegiance to Westminster orthodoxy, but it would not be required of professors at other Presbyterian seminaries. At New School Auburn

Seminary, organized in 1820 by the Synod of Geneva in New York, professors took essentially the same vow as all Presbyterian ministers "to receive and adopt the system of doctrine" in the *Confession*. Other New School oriented seminaries were the 1819 Southern and Western Seminary in Tennessee (Maryville College, 1842), Lane Seminary in Cincinnati (1832) whose president was revivalist Lyman Beecher, and Union Seminary in New York (1836). Old School seminaries included Union Seminary in Virginia (1824), Western Seminary, renamed Pittsburgh Seminary (1827), Centre College in Kentucky (1828) out of which came Danville Seminary (Louisville Seminary) in 1853 and the Theological Seminary of South Carolina and Georgia (1831) which was later called Columbia Seminary. Old School seminaries were answerable to their Synods, whereas, New School seminaries usually had independent boards of directors who were not under direct ecclesiastical authority. This difference underscored the conservative Old School perception that New School seminaries were not properly accountable and therefore could not always be trusted. Old School and New School seminary faculties sparred in the theological journals of the day, each party claiming it was the legitimate heir of the Presbyterian heritage.

OLD SCHOOL PRESBYTERIANS

By the 1830s two primary factions were present in the Presbyterian Church – a traditionalist Old School party and a more innovative New School party, divided by emphases in theology and practice. The focal point for much of the ongoing dispute was the question of faithfulness to the *Confession*. Old School advocates alleged that New School presbyteries were unwilling to discipline unorthodox ministers, hence the cure was enforcing strict adherence to doctrinal standards. The religious periodicals of the period were filled with debate over the meaning of confessional subscription. Some Old School men argued that if a consensus on this matter could be achieved, other issues with the New School could be resolved.

There was no monolithic Old School camp, neither was there absolute unanimity on the New School side. The professors at Princeton represented a group of moderate Old School men who critiqued the extremism of Nathaniel Taylor but accepted most New School Presbyterians as orthodox. The Princeton "peace men" believed there was not sufficient ground for ecclesiastical separation and appealed to the larger church to maintain a balanced perspective. On the volatile subscription issue, Charles Hodge argued against the two divisive extremes: strict "adoption of all the doctrines of the Confession" (Old School "ultras') and the latitudinarian "fundamental doctrines of the gospel" (extreme New School). Both positions represented the outer edges of each group. Hodge contended for the historic median position of professing to adopt the "Calvinistic system" of doctrine in the *Confession* as opposed to a Pelagian or Arminian view. Both Old School and New School contained a moderate middle group that agreed with Hodge, but vocal minorities tried to drown them out.

Professor Samuel Miller entered the fray in his pacific *Letters to Presbyterians* (1833) which attempted to assuage the tide of distrust sweeping through the church. Miller wrote sixteen open letters that were widely distributed, calling both parties to account for their faults in antagonizing the other wing of the church. According to Miller, the Old School had been overly rigorous in its demands and perpetually preoccupied with "heresy hunting." For its part, the New School appeared to "always sustain and acquit lax theology to whatever extreme it may go." Both practices were harmful to church unity, wrote Miller, who exhorted Presbyterians to avoid the extremes of either expecting perfect uniformity of views or resisting every censure of doctrinal error.[6]

Old School complaints about laxity in doctrine targeted cooperative arrangements with non-Presbyterian groups, revivalist theology, and New School publications that espoused teaching inconsistent with Reformed theology. Albert Barnes, pastor of First Presbyterian Church in Philadelphia, had charges filed against him in 1831 for the content of his sermon, "The Way of Salvation." Complaints were raised about receiving Barnes into Philadelphia Presbytery, and neither presbytery nor Synod could resolve the issue, so it was appealed to the General Assembly. The case was referred to a committee, chaired by Dr. Samuel Miller of Princeton, which recommended all proceedings against Mr. Barnes be suspended. The General Assembly concurred. Not satisfied with this outcome, Old School ultras continued to press their case through annual protests to the General Assembly. At the 1835 Assembly, Old School delegates used their majority to push through declarations on the duty of supporting Presbyterian missions, the necessity of examining ministers transferring from one presbytery to another and initiated a process to annul the 1801 Plan of Union. These actions were a direct assault on the New School, who pushed back with a vengeance the following year.

Southern Presbyterians had been sideline spectators of northern Old School / New School battles, sometimes wondering what all the fuss was about. Things began to change in the 1830s as the topic of abolition was reintroduced to General Assembly meetings. In 1818, the Presbyterian General Assembly had adopted a very strong anti-slavery statement which declared: "We consider the voluntary enslaving of one part of the human race by another, as a gross violation of the most precious and sacred rights of human nature; as utterly inconsistent with the laws of God, which requires us to love our neighbour as ourselves, and as totally irreconcilable with the spirit and principles of the gospel of Christ. ..." The declaration condemned slavery but also acknowledged the particular difficulty of the Southern situation. A moderate position of gradual emancipation had kept slavery out of General Assembly discussions for a number of years, but an 1835 petition from Ohio, calling for immediate abolition, brought the controversial subject back to center stage.

The American slavery situation had become intense in the 1830s. Radical abolitionist papers, Nat Turner's massacre of fifty-seven whites, and rumors of more slave uprisings had produced a hardened pro-slavery attitude in the South. In the Presbyterian Church abolitionism was identified with the New School and with revivals beginning with Finney who had helped spread radical abolitionist rhetoric throughout the North. The Ohio overture troubled Southerners in the Assembly who now looked more favorably upon Old School partisans inclined to keep abolition agitation out of General Assembly business. The 1835 General Assembly commissioned a Committee on Slavery, chaired by Samuel Miller, to report back to the Assembly the next year. Meanwhile, Southern Presbyterians supposed they were about to be "unchurched" by their denomination for slaveholding.

At the same time tempers were flaring over abolition, Albert Barnes again became the target of Old School conservatives. In 1835, Barnes had published a commentary on the book of Romans, which he had intended as a Sunday School resource. Immediately, Old School papers and periodicals began attacking *Barnes' Notes on Romans* as "unsound and dangerous." Charles Hodge offered a balanced review. While acknowledging there were some erroneous statements, he opined that there was much good in the book, and Barnes was not a heretic. Conservatives, determined to prosecute Barnes, brought charges against him for doctrines "contrary to the Standards of the Presbyterian Church." Barnes was acquitted by his presbytery in summer 1835, but when Synod reversed this decision and suspended him from the ministry, Barnes appealed to the General Assembly. Conservatives viewed the Barnes case coming before the 1836 Assembly as a referendum on New School doctrine that would determine the fate of the Presbyterian Church.

THE GREAT DIVIDE

The New School also viewed the upcoming Assembly as a test case for confessional boundaries in the Presbyterian Church. Determined to exonerate Barnes, whose convictions were shared by a number of New School men, the New School was irritated with the censorious spirit of Barnes' Old School attackers and was in no mood to negotiate. The 1836 New School majority pushed through their agenda on Barnes, missions support and slavery, completely alienating Old School conservatives by their unwillingness to compromise at any point. The General Assembly of 1836 cleared Barnes of all charges, refusing to censure any of his writings, and the Assembly backed the ABCFM, opposing a separate Assembly Board of Missions. Dr. Miller tried to broker moderate concessions to the Old School. He proposed censuring portions of Barnes' commentary and recommended a compromise on missions that would have endorsed both interdenominational missions as well as Presbyterian missions. Both of Miller's attempts to offer the Old School a palm branch failed. On the slavery question, a motion to "indefinitely postpone" any discussion passed, but vociferous New School protests to postponement sealed in the Southern mind a connection of abolition with New Schoolism.

As soon as the 1836 General Assembly concluded, Old School leaders began to organize for a response. They were now convinced that ecclesiastical separation from the New School was the only option left since discipline in church courts had failed. The perception among conservatives was that ministers from Plan of Union presbyteries had cast the deciding votes to exonerate Barnes. Professor Hodge of Princeton was dismayed by New School unwillingness to find middle ground but he firmly asserted this was inadequate justification for schism. He exhorted his fellow Old School men to trust New School claims of fidelity to the Westminster Standards. Princeton's influence was waning, and her pleas for peace went unheeded by resolute Old School conservatives who chided Princeton to get on board for an inevitable split.

In 1837, the conservative Old School party held a pre-Assembly Convention where they adopted a hands-off strategy on slavery and issued a declaration on the problems in the church: "hostility to the doctrines of the confession," toleration of the "heresies of Taylor" and the "policies of Finney." All of these errors were "virtually sanctioned" by the 1836 Assembly according to the Old School convention. When the 1837 General Assembly convened, an Old School moderator was elected on a close ballot. The Old School proceeded to systematically dismantle the church by officially abrogating the 1801 Plan of Union – which was interpreted as exscinding four New School synods – and ordering the investigation of errors in several presbyteries. An Assembly Board of Missions was appointed with a request that several voluntary societies cease operations in the Presbyterian Church.

After the Old School-dominated Assembly finished its ecclesiastical surgery, in the midst of strident New School protests, the New School members of the Assembly reconvened the next day at Albert Barnes' church. The New School challenged the accusations of heresy and condemned the Assembly's "unconstitutional measures." They directed all New School presbyteries to send delegates to the 1838 Assembly the next year, including those presbyteries exscinded by the dissolved Plan of Union. At a late summer convention in Auburn, New York, New School delegates officially responded to an Old School list of sixteen alleged errors by producing their own statement of "true doctrines" reflecting their genuine views. This "Auburn Declaration," as it came to be known, cited the 1729 Adopting Act with its allowance of "scruples" to substantiate their claims of Presbyterian orthodoxy. When the 1838 General Assembly opened, New School commissioners from the four excluded synods were not recognized, accordingly these delegates and those from twenty-nine other New School presbyteries elected their own Assembly officers and adjourned to another location.

NEW SCHOOL PRESBYTERIANS

The first act of the "true" Presbyterian Church (New School) was to adopt a resolution decrying the unconstitutional excision of the four synods and declaring the legal standing of the excluded synods. Declarations were issued in support of the voluntary societies; Lane, Auburn and Union (New York) seminaries were endorsed, and the rule requiring presbyteries to examine transferring ministers was rescinded. The New School Assembly also recommended the *Confession of Faith* and *Form of Government* for greater circulation among the presbyteries. A "Pastoral Letter" to the churches, explaining the schism and affirming commitment to the Presbyterian doctrinal standards, stated: "We love and honor the Confession of Faith of the Presbyterian Church as containing more well-defined, fundamental truth, with less defect, than appertains to any other human formula of doctrine, and as calculated to hold in intelligent concord a greater number of sanctified minds than any which could now be framed; and we disclaim all design past, present or future to change it."[7]

For the New School church, the 1840s were an era of developing self-identity and organizational growth. Property litigation with the Old School denomination was abandoned as the New School concentrated on its own mission, experiencing revivals of religion and increases of church membership by profession of faith. The New School established its own Boards and Publishing house but remained on the defense against relentless attacks in the Old School press. The New School journal, *The Presbyterian Quarterly Review* (1852), was often preoccupied with defending the "constitutional" Presbyterian Church as the genuine heir of the Presbyterian founding fathers.

In 1852 the editors of the New School journal described the New School mission as a calling to defend "old fashioned, Catholic, American Presbyterianism." The mission was described under four principles: religious liberty, living Calvinism, co-operative Christianity and an aggressive Christianity. "Living Calvinism" was understood as the "true line of succession" from the Log College and the New Side which emphasized the element of piety. The robust theology of Calvin needs to be infused with inward piety. The editors stated, "Without piety, it tends to formalism and a freezing orthodoxy or Antinomianism, as Arminianism degenerates into more nervous sentimentalism, or ungovernable enthusiasm for lack of substance."[8]

The 1840s and '50s were a period of American national expansion – statehood for Texas in 1845, the California gold rush and the Oregon territory coming under United States jurisdiction. The nation was at war with Mexico (1848), and fresh waves of immigrants from Ireland, Germany and China arrived on America shores. The first Chinese Presbyterian Church was organized in California in 1853. By mid-century Presbyterians had built churches and mission stations across the newly populated territories with established congregations giving faithfully to support home missions.

This was a time of increased strain between slave and free states as vocal antislavery men continued their unabated attack upon the South, while Southerners pushed back with hardened proslavery positions. The Fugitive Slave Act of 1850, the publishing of *Uncle Tom's Cabin* in 1851 by Harriet Beecher Stowe (daughter of New School Minister, Lyman Beecher), and the 1857 Dred Scott decision each added to the swelling tide. The 1850s mayhem in "bleeding Kansas" became an armed contest between proslavery and antislavery settlers. Militant abolitionist John Brown and six comrades executed five proslavery Kansas settlers in 1856. In 1859, Brown tried to initiate a slave insurrection at Harper's Ferry but was stopped by soldiers under Colonel Robert E. Lee.

Increasing fear about the "irrepressible conflict" made its way into churches, producing deep division among Christians. New School Assemblies during the 1850s were frequently troubled with the slavery question, unlike the Old School which had an unspoken agreement that slavery would not be discussed publicly. In 1853, the New School Assembly asked all its presbyteries to give a progress report on rooting out the evils of slavery; the mandate was ignored by Southern New School Presbyterians. By 1856, New School abolitionists urged disciplinary action, and Southerners, believing their liberty of conscience was being violated, departed to form a Southern New School church. The United Synod of the South, which was organized in Knoxville in 1858, consisted of 285 New School churches who vowed "political agitation" and "ultra abolitionist sentiments" would have no part in their new church. The United Synod immediately made overtures to the Old School for reunion discussions, but the Old School church was uninterested in 1858. This attitude would alter noticeably as the War Between the States progressed.

When the Civil War began in 1861 the New School (North) was firmly with the Union, having already purged itself of the southern contingent. The case was very different in the Old School which had been able to maintain ecclesiastical unity despite sectional pressures. Things changed at the 1861 General Assembly when Gardiner Spring of New York put forward a resolution urging Old School loyalty to the Federal Government. Under protest from Charles Hodge and the few southern delegates in attendance that year, the Spring resolution passed the Assembly easily (156 to 66). Irate Southerners interpreted this as excluding them from the Old School body and removed themselves to set up their own church. The Presbyterian Church in the Confederate States of America was established in 1861 by forty-one Southern Old School presbyteries assembled at First Presbyterian Church in Augusta, Georgia.

The Southern Old School church was characterized by traditional consistent Calvinism, an emphasis on parity of ruling and teaching elders, a doctrine of the "Spirituality of the Church" (no political involvement) and the defense of slavery. One of her ablest leaders was James Henley Thornwell of South Carolina who served the church as a pastor, seminary professor and college president. Thornwell's life was cut short (1812-1862), but he left the Southern Church a host of theological writings, including his infamous defense of slavery as sanctioned by the Bible. A gifted successor was Robert L. Dabney (1820-1898) of Virginia, a professor of theology and prolific writer who served as chaplain for General Thomas "Stonewall" Jackson (a Presbyterian deacon) during the war. When Old School and New School in the South began contemplating reunion, the Old School branch turned to Dabney for leadership.

In 1836 there was one Presbyterian Church in the United States, but by 1861 there were four Presbyterian bodies – an Old School and New School in both North and South. Theological and sectional differences had splintered the Presbyterian household in striking ways that produced long-term repercussions. The war years devastated the nation and consumed the energy of churches trying to carry on ministry in the midst of civil war. As the bitter contest continued, Presbyterians in the South reconnected, but in the North reunion discussions did not begin until the War Between the States was concluded. In both instances, the war had given Presbyterians a new perspective on ecclesiastical unity.

NINETEENTH-CENTURY REUNIONS

The United Synod of the South (New School) had initiated interest in reunion as early as 1858 only to be rebuffed by the Old School Church which was still undivided. Just three years later things had dramatically changed when a separate Old School Southern Church was born. This time the subject of reunion was raised from the Old School side. From its first General Assembly the Southern Old School Church had expressed a desire for closer communion with other Reformed churches in the South. A Committee of Conference was appointed in 1863 to meet with representatives of the United Synod, and a meeting was set for Lynchburg, Virginia with Dabney leading the Old School group and Dr. Joseph Stiles serving as chief spokesman for the New School. Dabney presented an opening speech with "entire fairness" and "the spirit of magnificent equity" according to Stiles, who declared that if Dr. Dabney's views represented those of the Old School, "the breach between us is healed."

Drs. Dabney and Stiles later met as a sub-committee to draw up articles for union. After full discussion and amendment by the joint committee, the articles were unanimously endorsed by both groups. The joint committee charitably and directly addressed the issues dividing the Old and New Schools, seeking to find common ground. The doctrinal articles were a series of counterbalancing statements that were both sensitive to New School emphases while also affirming traditional Old School theology. On the atonement, for example, the balanced statement declared:

> This atonement we believe, ... full and sufficient for the guilty of
> the whole world, and is to be freely and sincerely offered to every
> creature, inasmuch as it leaveth no other obstacle to the pardon of

all men under the Gospel, save the enmity and unbelief of those
who voluntarily reject it ... And, on the other hand, we hold that
God the Father doth efficaciously apply this redemption, through
Christ's purchase, to all those to whom it was His eternal purpose
to apply it, and to no others.[9]

On missions support, the statement encouraged churches to give
aid for missions "as their Christian conscience approve" whether that be
through "societies of voluntary and human origin" or through "branches
of Christ's visible church." Concerning the revival controversy, the
article stated:

> ... it is dangerous to ply the disordered heart of the sinner with
> a disproportionate address to the imagination and passions ...
> and to employ with him such novel and startling measures as
> must tend to impart to his religious excitement a character rather
> noisy, shallow and transient, than deep, solid, and Scriptural.
> ... But, on the other hand, we value, cherish, and pray for true
> revivals of religion, and wherever they bring forth the permanent
> fruits of holiness in men's hearts, rejoice in them as God's
> work, notwithstanding the mixture of human imperfection.
> And we consider it the solemn duty of ministers to exercise a
> Scriptural warmth, affection, and directness in appealing to the
> understanding, hearts, and consciences of men.[10]

A handful of the strict Southern Old School men resisted
the reunion because they believed the doctrinal articles were an
abandonment of Old School principles. Dabney ably defended the
reunion agreements before the 1864 Old School General Assembly in
Charlotte, North Carolina. Dabney told his Old School brethren: "A
right cause can be advocated in a wrong spirit; ... we should be willing
to confess that part of the guilt [for the schism] is ours."[11] The Southern
Old School Assembly overwhelmingly adopted the Plan of Union with
only seven dissenting votes; the Southern New School Assembly was
unanimous in favor of union. The reunited "Southern Church" had
affirmed a moderate Calvinism that was agreeable to the majority of
former Old School and New School ministers who now joined hands
as one Presbyterian Church in the South.

The road to Presbyterian reunion in the North took longer. The southern men had worked out a plan for union after one meeting but it would take several years of post-war negotiations to consummate union in the North. A number of factors paved the way for a climate favorable for union among the former Old School / New School adversaries. From the beginning of the war, the Northern New School Church was intensely loyal to the Federal Government. It abhorred slavery and the Southern rebellion that supported the evil institution. Southerners in both parties were now departed, and the northern Old School had been both devoted to the Federal Government and more critical of slavery as the war years progressed. Even with the removal of these obstacles, when reunion discussions began, both parties considered the other rigid and a compromiser of Presbyterian principles. It became clear very early that the question of confessional subscription would be the principal obstacle along the road to reunion. Meetings of the Joint Committee revealed, however, that there was more accord on this issue than either side realized.

One of the principle New School spokesmen was Henry B. Smith (1815-1877), professor of theology at New York's Union Seminary. Dr. Smith defended the New School's understanding of subscription against Old School attacks by articulating a clear traditional view, which Charles Hodge acknowledged as the same view he advocated. The New School had been accused of harboring "latitudinarian" subscription, that is, a broad "substance of doctrine" or "essentials of Christianity only" view which did not require adoption of the "system of doctrine" in the Confession as historically understood. Smith countered that the New School reject the extremes of either latitude or a strict "every proposition" view. Smith argued for a median position on subscription that he described this way:

> The right theory is found in a simple and honest interpretation
> of the ordination formula, 'that we receive the Confession of
> Faith as containing the system of doctrine taught in the Holy
> Scriptures.' This declares that the system of the Confession is
> the system taught in the Bible. The system of the Confession,
> as everybody knows, is the Reformed or Calvinistic system, in
> distinction from the Lutheran, Arminian, the Antinomian, the
> Pelagian, and the Roman Catholic. No one can honestly and fairly

subscribe the Confession who does not accept the Reformed or
Calvinistic system.[12]

After much give and take, a Joint Committee of Reunion proposed
a "Plan of Union" that was presented to the 1868 General Assemblies.
Both Assemblies adopted the Plan, but a protest was raised on the Old
School side about an "explanatory clause" in one article that appeared
to grant too much doctrinal latitude. New School men raised concern
about a controversial provision for re-examining ministers which had
been a sticking point for the New School, fearful that Old School
presbyteries might refuse admission of transferring ministers. Taking
into consideration these objections, a revised Plan was re-submitted
to both 1869 Assemblies meeting in New York City within walking
distance of one another. The Old School voted in favor of union with
only nine negative votes while the New School vote was unanimous.
By 1870 there were two main branches of American Presbyterianism,
which was now divided North and South rather than Old School and
New School. There were several unsuccessful attempts in the latter
decades of the nineteenth century to reunite the two bodies. It would
be more than one hundred years before Presbyterians were able to
reconnect the two major portions of the church that had been separated
since the Civil War.

THE CONNECTION

The nineteenth century was a period of great social/political strife
in the United States. The sectional division that ripped the national
fabric also penetrated church life. Old and New School parties went
separate ways, and by the middle of the century further schism divided
Presbyterians geographically. During the reunions, the Old School and
New School came to realize that their great difference had primarily
been one of emphasis and ministry practice rather than theology.
Unity did not require uniformity. Despite barriers which sometimes
seemed insurmountable, Presbyterians came to understand that they
needed one other. Commitment to both historic Calvinism and
contemporary ministry to a rapidly changing society were equal values;
ignoring either one could bring great peril to the church. A healthy

balance of theological integrity and missional effectiveness continue to characterize the best of twenty-first century American Presbyterianism.

The proliferation of para-church organizations (voluntary societies) in the nineteenth century had a keen impact on American Christianity. Presbyterians provided leadership in many of these multi-denominational organizations which focused on world missions, church planting, education and abolition. The spirit of cooperation that pervaded the societies became part of the Presbyterian ethos. Alongside strong support for distinctive Presbyterian programs, many believed that ecumenical approaches to spreading the gospel could be even more effective. Contemporary Presbyterians view the two approaches as complementary, encouraging monetary support for both Presbyterian missions and organizations such as Wycliffe Bible Translators, Campus Crusade for Christ (Cru), World Vision, Samaritan's Purse, etc.

Nineteenth-century Presbyterians learned a painful lesson on the dangers of aligning the church with social/political issues that compromise the faith. Many believers in the South defended race-based slavery because of social pressure to conform to the Southern culture. By doing this, Southern Presbyterians twisted Scripture to suit the predicament of the day as they understood it. Contemporary Christians have been tempted to do the same thing with abortion and homosexuality. Some have ignored the clear teachings of Scripture in order to support the societal value of "choice," which attempts to rationalize killing the unborn. Other Presbyterians have argued for the legitimacy of homosexual ordination and marriage, again bowing to contemporary social agendas rather than submitting to the Word of God.

9

FACING NEW CHALLENGES
Modernists Question Historic Christianity

"O Timothy, guard the deposit entrusted to you. Avoid the irreverent babble and contradictions of what is falsely called 'knowledge,' for by professing it some have swerved from the faith."
1 Timothy 6: 20, 21

"The movement [Modernism] is slowly secularizing the church and, if permitted to go unchecked and unchallenged, will ere long produce in our churches a new kind of Christianity, a Christianity of opinions and principles and good purposes, but a Christianity without worship, without God, and without Jesus Christ."[1]
Clarence E. Macartney, Presbyterian minister (1879-1957)

The reunion of the Old and New School Presbyterians was celebrated as a new era of brotherhood and common mission. With the War Between the States concluded, a new optimism for reaching a continent for Christ prevailed in the churches. Reconstruction in the South exacerbated residual sectional tensions, and though there were cries for a national Presbyterian reunion, it was not to be. Each Presbyterian body (North and South) faced new challenges during the post-war years of transition. Presbyterian influence in the nation continued to dissipate as Baptist and Methodist churches proliferated; these denominations were more amenable to the entrepreneurial, democratic spirit pervading much of evangelical Christianity in America, especially in the South.

The second half of the nineteenth century ushered in a period of seismic cultural and theological change in the United States. Millions of immigrants, many of whom were Roman Catholics or Jews, immigrated to large urban areas in the pre-Civil War years, changing the face of America forever. Ethnic and religious pluralism began to be an American reality. The former days of Anglo-Protestant hegemony were gone. Urbanization and industrialization shaped the new cultural landscape as city life reflected more and more diversity and distance from traditional Protestant values.

The new theory of evolution and higher criticism of the Bible began to erode the Christian principles that had influenced American society since before the founding of the Republic. Questions about the unique role of the Bible surfaced from those who viewed Scripture as just another piece of religious literature subject to human evaluation like any other ancient document. Evangelicals, who emphasized personal conversion and piety, held to a high view of Holy Scripture and shifted into an apologetic mode, defending the historic Christian understanding of the Bible. Liberals or "modernists" took another approach, choosing to accommodate Christianity to the new science and skepticism of the Bible's historicity and accuracy. Battle lines within the church were drawn as advocates of the two very different approaches squared off against one another in the courts of the church.

ENLIGHTENMENT AND EVOLUTION

The term "Modernism" described a new outlook in philosophy, science and religion that questioned traditional theology, contending that Christianity needed updating in the light of modern discoveries. Its seminal principles can be traced to the period known as the Enlightenment or "Age of Reason" of the seventeenth/eighteenth centuries in the Old World. Copernicus' (d. 1543) new cosmology with the sun at the center of the universe (not earth), Francis Bacon's (d. 1626) methods of experimentation and the devastating effects of European religious wars (Thirty-Years War, 1618-1648) set the stage for a revolution in intellectual pursuits. Building upon embryonic ideas from the Renaissance, Enlightenment philosophy and science fostered an optimistic anthropology which accentuated man's intellectual and moral capabilities. Rejecting ecclesiastical dominance, Enlightenment thinkers elevated the autonomous human's ability to discover universal natural laws. With man at the center of the universe (not God), truth or religion must be based upon reason not revelation. The revolution in philosophy may be traced to the father of modern philosophy, Frenchman René Descartes (d. 1650), who sought answers in man's ability to think (*"cogito ergo sum"*) and discover truth apart from divine revelation. English philosopher John Locke (d. 1704) argued for the reasonableness of Christianity, but others, like the Frenchman Voltaire (d. 1778), turned to Deism which aimed to reduce religion to universally valid "laws of nature" and human rationality. Scottish philosopher David Hume (d. 1776) embraced skepticism, believing that neither the rationality of Christianity nor Deism yielded certitude.

German philosopher Immanuel Kant (d. 1804) pursued a middle ground between skeptical rationalism and traditional Christianity by arguing for a special domain for religion. Kant believed that morality was the proper sphere of religion. His *Critique of Pure Reason* argued that realities lying beyond space and time cannot be known by empirical science. Man's "practical reason" (the moral dimension) is the realm of faith, a universal human moral experience that is rational and provides the "ought" of moral duty. Kant reversed the order of grace and works advocating that human beings should progress from virtue to pardoning grace. The person of Christ and the stories of the Bible should be understood in terms of moral virtue. Theology was grounded in morality for Kant, and man should look within to discern moral truth.

One of the important responses to Kant was the work of German theologian Friedrich Schleiermacher (1768-1834), known as the "father of modern theology." Born in Prussia, the son of a Reformed pastor, Schleiermacher read widely in Enlightenment philosophy and began to question certain doctrines of the Christian faith. Schleiermacher shared Kant's critique of rationalism. He also rejected the religious indifference of his age, symbolically displayed in the French Revolution's 1793 enthronement of the goddess of reason in Notre Dame Cathedral. He attempted to resolve the conflict between orthodoxy and rationalism by heralding religious experience as the true source of theology. In 1799, he wrote *On Religion: Speeches to its Cultured Despisers*, describing human "feeling" as the essence of religion not creedal propositions about God. According to Schleiermacher, Christianity is a consciousness of being "absolutely dependent" and theology is human reflection on religious experience of God. Schleiermacher redefined Christian doctrine in his systematic theology, *The Christian Faith* (1822). He denied the Bible as an exclusive source of belief, rejected the two natures of Christ as illogical and explained redemption as Christ communicating his God-consciousness to others. Schleiermacher's innovations laid the bedrock for late nineteenth-century liberal theology and its rejection of traditional Christian beliefs.

In America, Horace Bushnell (d.1876), a New England Congregational pastor who had studied under Nathaniel Taylor, initiated a new approach to the Bible in a "Dissertation on Language" included in his book *God in Christ* (1849). Bushnell claimed that all religious language is poetical not literal which implied that exact Christian systems of belief are invalid because spiritual realities cannot be expressed in definitive language. Modernist theologians utilized Bushnell's novel hermeneutical method to reinterpret Scripture in line with their new theology.

German scholar Albrecht Ritschl (d.1889), following the lead of Kant, stressed ethics as the core of Christianity, calling for a just and moral society emulating Christ's example and thus realizing the "kingdom of God." Berlin professor Adolf Harnck popularized Ritchl's theology in *What is Christianity?* (1900). He argued that the kernel of the Gospel is the commandment to love and establishment of a just social order based on the universal fatherhood of God and brotherhood of man. In the following decades this "Social Gospel" was advocated in the United States by New York Baptist minister Walter Rauschenbusch (d. 1918) whose *Christiantiy and the Social Crisis* (1907) criticized laissez-faire capitalism as the evil culprit of the growing gap between rich and poor in America.

Underneath these emerging "liberal" redefinitions of historic Christianity lay not only Enlightenment philosophy but also historical-critical methods of Biblical study. German theologian, David Strauss (d. 1874), in his *Life of Jesus*, had suggested that Jesus was not viewed as the Messiah in his own day. According to Strauss, the virgin birth, miracles and the resurrection were not historical but myths used by the Biblical writers to express how Jesus' life had influenced their lives. The so-called "quests for the historical Jesus" by critical scholars challenged the reliability of the Gospel accounts, declaring that Jesus was an ordinary human being who became the subject of legend. In Old Testament studies, Julius Wellhausen (d.1918) rejected traditional views of Israel's history, contesting Mosaic authorship of the Pentateuch and substituting a "documentary hypothesis" of multiple authors over many centuries. Theological liberals embraced these critical presuppositions because they believed Christianity was actually about human experience and morality, not outdated dogmas incompatible with modern science.

Another direct assault on conventional understanding of the Old Testament was Charles Darwin's theory of biological evolution. Darwin's *Origin of Species* (1859) postulated that animal life on earth was the product of natural selection over millions of years, rejecting the Genesis account of special creation. Evolutionary ideas influenced the new field of Comparative Religion which raised further questions about accepted views of Christianity. Descriptive study of world religions caused scholars to jettison convictions about Christian uniqueness as they concentrated on cultural development and the common elements in all religions. The fields of Psychology of Religion and Philosophy of Religion also appeared during this era, seeking philosophical and naturalistic explanations for religious behavior and experience, thus challenging traditional understanding of the Christian faith.

REACTION IN PRESBYTERIAN SEMINARIES

The Presbyterian churches, like all denominations in the United States, had to deal with the challenges of liberal thought as it began to exert influence in the late nineteenth century. The conservative professors at Princeton Seminary entered the battle with full force defending the faith against what they perceived as departures from orthodox Christianity. Charles Hodge addressed the theory of evolution in his book, *What is Darwinism?* (1873). For Hodge the evolutionary schema requiring long periods of time was not a big issue. He was open to a Day-Age interpretation of Genesis 1 – each day representing an age not necessarily a twenty-four hour day. What troubled Hodge was not the question of how God created the earth but the atheistic philosophy behind Darwin's theory. Theologian Benjamin Breckinridge Warfield

(Hodge's student), who began teaching at Princeton in 1887, believed that one could distinguish between the primal act of creation *ex nihilo* (Gen. 1, 2) and subsequent development of what was originally created. In 1901 B.B. Warfield wrote:

> What, then, is to be the attitude of the Christian man toward the modern doctrine of evolution? He is certainly to deny with all the energy given to him that the conception of evolution can take the place of creation as an account of the origin of the universe. Evolution offers no solution of the question of origins. ... On the other hand, the Christian man has as such no quarrel with evolution when confined to its own sphere as a suggested account of the method of the divine providence. [2]

In the Southern Presbyterian Church, evolutionary teaching on human origins by Columbia Seminary Professor James Woodrow resulted in his 1886 removal from the seminary by General Assembly action. The 1887 Southern Assembly, by a vote of 137 to 13, made this declaration: "Adam's body was directly fashioned by Almighty God of the dust of the ground, without any natural animal parentage." [3]

The Princeton professors also weighed in on the issue of Biblical authority. Warfield's predecessor, Archibald Alexander Hodge (son of Charles Hodge), in his years at Princeton, had emphasized the original autographs of Scripture as immediately inspired by God. In 1881, A.A. Hodge and Warfield collaborated on an article entitled "Inspiration," which declared the Scriptures to be entirely trustworthy and inerrant. Warfield carried the doctrine of inerrancy into the next generation in his exhaustive work, *The Inspiration and Authority of the Bible*, where he laid out an impressive array of arguments for the Scriptures' testimony to itself as the inspired Word of God. Critics of the Bible, said Warfield, began with anti-supernatural biases rather than hard facts, and it was this prejudice which led to denial of Biblical authority.

Not all of the Presbyterian seminaries shared Princeton perspectives on Scripture, and debate over the value of Biblical criticism eventually brought serious strife into the church courts. At the center of the ecclesiastical storm was Old Testament Professor Charles A. Briggs of Union Seminary in New York who began to publish materials supporting critical theories about Isaiah, Daniel and other Old Testament books. The catalyst for the Briggs crisis came in 1891 when he gave an inaugural address as he transferred to the new Biblical theology chair at Union Seminary. In his published speech Briggs declared: "It may be regarded as the certain result of Higher Criticism that Moses did not write the Pentateuch ... Isaiah did not write half of the book that bears his name."[4] The religious press condemned Briggs and the 1891 Presbyterian General Assembly received overtures from 63 presbyteries calling for action. By a vote of 449 to 60, the Assembly vetoed the appointment of Briggs to the new chair at Union exasperating the Union Board of Directors who in turn unilaterally annulled an 1870 agreement which had given the General Assembly veto power over Union faculty appointments. The Briggs case continued in appeal for several years with the Presbytery of New York acquitting him, but the 1893 Assembly finally suspended him from the ministry. Briggs remained at the seminary and joined the Episcopal Church in 1898.

The Briggs trial surfaced a church-wide discussion of the Presbyterian view of Holy Scripture, and the majority clearly sided with Princeton. The 1892 Assembly issued what came to be known as the "Portland Deliverance" which affirmed: "Our church holds that the inspired Word of God, as it came from God, is without error. . . All who enter office in our church solemnly profess to receive them as the only infallible rule of faith and practice. If they change their belief on this point, Christian honor demands that they should withdraw from our ministry."[5] There were however a number of ministers and seminary professors who agreed with Briggs' views and continued their push for a more inclusive attitude in the church. The Briggs affair, as well as several other "heresy" trials in the closing decades of the century, left a bad taste for some churchmen who preferred to concentrate on unity and ministry rather than theological debate.

REVISING THE CONFESSION OF FAITH

New School Presbyterians had expressed reservations about parts of the *Westminster Confession* for decades, objecting to the alleged harshness of predestination in chapter three (Decrees of God), and the phrase "elect infants" in chapter ten (Effectual Calling). By 1890, there were

134 out of 213 Presbyteries in the Northern Presbyterian Church that had indicated their interest in considering revision of the *Confession*. A committee was appointed to draft a revision with the directions not to propose "any alterations or amendments that will in any way impair the integrity of the Reformed or Calvinistic system of doctrine taught in the Confession of Faith."[6] The report came to the 1892 Assembly after input from the presbyteries. The proposed revisions were sent down to the presbyteries for a vote, but each of the recommendations failed to reach the two-thirds approval required for constitutional amendment.

Although the first effort at amending the doctrinal standards had failed, the issue was far from dead. By 1900, thirty-seven presbyteries requested revision or a new creed or both. Another committee was appointed to pursue input from all presbyteries and report back to the Assembly. What surfaced in this survey, in addition to objections in chapters three and ten, were questions about the designation of the Pope as anti-Christ, failure to affirm the universal love of God, inadequate treatment of the Holy Spirit, silence on the world-wide mission of the church and updating seventeenth-century terminology. Momentum toward a moderate revision of the *Confession* was so strong that when the report came before the Assembly it was approved with only two negative votes.

All the proposed modifications received the two-thirds vote required by presbyteries and the 1903 General Assembly completed the process of officially incorporating the changes into the church's constitution. The revisions included a "Declaratory Statement," which confirmed that the doctrine of election should be "held in harmony" with God's love for all humankind. Certain textual variations in a few chapters were made, including a statement declaring that all dying in infancy are saved by Christ. Two chapters were added: "Of the Holy Spirit" and "Of the Love of God and Missions." The previous Assembly (1902) had also adopted a "Brief Statement of Faith" with sixteen short articles. A few Presbyterians, e.g., Warfield, expressed reservations about these new statements but most embraced the additions believing the "generic Calvinism of the Standards" was still intact. In 1942, the more conservative Southern Presbyterian Church added essentially the same two chapters to the *Confession of Faith*.

One immediate by-product of the 1903 revision was a reunion overture from the Cumberland Presbyterian Church that heralded the new Confessional revisions as removing the "fatalism" in the doctrinal standards to which they had long objected. The Cumberland proposal was resisted by those opposed to compromise with Arminians, nevertheless, 194 of 241 presbyteries approved the reunion which was officially consummated in 1906. About a thousand Cumberland churches joined, but a remnant decided not to participate, preferring to maintain their distinct identity as the Cumberland Presbyterian Church.

THE CHURCH IN THE WORLD

The Presbyterian missionary commitment, whether it was evangelism at home or missions abroad, continued unabated in the second half of the nineteenth century. One of the most successful home mission leaders was Sheldon Jackson (1834-1909), a pioneer in church planting in Wisconsin and Minnesota early in his ministry. At one point Jackson had oversight of all Presbyterian mission work between Canada and Mexico and from Nebraska to Nevada, serving as editor of the *Rocky Mountain Presbyterian* from 1872-1882. As the "Alaska Apostle," his tireless ministry to the Eskimos included providing education, economic assistance and starting new churches. Under his leadership, eight Synods were established in the Northwest and over 150 churches were organized. In 1897, Jackson was elected moderator of the Presbyterian Church in the United States of America (Northern Church).

On the foreign field, the work of Ashbel Green Simonton (1833-1867) is noteworthy as the first missionary to Brazil under the auspices of the Presbyterian Board of Foreign Missions. Simonton moved to Rio de Janeiro in 1859 holding his first worship service in Portuguese the next year and leading the struggle for Protestant toleration in this predominately Roman Catholic country. The first Presbyterian Church in Brazil was established in 1862. Three years later the first presbytery in Brazil was organized with an ex-Catholic priest becoming the first native Brazilian pastor. Just before his death from yellow fever at age thirty-seven, Simonton founded the first Presbyterian seminary in Brazil. Today, Simonton's legacy, *Igresia de Presbyteriana de Brasil* (IPB), is a thriving church with a membership of about one million that maintains fraternal relations with conservative American Presbyterian bodies.

Korea was another fruitful mission field for Presbyterians with Horace Underwood (1859-1916), the first Presbyterian missionary to Korea, arriving in 1884. He built an orphanage and school for Korean children, founded the *Korean Religious Tract Society*, helped to translate the Bible and by 1889 had established a congregation. Korean Presbyterianism experienced significant growth over the succeeding decades, and by the end of World War II there were over eight hundred thousand communicant members in the Korean Presbyterian churches. By the 1970s, seventy percent of Protestants in Korea were Presbyterian. Today, the largest Presbyterian congregation in the World, the Young Nak Presbyterian Church in Seoul, has over thirty thousand members. Korean Presbyterians immigrated to America in large numbers in the 1970s and 80s, but the first American Korean Presbyterian church was established as early as 1906 in Los Angeles. A number of Korean immigrant congregations have chosen to affiliate with existing Presbyterian bodies in America; others have preferred to establish new denominations.

Part of the success story in Korea was the insightful missionary methodology of John Livingston Nevius (1829-1893), a Presbyterian missionary in China who undertook an 1890 Korean trip in order to consult with missionaries about appropriate missions strategy. The young Korean church needed to be independent, according to Nevius, and should therefore be self-supporting in church buildings in the native style and providing for her national pastors. Nevius' ideas were published in *Planting and Development of Missionary Churches* (1886) which was widely studied by missionaries. The other noteworthy book of Nevius was *Demon Possession and Allied Themes* (1894), published the year after he died. In this book, Nevius described his own experience in China with demonic activity that set itself against gospel proclamation.

American Presbyterians continued to be involved in public affairs in the early twentieth century. The most prominent Presbyterian politician of the era was President Thomas Woodrow Wilson (1856-1924), a Presbyterian elder and son of Presbyterian minister, Dr. Joseph R. Wilson. Woodrow Wilson was of Scots-Irish descent, his paternal grandfather, James Wilson, having immigrated to Philadelphia from Northern Ireland in 1807. His maternal grandfather and namesake,

Thomas Woodrow, was a Presbyterian minister and native of Scotland who came to America in 1835. Joseph Ruggles Wilson, father of Woodrow Wilson, served churches in Virginia, Georgia and North Carolina, as well as taught theology at Columbia Theological Seminary and Southwestern Presbyterian University. Joseph Wilson had been a staunch supporter of the Confederacy. The first General Assembly of the Presbyterian Church in the Confederate States of America (1861) convened at his church, First Presbyterian of Augusta, Georgia.

Woodrow Wilson enrolled at Davidson College in 1873 but had to withdraw for health reasons. Two years later, he attended Princeton University then completed doctoral work at Johns Hopkins University. Wilson returned to Princeton where he served as history professor and then as president of Princeton (1902-1910) – the first layman to serve as president. During his Princeton years, he published the five-volume *A History of the American People* (1902). With a growing reputation as a thinker and communicator, Wilson became Governor of New Jersey and then won the Democratic presidential nomination in 1912. He served the nation for two terms as the twenty-eighth President of the United States. Wilson's administration was preoccupied with the devastating effects of World War I (1914-1918). His vision for lasting peace through a League of Nations, though never realized, was a bold attempt to put his Christian principles into political practice for the cause of world peace. Woodrow Wilson has been called "the most God-centered man" ever to be president. During his years in the White House, he faithfully continued his personal Bible study, prayer and participation at Central Presbyterian Church in Washington, endeavoring to live out his faith while serving in public office.

Another Presbyterian with high public visibility was evangelist Billy Sunday (1862-1935) who preached to more people than any American preacher before Billy Graham. After his conversion, Sunday left his career as a major league baseball player becoming an itinerant evangelist in 1896 and leading preaching campaigns in over 200 major U.S. cities. In 1903, he was ordained as a Presbyterian minister. Known for his unconventional, energetic preaching style, Sunday proclaimed the Gospel to several million people with as many as 300,000 people coming to Christ as a result of his meetings. Sunday's wife, Helen Amelia Thompson, was the organizing genius behind these campaigns which catapulted Sunday into the national spotlight. He became very involved in current social issues supporting Prohibition, women's rights and helping raise millions of dollars to support the American military in World War I.

One American cultural battleground was debate over the theory of evolution and its place in public education. A crucial turning point in this dispute was the "Scopes Monkey Trial" of 1925 with the famous Presbyterian politician William Jennings Bryan (1860-1925) participating in the prosecution. Bryan served in the Wilson administration as Secretary of State and had been the Democratic nominee for President in 1900 and 1908. After politics, Bryan was heavily involved in social concerns, playing a significant advocacy role in the passage of the Eighteenth Amendment (1919) which prohibited the manufacture, sale or transportation of alcoholic liquors in the United States. Bryan attacked the dangers of evolution in his popular public lecture, "The Menace of Darwinism," arguing that it undermined morality which must be based on religious commitments. The teaching of evolution was illegal in Tennessee public schools, and John Scopes, a biology teacher in Dayton, was put on trial for violating the statute. Scopes was defended by lawyer Clarence Darrow who put Bryan on the stand, asking him scientific questions for which Bryan had no answer. While state law was upheld, Bryan and the "fundamentalist" cause were dealt a severe blow, being ridiculed in the press for stupidity. Bryan died just five days after the trial concluded.

MODERNISM IN THE PRESBYTERIAN CHURCH

By the early decades of the twentieth century, Enlightenment-inspired ideas had securely settled into American universities and were beginning to permeate society. Relativity was on the rise in religion and ethics even though only a handful of American theologians (at this point) fully accepted radical ideas. Nevertheless, growing numbers had begun to integrate the new philosophical and scientific principles into modified versions of the faith. In certain ecclesiastical circles, this accommodation to modernity was increasing, but evangelicals decided to fight back with firm public declarations of historic Christian belief. Tensions between liberals and conservatives in the Presbyterian Church (north) continued to grow as evangelicals voiced concern about "Broad

Churchism." The term used by conservatives to describe this drift from traditional orthodoxy was "Modernism," a word borrowed from Roman Catholics who had condemned "Modernism" by papal decree in 1907. The Fundamentalist movement was born as a reaction to inroads of liberal theology into American Protestant denominations. A burgeoning alliance of Protestant conservatives across denominational lines opposed the increasing liberal threat with the publication of a series of twelve paperback books, *The Fundamentals* (1910-1915), with contributors from multiple denominations including Presbyterians. The essays espoused traditional Protestantism by defending a high view of Scripture and offering an apologetic for evangelical doctrine and practice.

The method of defending the faith by focusing on "fundamental" elements made its way into Presbyterian doctrinal deliberations. In 1910, the General Assembly of the Northern Church issued a declaration of "Essential and Necessary Doctrines" which affirmed Christ's virgin birth, sacrifice to satisfy divine justice, bodily resurrection and miraculous ministry, supporting these Biblical truths with the assertion, "the Holy Spirit inspired the Scriptures which are free from error." The 1910 Assembly was clear that it was not intending to reduce the faith to these five points but declared that no candidate could be licensed to preach who would not affirm these truths. For a variety of reasons, there was resistance to imposing this minimal requirement on presbyteries; nevertheless, the General Assemblies of 1916 and 1923 reaffirmed its 1910 position. Modernists and conservatives continued to spar in church courts and periodicals, though there were no new heresy trials. One area of concern was missions for conservatives were convinced that modernism had infiltrated Presbyterian missions, diluting Christian witness.

The lightening rod for the Presbyterian "Fundamentalist-Modernist" battle in the 1920s was the gifted Baptist preacher, Harry Emerson Fosdick, whom ecumenically-minded First Presbyterian Church in New York had called as stated preacher. In 1922, Fosdick preached a sermon that was published as "Shall the Fundamentalists Win?" making a plea for toleration of liberal theology in the church. According to his sermon, the virgin birth, the inerrancy of Scripture and the bodily return of Christ were not essential to the Christian faith. When Clarence E. Macartney, pastor of Philadelphia's Arch Street

Presbyterian Church, preached a counter sermon published as "Shall Unbelief Win?," a firestorm ensued as Philadelphia Presbytery called for the General Assembly to bring New York's First Presbyterian pulpit into line with Presbyterian doctrinal standards. The fires were stoked as conservatives and liberals circulated materials to garner support for their positions heading into the General Assembly of 1923.

Debate on the Philadelphia overture took up five hours at the General Assembly which voted 439 to 359 to direct the Presbytery of New York to deal with Fosdick and report back. New York Presbytery expressed confidence in First Presbyterian Church, but complaints to the 1924 Assembly brought the Fosdick case before the Assembly again. Ultimately, it was concluded that the issue was whether or not Fosdick wanted to enter the Presbyterian Church and thus accept its doctrinal standards. Fosdick declined and resigned his position at First Presbyterian in New York.

In view of the Fosdick situation, the 1923 Assembly had reaffirmed the 1910 five "essential and necessary" doctrines. A group of ministers, reacting to this conservative reemphasis on "essential and necessary doctrines," met in Auburn, New York, and produced a reactionary document that came to be known as the "Auburn Affirmation" (1924). The affirmation claimed to "safeguard the unity and liberty of the Presbyterian Church" by rejecting the doctrine of inerrancy and pleading for "liberty in the interpretation of the Confession." Appealing to Presbyterian history, the ministers stated: "... we are opposed to any attempt to elevate these five doctrinal statements, or any of them, to the position of tests for ordination or for good standing in our church." According to the signers of the Affirmation, the Assembly's five points "... are not the only theories allowed by the Scriptures and our standards as explanations of these facts and doctrines of our religion, ..." The Auburn Affirmation was eventually signed by over twelve hundred Presbyterian ministers.[7]

Around this same time, Dr. J. Gresham Machen, Princeton professor of New Testament, wrote his book, *Christianity and Liberalism* (1923) in which he asserted that extreme versions of liberalism were no longer Christian in any real sense.[8] Machen argued that liberals should depart from the Presbyterian Church since they no longer believed historic Christian doctrines. Not all evangelicals in the Presbyterian Church shared Machen's stance. Many believed the two groups should work together in the church; nonetheless, many Presbyterians were concerned about the broadening of the church which appeared to be undermining basic tenets of Christianity and historic Presbyterianism.

Irregular licensures of two New York Presbytery candidates who denied the virgin birth produced complaints to the 1925 General Assembly which reminded the presbytery about the Assembly's unequivocal 1910 pronouncement on the virgin birth. Liberals, led by New York's Henry Sloane Coffin of Union Seminary, protested that imposing the five doctrines of 1910 was unconstitutional since it had never been approved by the presbyteries. In this tension-filled situation, moderator Charles Erdman (Princeton pastor and professor) tried to diffuse the situation urging the appointment of a special commission to study the current situation to assure the "purity, peace, unity and progress of the Church." The recommendation of Erdman was adopted, and the commission spent two years hearing from different corners of the church.

The commission reported to the 1927 Assembly, carefully clarifying the role of both presbyteries and the Assembly in ordination questions and interpretation of the *Confession of Faith*. The most important commission finding was its opinion that the General Assembly can only declare an article of faith "essential and necessary" by quoting a constitutional document, i.e., the *Westminster Confession of Faith*. This had been a major point made by the Auburn Affirmation signatories, who had protested the 1923 Assembly's attempt to amend the constitution with a list of "essential and necessary" doctrines without consent from presbyteries. The commission's report was unanimously adopted without debate. Through this Assembly action, the liberal wing of the church, hiding behind technical claims of constitutional integrity, gained ground in their resistance to the imposition of fundamental doctrines, all in the name of "Christian liberty." The net effect of these contentious years was to further open the door for presbyteries to allow ever-increasing divergence from the *Confession*, undermining Biblical authority and historic Christian theology.

WESTMINSTER SEMINARY AND THE OPC

Princeton Seminary had historically been on the conservative side of issues facing the Presbyterian Church, but there were moderates on the faculty (like Dr. Erdman) who, unlike Professor Machen, did not believe the liberals should be driven out of the church. Discord at the seminary centered upon Machen's election to the chair of apologetics and ethics and differences between faculty members and the seminary president. To address the Princeton problems, the General Assembly appointed an investigative committee which reported back to the 1927 Assembly. The report indicated that the seminary's organizational structure was contributing to the difficulties and recommended that the Board of Directors and Board of Trustees be combined into a single governing board. Conservatives and liberals again faced off in the church courts as conservatives perceived the reorganization proposal as a veiled attempt to stifle their majority on the faculty. Multiple reports came to the Assembly of 1929 attempting to resolve the impasse at Princeton; nevertheless, the General Assembly proceeded with plans to establish one board. The new singular Board of Trustees invited all faculty members to continue service at the seminary, but four declined the offer.

In September of 1929, Westminster Theological Seminary was opened in Philadelphia with eight professors and fifty-two students. Dr. Machen and the other professors were committed to keeping the conservative principles of "old Princeton" alive at their new seminary. Westminster was supported by numbers of prominent Presbyterians, and early graduates became active ministers in the Presbyterian Church. Though marginalized, Machen was continuing his ministry of theological training within the mainline Presbyterian Church. The issue of missions finally forced him out.

The publication of the book, *Re-Thinking Missions: A Layman's Inquiry after One Hundred Years* (1932), was the harbinger of more argument over missions. Lay authors from seven American denominations (including Presbyterians) participated in this study of foreign missions in multiple countries. The authors surmised that Christians should cooperate with non-Christian religions rather than try to uproot them, underscoring the relativity of Christian truth. Several controversial articles by Pearl S. Buck, who at the time was a Presbyterian missionary in China, also stirred up trouble. The Presbyterian Board of Foreign Missions came under scrutiny, but the General Assembly expressed confidence in the Board. A few Presbyterians did not share the Assembly's evaluation, and in 1933, an Independent Board of Presbyterian Foreign Missions was established with Machen as the president. Some of the Westminster Seminary supporters believed the new mission board was a mistake.

The General Assembly of 1934 decided to play hardball with the Independent Board and passed several resolutions: the Independent Board was to cease operations within the Presbyterian Church; all ministers and laymen connected with the Independent Board were to resign; presbyteries with jurisdiction over persons associated with the Board were to begin disciplinary process if resignations did not occur within ninety days. New Brunswick Presbytery suspended Machen from the ministry, and the Synod of Philadelphia, which had several cases referred to it, suspended five ministers. The hostility expressed toward the Independent Board was soon heaped upon Westminster Seminary as well. When the 1936 General Assembly upheld all the ministerial censures which had been appealed, a group of thirty-four ministers decided to proceed with plans for a separate Presbyterian Church in America, changing their name in 1939 to the Orthodox Presbyterian Church (OPC).

Within a year of the new Presbyterian denomination's founding, Machen died and there was a split within the church. Carl McIntire, who had been suspended like Machen for his association with the Independent Board, and J. Oliver Buswell Jr. (President of Wheaton College) wanted to take the young denomination in a more fundamentalist direction – embracing premillenialism and advocating abstinence from drinking and smoking. The majority favored traditional Reformed understandings of eschatology and Christian liberty. In 1937, a small group followed McIntire and departed to form what became the Bible Presbyterian Church and Faith Theological Seminary. With the fundamentalist element gone, the Orthodox Presbyterian Church's self identity as an orthodox Reformed church emerged in the ensuing decades. The OPC's emphasis on confessional heritage, rather than connections to the broader evangelical movement, solidified. Over the years, the OPC has been involved in several merger discussions with other Reformed bodies, but none of these has been successful. The

OPC has also declined to participate in the National Association of Evangelicals, but is a member of the North American Presbyterian and Reformed Council (NAPARC) that includes a number of conservative Reformed denominations. The OPC has over three hundred churches and mission work in forty-five states with nine active foreign mission fields.[9]

By the end of the 1930s Presbyterianism had splintered, some with-drawing to form the Orthodox Presbyterian Church and other evangelicals deciding to stay the course within the mainline. Most evangelicals still believed that the Northern Presbyterian Church was basically sound and their presence helped preserve her from wholesale apostasy, however more separations followed in the coming decades as liberalism permeated all the Presbyterian seminaries. Ministers trained in these schools spread their "modernist" doctrines, accommodating Christianity to the latest academic theological fad during the coming decades – neo-orthodoxy, process theology, secular theology, theology of hope, liberation theologies or narrative theology.[10] Presbyterianism in America was coming to a crossroads in her history. The question had moved beyond Presbyterian faithfulness to her unique heritage to the larger question: Would Presbyterianism continue to be Christian? By the end of the twentieth century, scores of evangelicals again chose to stay mainline, but progressively more were persuaded that the church was reaching a point of no return.

THE CONNECTION

Conservative Christians drew a line in the sand when parts of the American church began to drift toward a modernized reinterpretation of Christianity. The Presbyterian General Assembly declared that certain "essential and necessary" doctrines about the person and work of Christ were non-negotiable truths central to the Christian faith. Some "modernists" resisted the movement to define core beliefs, urging the church to embrace openness to new expressions of faith. These debates played out in Presbyterian seminaries and led to the founding of Westminster Theological Seminary whose self-identity was dedication to restoring historic orthodox faith to the Presbyterian family. It has been said, "As seminaries go, so goes the church," which has proven to be a rather accurate assessment of twentieth-century American Presbyterianism. The proliferation of conservative Presbyterian seminaries in the United States over the last eighty years confirms the importance Presbyterians place on training the next generation in Biblical Christianity.

Presbyterians faced a crisis when certain ministers began to question historic Christian belief in their public preaching and teaching. In a few instances, persons were removed from the ministry, but the whole process was exhausting and divisive. This is one of the most unpleasant parts of churchly life but one that is necessary to safeguard the purity of the church. Present-day Presbyterians are generally hesitant to pursue church discipline for heresy unless blatant deviation in doctrine makes correction compulsory. There is a balance to be found in these matters. Some may too easily be inclined to church discipline over issues not essential to the faith. On the other hand, others are so adverse to discipline that unashamed disavowal of core Christian beliefs is tolerated in the name of peace and unity. Presbyterian experience indicates that indeed some doctrines are "fundamental," and denying this reality is flirting with spiritual disaster.

The modernist-fundamentalist controversy in American Christianity again raised the old questions about faith and reason. How should the church understand the integration of faith and learning in the light of new research in the physical and social sciences? What is the relationship between human reason and God's revelation? Should scientific theories be allowed to trump the teachings of the Bible, or should Christians stand fast by the final authority of Scripture in everything it teaches? If all truth is God's truth, then should not believers be open to findings in all fields of intellectual inquiry? Presbyterians gave an assortment of answers to these questions which has produced unabated disagreement to the present day.

10

A HOUSE DIVIDED
Evangelicals Leave the Mainline Church

*"You are the salt of the earth, but if salt has lost its taste, how shall
its saltiness be restored? It is no longer good for anything except to be
thrown out and trampled under people's feet. You are the light of the
world. A city set on a hill cannot be hidden. ... let your light shine
before others, so that they may see your good works and give glory to
your Father who is in heaven."*

Matthew 5:13,14,16

*"[Evangelicalism is] Bible believing without shutting one's self off
from the full spectrum of life and in trying to bring Christianity into
effective contact with the current needs of society, government and
culture. It had a connotation of leading people to Christ as Savior, but
then trying to be salt and light in the culture."[1]*

Francis A. Schaeffer, Presbyterian philosopher (1912-1984)

The 1930s schism in the PCUSA (Northern Church) was the
beginning of the exodus from mainline Presbyterianism. While there
are numerous reasons for mainline demise in the twentieth century,
theological issues remained primary for conservatives frustrated
with revisionist theologies and the liberal social agenda advocated
by denominational leadership. Evangelicals in the PCUS (Southern
Church), while seemingly more hesitant to react than their northern
counterparts, were as committed to upholding historic orthodoxy. The

different timetable for schism in the North and South was the result of Machen's being defrocked by the Northern Presbyterian Church and the fact that theological pluralism in the PCUS surfaced more gradually in the years following World War II. Seminary faculties, North and South, imbibed the critical scholarship coming out of Europe, which undermined traditional faith. Conservatives in the mainline bodies tried to resist these trends and established networks supporting Biblical fidelity, but others, pessimistic about renewal efforts, began to contemplate separation from the mother church.

MAINLINE DECLINE

A major influence on American theology in the twentieth century had been the work of Karl Barth (1886-1968). His theology and that of others associated with him (Emil Brunner, Dietrich Bonhoeffer, Reinhold Niebuhr, et.al.) were part of the movement known as Neo-Orthodoxy. A member of the Reformed Church of Switzerland, Barth's Commentary on Romans (*Der Romerbrief*, 1919) marked a break with culture-affirming German liberalism when he charged old liberals with subverting the gospel by trying to make it respectable. In the 1930s, he was part of the anti-Nazi Confessing Church, helping to write the *Barmen Declaration*, a protest against the Nazi German church. Barth emphasized human sinfulness and God's grace in Jesus Christ, but his understanding of election implied universalism – Christ is the only elect one, and all will be saved in him. Barth accepted the results of higher criticism and accentuated God's subjective revelation to individuals through Scripture rather than an objective revelation in Scripture itself as the written Word of God. His scathing attack on liberalism was welcome, but many evangelicals were skeptical, considering Barth's theology a new version of Modernism. In 1962, Barth, at age seventy-five, lectured in the United States for seven weeks to high praise, even appearing on the cover of *Time* magazine.

The post-War years in America were a time of remarkable change for society and the church. The beginnings of the nuclear arms race, the Korean War, man in space, the sexual revolution, civil rights, Vietnam and the feminist movement all raised new theological and ethical questions. Increasingly, Presbyterian seminaries advocated adjustments in historic

Christian faith and practice to address these new questions. Mainline evangelicals, on the other hand, remained firm in their attachment to Biblically-informed Christian witness and found comrades in the larger evangelical movement. In the 1950s, evangelicalism (or, "neo-evangelicalism" to distinguish it from fundamentalism) received considerable momentum from the evangelistic ministry and influence of Billy Graham, whose 1949 crusade in Los Angeles initiated a revived evangelical presence in America. Donald Grey Barnhouse, pastor of Tenth Presbyterian Church in Philadelphia, was a mainline evangelical who gained a national platform through his radio program, "Bible Study Hour," and the founding of *Eternity* magazine. He was a conservative, unswerving in his loyalty to the PCUSA for the purpose of evangelical testimony, but in many ways he had melded into the larger evangelical community through his emphasis on fundamental Christian doctrines and his embrace of premillennialism.

Beginning near mid-century there was fresh interest among evangelicals for cooperative ministry with like-minded believers who shared a common commitment to a high view of Scripture. A key visionary of evangelical ferment during this era was Harold John Ockenga, a former student of Machen's at Westminster Seminary and close friend of Billy Graham. [2] A number of non-denominational organizations emerged attracting participants from across the evangelical spectrum: the National Association of Evangelicals (1942), Fuller Theological Seminary (1947), the Evangelical Theological Society (1949) and later Gordon-Conwell Theological Seminary (1969). Each of these organizations had widespread Presbyterian support around the country. Conservative Presbyterians experienced meaningful fellowship through these ecumenical evangelical associations as well as their own denominational renewal groups.

The mainline ecumenical movement also gained momentum during the post-WWII years creating denominational tensions because evangelicals believed these organizations clouded the clarity of the gospel through their minimalist version of Christianity and preoccupation with progressive social policy. The World Council of Churches (WCC) was constituted in 1948, and the National Council of Churches (NCC) was established through the merger of thirteen organizations in 1950; mainline Presbyterians were members of both WCC and the NCC. There were also merger discussions with other denominations which conservatives often resisted. In 1951, three-way discussions began between the PCUSA, PCUS and the United Presbyterian Church of North America (UPCNA) – the UPCNA was the result of the 1858 merger between the Associate Reformed General Synod and the Associate Synod of North America. The PCUS eventually dropped out of these union negotiations but the PCUSA and the UPCNA united in 1958 to form the United Presbyterian Church in the United States of America (UPCUSA) – the new name of the now larger Northern Church. In 1961, the UPCUSA, PCUS, Protestant Episcopal Church, United Methodist Church, United Church of Christ and others began the controversial Consultation on Church Union, later called the Church of Christ Uniting (COCU), which cynical evangelicals referred to as "cuckoo." Even Roman Catholics caught the mid-century ecumenical spirit when Vatican II (1962-65) referred to Protestants as "the departed brethren."

The evolving theology of the UPCUSA finally led to a new confession and revised ordination vows in 1967. The *Confession of 1967* (C-67) was neo-orthodox in orientation emphasizing "God's work of reconciliation" in the world and was noteworthy, not so much for what it said but for what it left unsaid – neglecting to address many historic Reformed doctrines. Modern Biblical scholarship was affirmed by C-67, which spoke of Christ as the "Word of God" rather than Holy Scripture, the emphasis of the *Westminster Confession*, chapter one. The new confession highlighted the importance of the church's social witness in the midst of American racism, nationalism, poverty and "anarchy in sexual relationships." All of this was a significant shift away from the old Calvinism of Westminster and was an omen of things to come.[3]

Alongside the new confessional statement, the UPCUSA adopted a *Book of Confessions* that contained numerous historic Reformed confessions, and ordination vows were modified to address this expanded confessional basis of the church. Presbyterian ministers promised to be "under the continuing guidance of the confessions of this Church," but evangelicals wondered if this vague oath had any meaning at all. A new ministerial vow concerning Scripture was unmistakably Barthian: "Do you accept the Scriptures of the Old and New Testaments to be the unique and authoritative witness to Jesus Christ in the Church catholic and by the Holy Spirit God's Word to you?" The PCUS moved in the same directions ten years later, adopting new ordination vows; however, the move for a new confession failed. The new confessional document, *A Declaration of Faith*, and a proposed *Book of Confessions* were both narrowly defeated by the PCUS in 1977. Presbyterians were clearly moving toward a much looser perspective on confessional standards and the doctrinal commitment expected of clergy. [4]

In the 1970s and 80s, the UPCUSA and PCUS pursued their social justice witness by keeping before the church the issues of racism, poverty and international economic justice. While these mostly admirable kingdom pursuits consumed much mainline energy, debate over funding abortion and human sexuality became significant distractions into the 80s. An early 1978 UPCUSA study on homosexuality advocated new ways of reading what the Bible has to say about homosexuality, emboldening gay and lesbian Presbyterians who relentlessly started pushing their cause at annual General Assembly meetings. Feminist ideology, with its revisionist account of Christian history, was taking root in some corners of the church. An extreme example of radical "feminist theology" was the infamous "Sophia" conference in 1981 where a gathering, which included Presbyterian women, participated in bizarre rites of worship directed to a female deity causing no little controversy. Escalating numbers of denominational officials and seminary professors openly sanctioned universalism. Traditional Reformed theology was all but abandoned in the Presbyterian seminaries as faculty members seemingly welcomed the innovations of the latest progressive theology in vogue. In 1981, Mansfield Kaseman, pastor of United Church of Rockville, Maryland (Capital Union Presbytery), denied the deity of Christ; he was brought to trial but exonerated by the UPCUSA.

In practice it seemed to conservatives that there was no longer authentic doctrinal accountability in the mainline Presbyterian churches, yet many evangelicals sustained their allegiance to the church. These pastors and churches worked for change, prayed for revival and sometimes chose to focus on local ministry and ignore the larger issues of the denomination. A number organized themselves politically to fight the liberal program in the church courts. Others formed renewal organizations that concentrated on revitalizing local congregations and encouraging conservative pastors. Organizations like Presbyterians United for Biblical Concerns, Covenant Fellowship of Presbyterians, Presbyterians for Renewal, et.al, provided a vital network of fellowship and collaboration for mainline evangelicals who found themselves marginalized by the church bureaucracy's activist agenda. A number of evangelicals who participated in these Presbyterian ministries eventually lost all hope for a return to Biblical faithfulness. These conservative Presbyterians faced a painful crisis in their faith journey as they began to ponder the question: Is it time to leave the denomination and establish something new?

PRESBYTERIAN CHURCH IN AMERICA

Southern evangelicals in the PCUS, responding to encroaching liberal theology, started a new periodical, the *Southern Presbyterian Journal* (1942), as a voice of conservative concern. Under the leadership of L. Nelson Bell, the *Presbyterian Journal*, as it was later renamed, became a rallying point for addressing the diminishing faithfulness of the PCUS. Dr. Bell had been a Presbyterian medical missionary in China in the years before WWII but was forced to leave the country and return to the United States. He became a prominent American evangelical leader in the post-war decades because of his famous son-in-law, Billy Graham, and his part in founding *Christianity Today* magazine (1956).

Evangelical angst over creeping universalism, which undermined the priority of the great commission, motivated the organization of Presbyterian Evangelistic Fellowship (PEF) by Bill Hill in 1964 to support both home and foreign missions. PEF leadership became instrumental in the impending conservative push to leave the Southern Church. Some southern conservatives were concerned enough about the theological direction of the Presbyterian seminaries that they thought it was time to consider starting a new school for ministerial preparation. One catalyst for these discussions was an article in the *Presbyterian Survey* wherein the PCUS seminary presidents indicated that none of their schools taught the doctrine of Biblical inerrancy. A handful of laymen and ministers prayerfully began to set plans for a new seminary that opened in 1966 as Reformed Theological Seminary in Jackson, Mississippi. Sam Patterson, the first president, along with two professors and seventeen students made for a meager beginning which in time would expand to eight campuses, becoming one of the largest seminaries in the United States. Within a few years, a number of Reformed Seminary graduates participated in the movement to establish a new Presbyterian denomination.

In the late 1960s, things began to stir as both society and the church underwent a massive upheaval. Ever-increasing numbers of ministers and laypersons in the Southern Church watched in dismay as the PCUS slipped further down the slope of cultural and theological compromise. Many became convinced that separation from the PCUS was inevitable. Evangelical churches had already begun discarding denominational literature and substituting non-denominational Sunday school curriculum. Giving to missions outside the PCUS had grown due to concern about equalization of funds, whereby money given to General Assembly missions might be transferred somewhere else. When the schism finally arrived, in many ways, it was simply formalizing a reality that had already existed. Many conservatives felt that the ever-changing denomination had left them while their convictions had never wavered. They desired a continuing Presbyterian church committed to evangelism and the historic Reformed tradition – something that, from their perspective, had ceased to exist in the mainline church.

At a 1971 meeting in Atlanta, conservative leaders issued "A Declaration of Intent" stating their desire for a church "Presbyterian in government, Reformed in doctrine, fervent in evangelism and concerned for human welfare." In May of 1973, a Convocation of Sessions met in Atlanta, to set in motion plans for a new Presbyterian denomination comprised of churches out of the PCUS (Southern Church). In December of that year the first Assembly of the National Presbyterian Church convened at Briarwood Presbyterian Church in Birmingham (pastor, Frank Barker) with representatives from 212 churches. The next year the name of the new denomination was changed to Presbyterian Church in America (PCA). The 1973 Assembly issued a statement setting out its justification for separation from the mother church citing these issues: "... a diluted theology, a gospel tending towards humanism, an unBiblical view of marriage and divorce, the ordination of women, financing of abortion ..., and numerous other non-Biblical positions ... all traceable to a different view of Scripture from that we hold and that which was held by the Southern Presbyterian forefathers."

The founders of the PCA were intentional about returning to a former era of Presbyterian faithfulness. In their zeal to establish a "continuing church," they adopted an earlier version of the Westminster Confession and Catechisms endorsed by the nineteenth-century Southern Presbyterian church in 1861. The PCA's polity also revisited historic Presbyterian practice by limiting church office (ministers, elders and deacons) to men. From the beginning, the PCA wanted to be a grass-roots movement that avoided the clergy-run centralized bureaucracy they had experienced in the PCUS. Therefore, parity of teaching and ruling elders was required by church polity, and denominational structure would be organized by committees answerable to the General Assembly rather than independent boards.

The first moderator of the PCA was layman W. Jack Williamson, and the stated clerk was Dr. Morton Smith who had been a theology professor at Reformed Seminary. The group of ministers that shaped the PCA was roughly divided into two groups – those who had a vision of the PCA as a truly Reformed Presbyterianism and a larger group who found their primary identity in being evangelical and were driven by evangelism and world missions. These diverse emphases were not mutually exclusive but were the cause of ongoing stress in the young denomination as it struggled to define its unique place among the Presbyterian family of churches.

Theological debates within the PCA on certain controversial topics have highlighted the existence of various parties in the church. In the late 1970s and early 1980s, the PCA dealt with the conflict-ridden subject of theonomy (God's law). Christian Reconstruction (or "theonomy") refers to applying Old Testament law to the New Testament church and social structures (politics, economics) in ways most Presbyterians believe transgress the separation of church and state. The PCA General Assembly never officially endorsed theonomy but ruled in 1979 and 1983 that this minority view could be tolerated. Another contentious topic in Old Testament studies has been the long debate over the days of creation in Genesis chapter one. While the *Westminster Confession* speaks of God creating the earth "in the space of six days," Presbyterians have traditionally allowed disagreement on interpreting the "days" as either a figurative expression, a designation of long periods of time or literal twenty-four-hour days. The 2001 Assembly sanctioned historic American Presbyterian liberty on this topic by affirming the essential historicity of the Genesis account of creation, including a literal Adam, but leaving the debated particulars of the creation story as open questions.

The PCA was forced to address the old question of subscription to the *Westminster Confession and Catechisms* in the 1980s and '90s due to rancor in some segments of the church. A few vocal activists urged "full subscription" to the doctrinal standards as the legitimate Presbyterian position. Others were equally convinced that the historic principle of allowing "scruples" (exceptions) to the Confession ("good faith subscription") had been Presbyterian practice for generations and saw no need to modify it. In 2003, the Assembly answered this question by requiring presbyteries to ask ministry candidates to put their exceptions in writing. Each presbytery was then to judge if these "scruples" violated the "fundamentals of the system of doctrine" found in the standards.

One of the most significant events in the PCA's short history was the "joining and receiving" of the Reformed Presbyterian Church, Evangelical Synod (RPCES) into the PCA in 1982. The RPCES was a denomination formed by the 1965 union of the Evangelical Presbyterian Church (formerly, Bible Presbyterian Church, 1937-1961) and the Reformed Presbyterian Church in North America, General Synod (Scottish Covenanters). Originally, there was a three-way discussion between the PCA, OPC and the RPCES, however, the OPC finally voted not to participate. When the RPCES united with the PCA, she brought to the union Covenant College in Lookout Mountain, Georgia, and Covenant Seminary in St. Louis, acquisitions that gave the young denomination an immediate institutional presence. Both of the schools have grown substantially since the merger, training hundreds of students for ministry and equipping men and women to serve vocationally from the framework of a Christian worldview.

The PCA is the second largest Presbyterian denomination in the United States with about fifteen hundred churches. Denominational offices are in Atlanta, Georgia, where the PCA has a publishing division, Great Commission Publishing (a joint effort with the OPC), which provides educational materials and resources. The Mission to North America committee has supported an aggressive church planting movement in the PCA, making it one of the faster growing denominations in the United States. Perimeter Presbyterian Church, under pastor Randy Pope, has started over twenty PCA mission churches in the greater Atlanta area. Mercy ministry, by congregations such as Redeemer Presbyterian in New York and Desire Street Ministries in New Orleans, reflect the PCA's ministry to the urban poor. The PCA's foreign mission endeavors are implemented through Mission to the World, supporting about six hundred missionaries in sixty countries.[5]

When the PCA was established in 1973, there were still many conservatives in the PCUS who believed the time for division had not yet come. A number thought there might be hope to turn things around; others could not bring themselves to separate out of conscience, believing that some blatant act of apostasy was required to justify separation. Since there were still so many evangelical congregations in both the PCUS and UPCUSA, a few voices suggested the combined strength of conservative Presbyterians in both bodies might be an effective change agent if the PCUS and UPUSA consummated formal reunion.

REUNION IN 1983

Reunion between the Southern and Northern Presbyterian churches had been the dream of a large number of Presbyterians ever since the failed attempts in the years following the Civil War. In the early decades of the twentieth century union discussions had made little progress until 1943 when a formal plan of union was placed on the table. Conservatives in the PCUS were generally opposed to reunion because of northern liberal theology and polity differences. There were delays in the process but liberals favoring reunion (in both churches) kept the issue a priority. The proposal for reunion was sent down to PCUS presbyteries for a vote in 1954 but was defeated with forty-two presbyteries in favor and forty-three opposed. It required a two-thirds majority vote for reunion to pass.

Reunion was an ultimate goal that liberals were never willing to abandon. By 1969, the two Presbyterian bodies adopted a plan for "union presbyteries" which allowed presbyteries in the PCUS and UPCUSA to be members of both denominations. The two denominations also decided to hold their General Assemblies in the same city in alternate years in another attempt to foster fraternal relations. Conservatives viewed union presbyteries as "reunion through the back door" and resented it. In the late 1970s, reunion discussions between the PCUS and UPCUSA were on a fast track and conservatives were torn about the prospects for what a reunion might bring. Some evangelicals believed reunion would be a good thing; combining the conservative influence in both churches would produce a stronger voice for Biblical faithfulness. Other evangelicals viewed the reunion as another minimalist attempt to advance Christian union at any cost. They believed this would further dissolve whatever genuinely Christian elements remained in the Presbyterian church. A handful of conservative ministers and churches began discussing their options as the intensity of reunion negotiations indicated that the consummation of the union was almost certain.

In an adroit ecclesiastical move, Southern Presbyterian conservatives were able to secure a special arrangement in the Plan for Reunion for PCUS churches to have the option of withdrawing from the reunited church. This provision, known as "Article Thirteen," gave Southern churches up to eight years after reunion to choose dismissal to another Reformed body with their church property. The Plan for Reunion stipulated: "If two thirds of those present and voting vote to request dismissal, this particular church will be dismissed under the special provisions of Article Thirteen of the Articles of Agreement, and will retain all of its property, subject to any existing liens and encumbrances, but will surrender its membership in the Presbyterian Church (U.S.A.)."[6] The church property component of Article 13 was the key provision because state courts had historically given different interpretations to the Presbyterian constitution's understanding of property ownership during the 1970s when the PCA was formed. Under this exclusive arrangement to appease southern conservatives, the evangelical PCUS churches would be more likely to vote in favor of reunion, knowing that they would have unencumbered freedom to withdraw if the reunion proved unsatisfactory.

The property question had always been a thorny issue in the Presbyterian connectional system. A number of Presbyterian churches wanting to be dismissed to the PCA had presbyteries challenge local church property ownership, landing the disputing parties in state courts. A 1979 Supreme Court ruling favored local churches, and the PCUS and UPCUSA both moved to strengthen constitutional provisions making explicit denominational ownership of property. While the

Plan for Reunion granted the right of property ownership to southern congregations who might choose not to remain in the united church, it also strengthened denominational ownership of all church properties for the rest of the churches. The Plan for Reunion granted liberals control over property assets in all former UPCUSA congregations as well as any PCUS congregation that chose to stay in the church past the eight year "window" of Article Thirteen. The compromise was a double-edged sword, for while it provided an "escape clause" for some, it made departure more difficult for others.

The Plan for Reunion circulated in both churches for several years and at long last was approved in 1983 with only eight PCUS presbyteries (five in SC) voting against the Plan. The reunited church took the name Presbyterian Church (U.S.A.), redrew presbytery lines, united all organizations within the two previous bodies and moved denominational headquarters to Louisville, Kentucky. The mainline church had finally mended the breach that had divided them since 1861. The reunited PC(U.S.A.) now contained over three million members, thirteen thousand churches and twenty-one thousand ministers, however, major decline in numbers had been taking place for three decades and would continue after reunion. In 1950, Presbyterians had been the fourth largest denomination in America with over four million members, but statistical records show that by 2002 the mainline Presbyterian church had lost almost 2.5 million members since its highpoint in the 1960s. The PC(U.S.A) has about two million members in over ten thousand congregations.

In the decades following the 1983 reunion, the question of homosexual ordination has been a constant provocation throughout the PC(U.S.A.). A 1991 Human Sexuality Report set the stage for this prolonged contest with its attempt to shift the discussion away from sexual morality to justice for homosexuals. Rather than looking intently at Biblical texts that specifically address homosexual behavior, the report declared: "... the pressing moral problem, as we have argued, is not homosexuality, but rather the unjust treatment of gay and lesbian persons and their devaluation as sexual-spiritual persons in our midst."[7] In 1997, conservatives were able to secure a modification to the PC(U.S.A.) *Book of Order*, adding a requirement for clergy to live in "fidelity within the covenant of marriage between a man and a woman, or chastity in singleness." Progressives would not let the issue die, and by 2006 a "Peace, Unity and Purity" Task Force, seeking middle ground in the ongoing homosexual debate, recommended allowing exceptions to the "fidelity and chastity" standard. In 2011, the "fidelity and chastity" constitutional language was jettisoned by a majority vote of the presbyteries, which has opened the door to homosexual ordination in the Presbyterian Church.

Anticipating that ordination of practicing homosexuals would inevitably be approved by the PC(U.S.A.), a significant exodus of conservative congregations and ministers began in 2007. Scores of evangelical churches departed from the mainline church by means of negotiated monetary settlements, abandonment of buildings or legal action to determine property ownership. The destination for most of these congregations was the Evangelical Presbyterian Church.

EVANGELICAL PRESBYTERIAN CHURCH

A handful of conservative ministers and churches (PCUS and UPCUSA), during the latter years of the reunion negotiations, began discussing the possibility of forming a new Presbyterian body. In 1980, a convention led by Bartlett Hess and Andy Jumper convened in St. Louis to set in motion plans for establishing The Evangelical Presbyterian Church (EPC). A Steering Committee was directed to edit provisional constitutional documents and report to the first General Assembly (1981) which convened at Ward Presbyterian Church near Detroit Michigan. The first EPC Assembly consisted of representatives from fifteen churches. After 1983, additional congregations were added from the old Northern Church and former PCUS congregations who withdrew under provisions of Article Thirteen. A few independent churches and new church plants also joined the new denomination. The first EPC Assembly adopted a *Book of Government*, ordained six ministers and received a new congregation. Dr. Francis Schaeffer spoke to the first Assembly, challenging them with the message, "To Be God's Church in the Midst of the Twentieth-Century Confusion."

The EPC leaders created a niche for themselves as a middle-ground Presbyterian body that rejected the liberalism of the mainline but was broader than either the OPC or the PCA. Three factors distinguished the EPC – its position on women officers, openness to the charismatic movement and moderate Calvinism. These unique characteristics were attributable to several historic factors related to evangelical experience in mainline denominations since the 1950s. Evangelicals who had remained in the mainline (PCUS and UPCUSA) through the 1970s had become accustomed to working with liberals and were able to stay with a clear conscience because of their broader perspectives. These evangelicals attempted to be as tolerant as possible within the liberal church while retaining their own convictions, but this posture became more difficult to preserve as the years passed. By the 1970s, renewal-minded mainline evangelicals were primarily concerned about the church keeping some semblance of essential Christian belief as liberals continued to challenge all aspects of historic Christian faith and practice. These conservatives could be characterized as moderate Calvinists who perceived themselves as evangelicals first and secondarily identified as Presbyterian and Reformed. Ministers and churches with this frame of reference were the principal founders of the EPC.

The EPC tackled the women's ordination issue head-on from the beginning. Women's ordination as ministers had been a given in the mainline church for decades – 1956 in the Northern Church, 1964 in the Southern Church.[8] Evangelicals in the mainline had come to terms with this situation believing it was no grounds for separation and some were convinced that Scripture allowed for women to serve in ordained church office. While rejecting the gender-rights quota system advocated by feminists, they viewed women's ordination as a legitimate expression of leadership gifts in the church. Numerous conservative Presbyterian churches (north and south) had women officers and wanted to preserve this practice in the EPC. The denomination staked out new territory by neither requiring nor forbidding women officers, believing women's ordination was a nonessential issue about which faithful believers have honest differences of Biblical interpretation.

Decisions about ruling elders were a local option left to the discretion of individual congregations with no coercion from the denomination. Women ministers must be approved by presbyteries which produced strain in a few presbyteries that were divided on the question. Wishing to preserve its original commitment to women's ordination as a "non-essential," the 2011 General Assembly modified the *Book of Government* allowing a congregation to transfer to a bordering presbytery if a female candidate/minister is prohibited from admission in a presbytery predominantly opposed to women clergy. The compromise retained the EPC's neutrality on women's ordination by providing constitutional safeguards that affirmed both the local church's liberty to call a minister of its choosing and presbytery's authority to determine its own membership.

The EPC founders also addressed the controversial charismatic movement that had been part of the wider evangelical experience but had created division. In the 1960s and 1970s a number of mainline Presbyterian churches had been touched by the charismatic renewal sweeping the United States. Ministers, as well as stagnant church members, were either genuinely converted or revitalized by this effusion of the Spirit. While distinct from Pentecostalism, tongues and "prophetic gifts" were sometimes associated with the movement, but the emphasis was on true conversion, committed discipleship and evangelism. The EPC leadership wished to affirm legitimate parts of the charismatic renewal but also to maintain their Reformed commitment to the priority of Scripture. In the early years, the EPC Assembly adopted a "Position Paper on the Holy Spirit" and in 1992 added further interpretive statements which expressed a balanced Reformed understanding of the Spirit's work by carefully defining "the baptism in the Spirit" as regeneration and not a second work of grace. On the other hand, the EPC declared, "As a Reformed denomination, we adhere strongly to our belief in the sovereignty of God, a belief that does not allow us either to require a certain gift or to restrict the Spirit in how He will work."[9] This judicious treatment of a potentially divisive subject satisfied the EPC membership which included both charismatic and non-charismatic churches and ministers.

The founding fathers of the EPC desired to be broadly Calvinistic and yearned to reconnect with traditional Reformed theology that had been suppressed in the mother church. They did this constitutionally by adopting a modern-language version of the Westminster Confession and Catechisms which included the 1903 chapters on the Holy Spirit and missions. Several position papers on topics such as abortion and homosexuality have been adopted to affirm commitment to traditional Christian ethics. The name of the new denomination as well as her motto, "In essentials unity; in non-essentials liberty; in all things charity," exhibited a winsomely-Reformed ethos. The first Assembly adopted a "Statement of Faith," subsequently re-titled "Essentials of the Faith," a brief declaration of catholic faith that unequivocally proclaimed adherence to historic Christian orthodoxy as opposed to the ever-shifting evasive theology of liberal mainline Protestantism.

The function of the "Essentials" statement would cause dissension in future years due to early confusion about its purpose. The origins of the "Essentials" lay in a request from several ministers to define the "fundamentals" described in the fourth ordination vow requiring ministers (after ordination) to report any changes in their views on "fundamentals of the faith." Misunderstandings began to surface at the second General Assembly when the fourth ordination vow was modified to substitute the words "essentials of the faith" for "fundamentals of faith" – this change led some to identify the "Essentials" statement with the ordination vow. Alongside this confusion was a view shared by a few EPC ministers that the "Essentials" were the minimal standard of belief for ordination rather than assent to the Westminster Standards. One of the problems with this idea was that "Essentials," though adopted by the first General Assembly, had never officially been part of the constitution. The denomination's Theology Committee did a thorough study in 1998 to clarify the function of "Essentials." The report did not ultimately resolve the matter, so the Assembly established a special committee with representatives from each presbytery to meet over a two-year period and bring back recommendations. The result was that in 2002 the EPC officially inserted a reference to the "Essentials" statement into an ordination vow but then added "An Explanatory Statement to 'Essentials of Our Faith'" in the *Book of Order* which explained, "The *Westminster Confession of Faith* is our standard of doctrine . . .'Essentials of Our Faith' is an irenic statement of historic evangelicalism . . .It is not to be construed as a substitute for the *Westminster Confession of Faith*." These amendments satisfied the whole church and strengthened the EPC's Reformed identity.

On the practical questions of polity, the EPC determined to safeguard rights of congregations and protect the young denomination from creating another clergy-dominated bureaucracy. The EPC *Book of Order* stipulated that congregations had certain "rights held in perpetuity" – the right to elect her own officers, the right of property ownership and the right of each congregation to determine where her benevolent dollars would be spent. Participation of the laity at all levels of the church was mandated by a two to one ratio rule for ruling elders and teaching elders at Presbytery and General Assembly meetings. While not always realized, the EPC's aim was to have widespread participation by laypersons at every level of the church's work.

Since 2000, being a "missional church" has become a priority for the EPC, which evaluated its structure and resources in light of that commitment. Over the years church planting has been initiated by several larger churches, presbyteries and the denomination's National Outreach Committee. The EPC has shared a church planters assessment program with the Associated Reformed Presbyterian Church (ARP). In global missions, the World Outreach Committee of the EPC supports forty-eight missionary units (singles, couples, families) in twenty-six countries with particular attention to the Muslim world. In South America the EPC has provided significant resources to strengthen seminaries of the Presbyterian Church of Brazil and has helped establish indigenous presbyteries in Argentina. The EPC does not have its own college or seminary but has established cordial relationships with a number of institutions that have provided education for its college students and ministers.

Maintaining appropriate ecumenical connections has been an EPC objective, choosing to participate in the larger evangelical movement as well as maintaining relationships with other Reformed denominations (liberal and conservative). The EPC is a member church of the National Association of Evangelicals (NAE) and the evangelical World Reformed Fellowship (WRF). In another direction, the EPC joined the mainline-oriented World Alliance of Reformed Churches (WARC), since 2010 called the World Communion of Reformed Churches (WCRC), which includes over two hundred church bodies in over one hundred countries. Membership in WARC has not been without debate due to its theological positions on numerous social issues.

When a new wave of PC(U.S.A.) churches began inquiring about membership in the EPC, the denomination became concerned about being overwhelmed by a large influx of new congregations. The EPC adopted an innovative structure in 2007 called a "Transitional Presbytery" wherein churches might be received into a transitional non-geographic presbytery that would only exist for five years. During these five years, churches and pastors received into an EPC transitional presbytery would make application to be received by a permanent geographic presbytery. After the five years has concluded, a church that has not been received into an existing EPC presbytery will be dismissed to independency. The purpose of the five-year structure was to give adequate time of deliberation to the congregation wishing to join and to geographic presbyteries in order that both parties could make a fully informed decision. A support network of conservative PC(U.S.A.) churches called "New Wineskins" had a number of its member congregations vote to be dismissed from the PC(U.S.A.) into the EPC transitional presbytery. During the years 2007-2012, the EPC received over 200 churches from the PC(U.S.A.).[10]

EVANGELICAL COVENANT ORDER

As the EPC was receiving numerous former PC(U.S.A.) congregations into her ecclesiastical fold, another cluster of Presbyterians was planning a substantial departure from the mother church. In January 2012, the Fellowship of Presbyterians, a PC(U.S.A.) evangelical group, sponsored a Covenanting Conference attended by representatives from over five hundred congregations. Responding to constitutional changes allowing for gay ordination and years of frustration with the direction of the denomination, the purpose of the meeting was to launch a new Presbyterian body – ECO: A Covenant Order of Evangelical Presbyterians. The new denomination is committed to Biblical authority and a "missional centrality" focused on growing and planting flourishing congregations. The name ECO points to three priorities: "to make disciples of Jesus Christ (Evangelical), connect leaders through accountable biblical relationships founded in God's grace (Covenant), and commit to a shared way of life together (Order)."

Theologically, ECO has distinguished itself by its endorsement of the PC(U.S.A.) *Book of Confessions* which includes ancient creeds, Reformation-era confessions and the twentieth-century Barthian-influenced *Barmen Declaration and Confession of 67*. This is in contrast to the conservative Presbyterian churches (OPC, PCA, EPC) who had all adopted the *Westminster Confession* and Catechisms, the historic creed of American Presbyterians. ECO is committed to an "egalitarian ministry," making this an essential element of the denomination's ethos, thus mirroring mainline feminist practice and setting itself apart from the other evangelical Presbyterian denominations on women's ordination.

Evangelical mainline Presbyterians have multiple alignment options: some will choose to remain in the PC(U.S.A.) and align with the Fellowship of Presbyterians; others are leaving the PC(U.S.A.) to join ECO which will also be a part of the Fellowship of Presbyterians. Leaving the PC(U.S.A) for ECO will certainly include battles over property similar to those experienced by congregations being dismissed to the EPC. It remains to be seen how many churches will opt for ECO in the coming years. There are about fifty churches that have joined ECO thus far and it appears that a significant number of mainline congregations are still considering some kind of realignment with the EPC, ECO or the Fellowship of Presbyterians.[11]

CHRISTIANITY AND CULTURE

The story of twentieth-century American Presbyterianism is a narrative about the array of answers Presbyterian groups have given to the question: What does Christ have to do with culture? Mainline Presbyterianism progressively mirrored the values of post-modern American culture, embracing each new social trend – sexual liberation, abortion, feminism, homosexuality, as though it were the next stage in advancing the kingdom of God. According to mainline leadership, the church's calling is to affirm all persons, lifestyles and beliefs. This Christianity of culture approach made the faith less and less like historic Christianity and more like a syncretistic religion always seeking to find God but never certain about anything. In its extreme forms, relativistic post-modern "Christianity" appeared at times to accommodate itself to neo-pagan ideas. Admittedly, only a minority of mainline Presbyterians ever embraced the most radical concepts, but the majority has been tolerating heterodox theology for many years. Evangelicals still strive for mainline renewal, but some, believing reclamation is all but impossible, focus on faithfulness in their congregations and communities.

While thousands of mainline evangelical Presbyterians struggled to keep their personal integrity in the midst of a declining church, other evangelicals followed an alternative path and formed new denominations. These evangelicals approached the question of culture from a different paradigm, believing the gospel could be relevant without being compromised by the confusions of secular culture. They understood the message of Christ as light in the darkness, not accommodation to the deceptions of lost humanity. The evangelical Presbyterian denominations were relegated to the fringes of culture, but from that vantage point, they have been able to proclaim the Biblical good news of hope to the perishing. Through church planting, evangelism and outreach, the conservative branches of Presbyterianism continue to grow. If these trends continue, the twenty-first century may witness the conservative churches becoming "mainline" Presbyterianism.

THE CONNECTION

The second half of the twentieth century was a time of restoring historic Presbyterian identity for the new conservative Presbyterian bodies. These believers found themselves rediscovering what it meant to be "Presbyterian." Defining moments arrived when the PCA and EPC were established, revisiting the old Presbyterian paths that had oftentimes been abandoned by the broader mainline church. Reconnecting with the earlier American Presbyterian heritage, the conservative denominations recommitted themselves to traditional Reformed theology and unequivocal witness to the gospel as the only hope of human salvation.

Social issues in American society will continue to be complicated questions for Presbyterians. While there is a rather rigid line between conservative and liberal stances on volatile issues such as abortion and homosexuality, the lines are not so clear in areas like social justice, gender roles and ecology. Many conservatives, while not identifying social justice as the central concern of Christ's kingdom, do believe it is a vital area of ministry for all believers. Numerous evangelical Presbyterians are convinced there is Biblical warrant for women to serve in all church leadership roles; others hold more traditional views of male headship. Numbers of conservatives are interested in addressing the environmental woes that plague the planet. The stance of evangelicals is that Holy Scripture always sets the agenda. Whatever questions arise in society, the evangelical Christian always turns to the Bible to inquire if God's infallible Word has specific directives or general principles that must be applied.

Each generation of believers must answer the Christianity and culture question, grappling with its role to be salt and light in the midst of a sin-infested culture. Evangelicals in the mainline also believe they are called to be salt and light within their denominations. The prospect of denominational renewal sometimes appears doubtful, nonetheless, the Spirit may choose to intervene according to his sovereign purposes. From earliest times on America's shores, Colonial Presbyterians found themselves surrounded by darkness but always believed the gospel was brighter. Each new generation of Presbyterians must reaffirm that gospel-centered optimism as it encounters its own culture. Jesus Christ, the head of the Church, will build his kingdom, and in steadfast love has included Presbyterian churches in his redemptive plan for humanity.

EPILOGUE:

QUESTIONS FOR THE FUTURE

What is the final authority for doctrine and practice in the Church? This is a fundamental question for the Church in all ages. Church fathers pointed to the canon, the creeds and the authority of bishops. At the time of the Protestant Reformation, this question was again raised, and the answer, while not denying the importance of ancient creeds and church structure, emphasized the final authority of Holy Scripture on all matters to which it speaks. English-speaking Calvinists reiterated that commitment in the first chapter of the *Westminster Confession*: "The Holy Spirit speaking in the Bible is the supreme judge of all religious controversies, all decisions of religious councils, all the opinions of ancient writers, all human teachings, and every private opinion."[1] Presbyterians in America have publically made that same commitment in all their statements of faith. A question for the future: Will the Bible remain the final court of appeal or will Presbyterians be tossed about by innovative theological winds that blow?

Building upon a foundational commitment to the authority of Scripture, Calvin and the other Reformers tended to emphasize the core elements of catholic faith. Creeds and confessions were of vital importance to Calvin, especially the Apostles' Creed but he also saw the place for larger Confessions, writing the *French Confession* ("Gallican Confession") in 1559 to provide a statement of faith for the persecuted Huguenots. The Dutch, German, and Swiss Reformed Churches, along with the Scottish Presbyterians and English Puritans, all wrote their confessions and catechisms. Reformed churches have always believed that doctrinal truth matters and Christian unity is founded in the truth.

Colonial Presbyterians adopted the *Westminster Confession and Catechisms* of the seventeenth-century Puritans. In the preamble to the 1729 Adopting Act, the Americans stated why it was necessary to adopt a formal creed: "We are undoubtedly obliged to take care that the faith once delivered to the saints be kept pure and uncorrupt among

207

us, and so handed down to our posterity." Elder Christian statesman, Chuck Colson, in his book *The Faith*, has issued a wake-up call to Christians about the neglect and overall ignorance of the essential doctrines of the faith. Colson illustrates this by pointing to statistics on Biblical illiteracy, acceptance of the myth that all religions are alike and increasing confusion in sexual ethics among Christian young people and adults. [2] Will Presbyterians pass on the authentic faith to the next generation, or will revisionist Christianities gain the hearts and minds of the young?

For two thousand years, God's people have interpreted the Bible as teaching the absolute necessity of being committed to a local body of Christ and being in submission to church shepherds who are responsible for the feeding and care of one's soul. All Christians are members of the invisible church, but that reality must have a visible expression in the earth – that has always been Christian teaching without exception. The Reformed and Presbyterian churches have implemented this connectional principle through a church polity that includes membership, church officers and a system of graduated church courts that oversee the life of God's people in community. Some contemporary Christian practice seems to imply the novel idea that Church membership is optional as long as one has a personal relationship with Jesus. People are short-circuiting their spiritual lives when they neglect the church, and one is not doing them any favors by not telling them the truth about Christ's body. Will Presbyterians maintain their high view of the church or will they succumb to contemporary attitudes which suggest the church may be unnecessary?

Presbyterians have been deeply influenced by the evangelical ethos in America, but one wonders why the old evangelical passion for holiness has so drastically deteriorated. The lives of many professing Christians look very similar to those of their unbelieving neighbors – divorce, materialism, cheating on taxes, unethical business dealings, sexual immorality, absence at public worship, prayerlessness, neglect of regular Bible reading and little concern for the poor. Presbyterians in earlier times took personal holiness seriously and were known for strictness of life in obedience to the commands of Scripture. Can Presbyterians recover the old piety that once was a hallmark of their identity?

The church from its infancy as recorded in the book of Acts

was missional – that is, focused on reaching those who had not yet heard or embraced the good news about Jesus Christ. The story of Christianity is full of martyrs and missionaries who boldly testified for Christ in ways that were often costly. Monks brought the message to our ancestors whose descendants then brought the Gospel to the New World. Presbyterians in America actively participated in the First and Second Awakenings as well as providing leadership in evangelistic and missionary activity both at home and around the globe. That historic missional ethos is something each generation must take on afresh and renew its own commitment to spread the gospel.

In the contemporary cultural context, there are serious threats to the missional mindset that is other-focused, and among these threats is Christian complacency. On the other hand, the politically-correct religious pluralism of Western societies makes evangelism and missions offensive, since all religions are supposedly equal paths to relationship with God. Can Islam be an equally authentic pathway to God alongside Christianity, or is faith in Christ the only means of salvation from human sin? Will Presbyterians hold fast to the historic Christian urgency of proclaiming the gospel, or will they bow to the inclusivity of the age?

The major future dividing line in the worldwide church will likely be the issue of homosexuality. Roman Catholics and the Orthodox are firm in their commitment to historic Christian sexual ethics, but this is not the case among all Protestants. As increasing numbers of mainline denominations have become advocates of ordaining non-celibate homosexuals and the blessing of same-sex marriages, the mainline churches face a crisis. Will the culture set the church's agenda or will Scripture alone be the final authority for acceptable standards of Christian sexual expression? What will this mean for one's denominational affiliation? Will evangelicals in good conscience be able to maintain mainline ecclesiastical fellowship if the church will not renounce homosexual ordination and same-sex marriage? These will be difficult questions for many Presbyterians to answer.

A great irony of the twenty-first-century church is the reality that conservative Protestants often find themselves closer in sentiment to Roman Catholics and the Orthodox than to fellow Protestants who have departed from traditional Christian faith and practice. This commonality is rooted in the ancient church – the ecumenical creeds and historic Christian ethics which have defined the legitimate boundaries of authentic Christianity for two millennia. The huge worldwide Pentecostal tradition likewise shares these common historic commitments and boundaries. One wonders if old liberal Protestantism will eventually fade into oblivion as the global church distances itself from these departures from authentic Christianity. The Reformers probably never dreamed that some of their ecclesiastical children would become more corrupt than the Roman Church. What will this situation mean for future ecumenical relations among the variety of Christian bodies that continue to embrace traditional Christian orthodoxy? Should there be more ecclesiastical fellowship and cooperation between the ancient churches (Roman Catholic, Orthodox) and evangelical Protestants?

Disunity among Christians has given the world an excuse to ignore the gospel. The Presbyterian story reminds us that schism among brethren is a scandal, and sometimes it is self-righteous, judgmental and full of misunderstanding; at other times, it may be justified when essential doctrine and practice have been compromised. At the 1758 reunion of Old Side and New Side Presbyterians, after officially ending the separation, the presbyters issued a joint statement about their commitments as they moved forward in the reunited church. This declaration captures the historic Presbyterian ethos which is worthy of emulation. The Synod stated:

> ... we unanimously declar[e] [our] Serious and fixed Resolution,
> by divine Aid, to take heed to ourselves, that our hearts be
> upright, our Discourse edifying, and our Lives exemplary for
> Purity and Godliness – to take heed to our Doctrine, that it
> be not only orthodox, but evangelical & Spiritual, tending to
> awaken the Secure to a Suitable concern for their Salvation, and to
> instruct and encourage Sincere Christians; ...[3]

Times change but basic Christian commitments do not because the gospel is timeless. God calls every new generation to faithful obedience to the truth revealed in Holy Scripture. Our Presbyterian forefathers and mothers through many trials have shown us the way if we will have ears to hear their story.

GLOSSARY

Anabaptists

A group of early sixteenth-century sects that practiced rebaptism. Anabaptist means "one who baptizes again." Infant baptism was not recognized as valid and the Catholic Mass was rejected. They believed in non-violence and opposed any relationship between churches and the state.

Anathema

In the New Testament, Paul used the term to indicate separating one from the Christian community due to sin (Gal. 1:8) or for not loving the Lord (1 Cor. 16:22). In church history it came to mean a formal ecclesiastical curse involving excommunication.

Apostle

Someone sent with a special message or commission. Jesus is called the apostle and high Priest of our confession in Hebrews 3:1. The twelve apostles of Jesus were Simon Peter, Andrew, James the son of Zebedee, John, Philip, Bartholomew, Thomas, Matthew, James the son of Alphaeus, Thaddaeus, Simon the Zealot, and Judas Iscariot who was replaced by Mathias (Acts 1:26). Paul became an apostle after Jesus' resurrection (2 Cor. 1:1), along with Barnabas (Acts 14:14), and others. Apostles established churches (Rom. 15:17-20), exposed error (Gal. 1:6-9), and defended the truth of the gospel (Phil. 1:7,17). Some were empowered by the Holy Spirit to perform miracles (Matt. 10:1,8) and they were to preach the gospel (Matt. 28:19,20).

Arianism

An ancient theological error that appeared around the year 320. It taught that God could not appear on the earth, that Jesus was not eternal and could not be God. Additionally, it taught that there was only one person in the Godhead: the Father. Jesus, then, was a creation. It was condemned by the Council of Nicea in A.D. 325.

Arminianism

A theological system that was begun by Jacobus Arminius, a Dutch pastor and theologian. There are five main tenets of Arminianism: 1) God elects or reproves on the basis of foreseen faith or unbelief, 2) Christ died for all men and for every man, although only believers are saved, 3) Man is so depraved that divine grace is necessary unto faith or any good deed, 4) This grace may be resisted, 5) Whether all who are truly regenerate will certainly persevere in the faith is a point which needs further investigation. (Compare with Calvinism.)

Calvinism

A comprehensive Christian theology formulated by John Calvin in his *Institutes of the Christian Religion.* It is a distinct theological system often contrasted with Lutheranism and Arminianism. The "five points of Calvinism" were developed by the Dutch Reformed church at the Synod of Dordt (1618-19) in response to the Arminian position. Calvinism teaches: 1) Total depravity: that man is touched by sin in all parts of his being: body, soul, mind, and emotions, 2) Unconditional Election: that God's favor to man is completely by God's free choice. It is completely undeserved and is not based on anything God sees in man (Eph. 1:1-11), 3) Limited atonement: that Christ did not bear the sins of every individual who ever lived, but instead only bore the sins of those who were elected into salvation (John 10:11,15), 4) Irresistible grace: that God's call to someone for salvation cannot be resisted, 5) Perseverance of the saints: that it is not possible to lose one's salvation (John 10:27-28).

Catholic (lower case)

The Greek word means "universal." It is used of the universal church as distinguished from local congregations. Sometimes it refers to the faith of the universal church or "orthodox" as opposed to heretical beliefs.

Catechism

A manual for catechizing; specifically : a summary of religious doctrine often in the form of questions and answers.

Christology
Theological interpretation of the person and work of Christ with special attention to the relationship of the human and divine natures in Jesus Christ.

Conciliar Movement
This was a late medieval attempt by the bishops to reform the church through General Councils. As medieval popes claimed more authority and there was increasing schism over the papacy, the bishops claimed that supreme authority in the church rested in a General Council and not the papacy. The movement failed and was one of the factors leading to the Protestant Reformation.

Covenant
An agreement between two parties. The agreement, according to Ancient Near East custom, consists of five parts: 1) Identification of parties, 2) Historical prologue where the deeds establishing the worthiness of the dominant party is established, 3) Conditions of the agreement, 4) Rewards and punishments in regard to keeping the conditions, and 5) Disposition of the documents where each party receives a copy of the agreement (e.g. the two tablets of stone of the 10 Commandments). Ultimately, the covenants God has made with man result in our benefit. We receive eternal blessings from the covenant of grace. (For further study see Gen. 2:16-17; 9:1-17; 15:18; Gen. 26:3-5; Gal. 3:16-18; Luke 1:68-79; Heb. 13:20).

Covenant Theology
Covenant Theology is a system of theology that views God's dealings with man in respect of covenants rather than dispensations (periods of time). It represents the whole of Scripture as covenantal in structure and theme. The two main covenants are the covenant of works in the Old Testament made between God and Adam, and the covenant of grace between God and sinners to whom he offers salvation through Christ by faith. Some theologians add a third Covenant of Redemption between the Father and the Son where the Father promised to give the Son the elect and the Son must redeem them.

Docetism
A Gnostic heresy that was condemned by the early church, with several variations concerning the nature of Christ. Generally, it taught that Jesus only appeared to have a body, that he was not really incarnate, (Greek, dokeo = "to seem"). This error developed out of the dualistic philosophy, which viewed matter as inherently evil, that God could not be associated with matter, and that God, being perfect and infinite, could not suffer.

Deism
The belief that God exists but is not involved in the world. It maintains that God created all things and set the universe in motion and is no longer involved in its operation. (Compare to Theism.)

Donatism
The error taught by Donatus, bishop of Casae Nigrae in North Africa, that the effectiveness of the sacraments depends on the moral character of the minister. In other words, if a minister who was involved in a serious enough sin were to baptize a person, that baptism would be considered invalid. Donatists separated themselves from the catholic church, rebaptizing their adherents and claiming themselves to be the true church.

Erastianism
The sixteenth-century Swiss thinker, Thomas Erastus, argued that the state should have ascendancy over the affairs of the church. According to his theory, civil authorities in a state with one religion should regulate ecclesiastical matters in their domain, including the final approval of excommunications from the church.

Excommunication
Excommunication is the act of discipline where the Church breaks fellowship with a member who has refused to repent of sins. Matthew 18:15-18 is generally used as the model of procedures leading up to excommunication. Those excommunicated are not to partake in the Lord's Supper. In the Bible, serious offenders of God's law, who were supposed to be Christian, were "delivered over to Satan for the

destruction of the flesh," (1 Cor. 5:5; 1 Tim. 1:20). However, upon repentance, the person is welcomed back into fellowship within the body of Christ.

Filioque

The Latin term means "and the Son." This is the doctrine that the Holy Spirit proceeds equally from both the Father and the Son. This "double procession" of the Spirit is contrasted with the original language of the Nicene Creed which only spoke of the Spirit proceeding from the Father. This became a dividing point between the churches of the east and west; the Eastern Orthodox churches object to adding the "filioque clause" to the creed.

Gnosticism

A religious movement that began to appear just after the time of Christ and became widespread by the second century. Generally speaking, Gnosticism taught that salvation is achieved through special knowledge (gnosis). In "Christian" versions of Gnosticism Christ is the messenger who brings the secret knowledge concerning the individual's relationship to the transcendent being. It denied the incarnation of God as the Son. In so doing, it denied the true efficacy of the atonement since, if Jesus is not God, He could not atone for all of mankind and we would still be lost in our sins. Gnosticism was a school of thought rather than a collection of churches. A number of Gnostic teachers wrote their own "gospels" which they claimed were of apostolic origin.

Heresy

A doctrinal view that deviates from the truth as defined by Scripture and the orthodox Christian church. The church is warned against false teachers throughout the New Testament (Acts 20:29-32, Phil. 3:2, 1 Tim. 1:3-7, 2 Pet. 2). Heresies include teachings that deny the person and work of Christ as well as immoral living. To combat heresy, the church fathers formulated "rules of faith" as summaries of orthodox belief. These early statements of faith were eventually formulated into creeds (Apostles, Nicene, etc.) which served as bulwarks against heretical teaching.

Heterodoxy
A set of beliefs or opinions that are not in agreement with accepted doctrinal beliefs of the church. See Orthodoxy.

Homoiousios
The Greek word Homoiousios means "of similar substance," "of similar essence." It was a term used in the fourth century by one group to describe the relationship between the Father and the Son. This is an improper term to use when describing the relationship between the Father and the Son. They are not of similar essence. Rather, they are of the same essence (Homoousious). In other words, according to the correct doctrine of the Trinity, the Father and the Son (and the Holy Spirit) share the same essence.

Homoousios
The Greek word Homoousios means "of the same substance," "of the same essence." Homo means "same" and ousia means "essence." The term was used by Athanasius in his correct teaching of the oneness of the Father and the Son in that they are the same substance, the same essence of divinity. The term was used in the Nicene Creed (and creeds thereafter) when it described Jesus as being of the same substance as the Father in its affirmation of the Trinity.

Humanism
An intellectual movement undergirding the fifteenth-century Renaissance which sparked new interest in the achievements of antiquity both pagan and Christian. It was foundational for renewed attention to the early church fathers' writings in the Reformation era. This movement is to be distinguished from modern "secular" humanism which is an atheistic philosophical system of thought that focuses on human value, thought, and action. Humans are considered basically good and rational creatures that can improve themselves through natural human abilities of reason and action. Secular Humanism is a late development emphasizing objectivity, human reason, and human standards that govern art, economics, ethics, and belief.

Indulgence
In Roman Catholicism, a means by which the church takes away some of the earthly punishment due the Christian in this life and/or purgatory because of his sin. Plenary indulgences were offered to those who participated in the Crusades. In the sixteenth-century the corrupt practice of selling indulgences was introduced in order to rebuild St. Peter's bascilica. The granting of indulgences is usually confined to the pope.

Independent
In seventeenth-century England, this referred to congregations that were autonomous with no ecclesiastical connections like Catholics, Anglicans or Presbyterians. The congregations were typically Puritan Calvinists who practiced infant baptism but did not agree with either episcopacy or Presbyterianism in church government. It was another name for "Congregationalists."

Interdict
In the Roman church, the term usually refers to an ecclesiastical penalty which excludes the faithful from the administration of the sacraments. Interdicts may be personal, local or general. A personal interdict penalizes named persons. A local interdict, (no longer part of canon law) suspends all public worship and withdraws the church's sacraments in a particular area. A general interdict against a country was the equivalent of excommunication against an individual. It would cause all the churches to be closed, and almost all the sacraments to be disallowed (i.e. preventing marriage, confession, anointing of the sick, and the Eucharist). Certain exceptions allow for baptism, anointing of the sick, and sacraments on Christian holy days. Interdiction was used by the pope during the middle ages as a way to influence rulers.

Inerrancy
A nineteenth-century term that means the Bible is without error. In Christianity, inerrancy states that the Bible, in its original documents, is totally true and without mistakes as a special revelation from God. The term is sometimes contrasted with "infallibility" which refers to the full trustworthiness of Scripture that will not deceive. Inerrancy does not extend to the transmission of Biblical manuscripts which may contain copyist errors.

Latitudinarian

A pejorative term applied to a group of seventeenth-century English Arminian theologians who believed in conforming to official Church of England practices but who felt that matters of doctrine, liturgical practice, and ecclesiastical organization were of relatively little importance. The term is sometimes used generically to refer to persons or groups who are extremely broad or loose in theology and/or practice.

Liberal Protestantism

A group of nineteenth-century German theologians who emphasized the universal fatherhood of God. Liberals revised traditional Christianity, arguing for human potential to realize the kingdom of God upon the earth. Christianity and culture were understood to be in continuity with one another. Jesus Christ was the exemplary man who serves as the model for humanity. Friedrich Schleiermacher is considered the "father" of Protestant liberalism or modern theology.

Neo-orthodoxy

A term generally applied to a twentieth-century theology which rejected liberal Protestantism's optimism about man and returned to the Reformed emphasis on human depravity and the need for saving grace. These theologians emphasized existential aspects of religious experience, and accepted much of higher criticism's denunciation of Biblical literalism. Experience with the divine is what makes Scripture real, not Biblical revelation, not reason. This school of thought is mostly identified with Karl Barth and several of his contemporaries; the movement was very diverse.

Orthodoxy

This term is used in three different ways: 1) Accepted or right doctrines as opposed to heresy, 2) Eastern churches such as the Greek or Russian Orthodox Church, 3) A seventeenth-century movement that emphasized the importance of Protestant doctrinal definition – e.g., Reformed orthodoxy or Lutheran orthodoxy.

Papal Bull
An official letter issued by the Pope that deals with important issues related to the Roman Catholic Church. It can deal with excommunications, sainthood, doctrine, etc. "Bull" is derived from the seal (Latin, *bulla*) that is added to the end of a document to make it authentic.

Pre-millennialism
A teaching concerning the end times (eschatology), which asserts that there is a future millennium (1000 years) where Christ will rule and reign over the earth. At the beginning of the millennium Satan and his angels will be bound, and peace will exist on the entire earth. At the end of the 1000 years, Satan will be released in order to raise an army against Jesus. Jesus will destroy them and the final judgment will take place followed by a new heavens and the new earth.

Protestant
The term Protestant refers to a person or group who holds to one of the systems of doctrine (i.e. Lutheran, Reformed, Anglican) that resulted from the sixteenth-century Reformation. Originally, these groups stood in opposition to the Roman Catholic Church, and held in common belief in Scripture as the final authority and justification by faith alone. Soon after they departed from the Roman church they began to divide among themselves over numerous issues (e.g., polity and sacraments).

Simony
Paying for holy offices or positions in the hierarchy of a church, named after Simon Magus who appears in Acts 8:18-24. Simon Magus offers the disciples of Jesus, Peter and John, payment so that anyone on whom he placed his hands received the power of the Holy Spirit. This is the origin of the term simony but it also extends to other forms of trafficking for money in "spiritual things."

Semi-Pelagianism

A Christian theological understanding about salvation; that is, the means by which humanity and God are restored to a right relationship. Semi-Pelagian thought stands in contrast to the earlier Pelagian teaching about salvation (in which man is seen as effecting his own salvation), which had been dismissed as heresy. Semi-Pelagianism in its original form was developed as a compromise between Pelagianism and the teaching of Church Fathers such as Saint Augustine, who taught that man cannot come to God without the grace of God. In Semi-Pelagian thought, therefore, a distinction is made between the beginning of faith and the increase of faith. Semi-Pelagianism teaches that man must act first, then God comes to his aid with the offer of grace. It too was labeled heresy by the Western Church in the Second Council of Orange in 529.

Sola Fide

The teaching that faith alone (without works) saves a person, when he places his trust in the sacrificial work of Christ. Believers are justified by faith alone which is the means for receiving the grace of God.

Sola Gratia

The teaching that God pardons sinners apart from any merit of their own which would make them worthy to receive God's grace. Believers are saved by grace alone solely based upon God's mercy in Christ, leaving nothing to the human will. Even faith is a gift of grace.

Sola Scriptura

The teaching that the Scriptures contain all that is necessary for salvation and proper living before God. The Scriptures of the Old and New Testaments are the final authority in all that they address, and that tradition, even so-called Sacred Tradition, is judged by those Scriptures. Sola Scriptura does not negate past councils or traditions. Instead, it is above them and they are to be judged by Scripture.

Soli Deo Gloria

Latin for "glory to God alone." It is the Reformation teaching that all glory is to be given to God alone. This is because the Reformers believed that salvation, sanctification and glorification are all accomplished through God's will and action, not man's effort, including good works (Eph 2:10).

Solus Christus

The teaching that salvation comes through Jesus Christ alone.

Substitutionary Atonement

Christ's death on the cross was substitutionary in that he suffered in our place, taking upon himself the judgement that human beings deserved for their sin. He was our representative in his work of atonement, turning away the wrath of God through the cross and reconciling believers to God.

Theism

The teaching that there is a God and that He is actively involved in the affairs of the world. This does not necessitate the Christian concept of God, but includes it. (Compare to Deism, which is the teaching that God exists but is not involved in the world.)

Theology

In the early church, "theology" (Greek: *theologia*) primarily referred to teaching about the Godhead. In medieval universities, the term was used more broadly of a field of study and teaching as distinguished from philosophy. In the modern context, the word is used comprehensively of multiple disciplines related to the study of God and the Christian faith.

Theonomy

The word theonomy derives from combining the Greek words *theos* (God) and *nomos* (law). The basic belief is that civil states should be governed by the law of Moses, including the penalties prescribed for violations of that law. This means that homosexuality, adultery or blasphemy could be punishable by death. Theonomists or "Christian Restructionists" are typically postmillennial in eschatology, believing that one day Christianity will dominate all earthly human cultures and at this point God's law should prevail in the state. Opponents argue that God's relationship to Israel was unique, and in light of New Testament teaching, it was not God's intention that Jewish law be imposed on all the nations. Theonomy has caused dissention among some conservative Reformed thinkers in the twentieth century.

Unitarianism
A theological error that holds to the unity of God by denying the Trinity, the deity of Jesus, and the deity of the Holy Spirit. In the sixteenth century, Socinians were an early unitarian group that organized themselves in opposition to orthodox Christianity. Unitarian views emerged in eighteenth-century England and in New England leading eventually to the formation of the Unitarian Universalist Association formed in 1961.

Universalism
The teaching that all people will eventually be saved through the universal redemption of Jesus. Some universalists teach that even the devil, after a time of punishment, will be redeemed.

APPENDIX

American Presbyterian Chronology

THE COLONIAL ERA

1640 Southhampton Church on Long Island is one of the oldest Presbyterian congregations.

1706 Francis Makemie initiates the first American presbytery, with seven ministers.

1717 The Synod of Philadelphia is organized with seventeen Presbyterian congregations.

1727 William Tennent founds the "Log College" in order to train young revival preachers.

1729 The *Adopting Act* compromise endorses the *Westminster Confession* and *Catechisms*.

1741 Old Side and New Side Presbyterians divide over the Great Awakening.

1745 Jonathan Dickinson helps establish the pro-revival Synod of New York.

1758 The reunion of Synods of Philadelphia and New York is led by Gilbert Tennent.

1768 John Witherspoon becomes the fifth president of the College of New Jersey.

1788 Presbyterians ratify a constitution, including a new *Book of Government*.

1789 First General Assembly includes 177 ministers and over 400 congregations.

OLD SCHOOL/NEW SCHOOL PERIOD

1801   The Plan of Union unites Presbyterians and Congregational churches for mission.

1810   Cumberland Presbyterians establish their own denomination on the frontier.

1812   Princeton Seminary is founded, with Archibald Alexander as the first professor.

1818   The General Assembly declares slavery, "irreconcilable with the gospel of Christ."

1831   Presbyterian minister Albert Barnes is exonerated at his first General Assembly trial.

1837   The New School issues the "Auburn Declaration," responding to accusations of error.

1838   Old School/New School schism divides Presbyterians into two denominations.

1858   The United Synod of the South separates from the northern New School over slavery.

1861   Old School churches in the Confederacy leave the northern church when the War begins.

1864   The Old School/New School churches in the Confederacy reunite.

1870   The reunion Old School/New School churches in the North takes place after the War.

1893   Professor Charles Briggs of Union Seminary is suspended from the ministry.

THE TWENTIETH-CENTURY

1903   Presbyterians add two new chapters to the *Westminster Confession of Faith*.

1906   Many Cumberland Presbyterians reunite with the Northern Presbyterian church.

1910   The General Assembly issues a declaration of five "essential and necessary doctrines."

1924   The "Auburn Affirmation," signed by over 1,200 ministers, challenges the five essential doctrines.

1925   Presbyterian politician William Jennings Bryan participates in the Scopes Monkey Trial.

1929   Westminster Theological Seminary is founded by J. Gresham Machen.

1936   The Orthodox Presbyterian Church is established as a new Presbyterian denomination.

1958   The UPCNA and Northern Presbyterians (PCUSA) unite to form the new UPCUSA.

1964   The Ordination of Women is endorsed by the Southern Presbyterians (PCUS).

1967   A *Book of Confessions* and a new *Confession of 1967* are adopted by the UPCUSA.

1973   Southern evangelical Presbyterians found the Presbyterian Church in America (PCA).

1982   The Reformed Presbyterian Church, Evangelical Synod joins with the PCA.

1981   Mainline Presbyterian evangelicals establish the Evangelical Presbyterian Church (EPC).

1983   The UPUSA and PCUS reunite to establish the Presbyterian Church (U.S.A.).

2012   ECO: A Covenant Order of Evangelical Presbyterians holds its first organizational meeting.

Study Guide

Many of God's people have not been exposed to the full story of Christianity and are spiritually poorer for it. This book is an attempt to address this situation for Presbyterians by highlighting the Reformed Tradition and the Presbyterian heritage in America within the larger context of church history. There are many treasures in this narrative that continue to inform what we believe and how we practice the faith.

The purpose of the Study Guide is to assist the reader in considering how the whole scope of *The Presbyterian Story* is pertinent for the practice of the modern church. Individuals and group leaders who use this book are encouraged to make the material relevant by constantly asking the "So what?" question as they read each chapter. Some general questions to consider for each chapter: **Are there things this era tells us are important? Are there errors to avoid? Are there principles to emulate? In what ways were these saints faithful to God's call in their generation? How can we be faithful in our time?**

For each chapter the Study Guide provides discussion questions that attempt to apply the material to the contemporary church. In addition, there is a list of Scripture passages that relate to the themes of that chapter along with further questions for reflection. Also included is a reading list for further study.

CHAPTER ONE: CHURCH HISTORY MATTERS

Questions to Consider

• Why do some believers have such a negative view of "tradition"? How has this attitude shaped contemporary Christianity?

• If we carefully considered what ancient Christians believed and how they lived, how would it make a difference in our lives?

• How does church history help clarify our self-identity as followers of Christ?

• Have we become too accustomed to division among believers? What are some tangible ways Christians can express an ecumenical spirit towards those in other denominations?

Reflection on Scripture

Read: *Joshua 4:19-24*

• Do members of your congregation know the basic story of Christian history? If not, how can you help remedy this situation?

Read: *2 Thessalonians 2:13-17*

• In what ways have modern congregations failed to "stand firm and hold to the traditions"? How has this neglect weakened the life of the church?

Read: *Hebrews 11:32-12:2*

• Have you read any Christian biographies in recent years? How might you be encouraged by the testimonies of the saints in heaven?

For Further Study

131 Christians Everyone Should Know. Editors of *Christian History* magazine. Nashville: Broadman & Holman Publishers, 2000.

Cutsinger, James S. *Reclaiming the Great Tradition: Evangelicals, Catholics and Orthodox in Dialogue.* Downers Grove: InterVarsity Press, 1997.

Hall, Christopher A. *Reading Scripture with the Church Fathers.* Downers Grove: InterVarsity Press, 1998.

Mathison, Keith A. *The Shape of Sola Scriptura.* Moscow, Idaho: Canon Press, 2001.

McGrath, Alister. *Historical Theology: An Introduction to the History of Christian Thought.* Oxford: Blackwell Publishers, 2001.

Noll, Mark A. *Turning Points: Decisive Moments in the History of Christianity.* Grand Rapids: Baker Books, 1997.

Shaw, Mark. *Ten Great Ideas from Church History: A Decision-Makers Guide to Shaping Your Church.* Downers Grove: InterVarsity Press, 1997.

Williams, D.H. *Retrieving the Tradition & Renewing Evangelicalism: A Primer for Suspicious Protestants.* Grand Rapids: William B. Eerdmans Publishing Company, 1999.

Woodbridge, John. Ed. *Great Leaders of the Christian Church.* Chicago: Moody Press, 1988.

CHAPTER TWO: EARLY CHRISTIANITY

Questions to Consider

• Early Christianity grew significantly in the midst of persecution. In what ways is the modern global context similar to that of early Christianity? How is it different?

• Who are the intellectual attackers of Christianity today? What are their criticisms of the Church? Who is answering them?

• Cyprian, bishop of Carthage said: "You cannot have God for your father unless you have the church for your mother." What do you think about this statement? Why do you think some contemporary believers appear to view church membership as optional?

• What is the value of the Apostles Creed for the twenty first-century church?

Reflection on Scripture

Read: *Matthew 10:16-39*

• How do Christians in America suffer persecution in the midst of a neo-pagan culture? Do you currently pray for the persecuted church in the world? What practical steps are you willing to take to make this a priority in your prayer life?

Read: *Acts 1:6-11*

• Name ways that Christians can witness by their lives? Are you praying for any unbelievers? In what ways are you trying to share Christ with them?

Read: *Acts 2:42-47*

• What's your impression of church life described in the book of Acts? How does your congregation's practice compare to the description in Acts 2?

For Further Study

Bettenson, Henry. Editor. *Documents of the Christian Church*. Third Edition. New York: Oxford University Press, 1999.

Cross, F.L. and E. A. Livingstone ed. *The Oxford Dictionary of the Christian Church*, Reprint ed. Oxford University Press, 1990.

Dowley, Tim. Editor. *Introducton to the History of Christianity*. Reprint. Grand Rapids: Minneapolis: Fortress Press, 1995.

Ferguson, Everett, ed. *Encyclopedia of Early Christianity*. New York: Garland Publishing, Inc., 1990.

Kelly, J.N.D. *Early Church Doctrines*. Reprint ed., San Francisco: Harper Collins, 1978.

Lightfoot, J.B. *The Apostolic Fathers*, Grand Rapids: Baker Book House, Reprint, 1976.

Maier, Paul. Editor. *Eusebius: The Church History*. Grand Rapids: Kregel, 2007.

The New Encyclopedia of Christian Martyrs. Compiled by Mark Water. Grand Rapids: Baker Books, 2001.

White, James F. *Christian Worship: A Brief History*. Nashville: Abingdon Press, 1993.

Williams, D.H. *Evangelicals and Tradition: The Formative Influence of the Early Church*. Grand Rapids: Baker Academic, 2005.

CHAPTER THREE: CHURCH FATHERS

Questions to Consider

• What are some current counterfeit ideas in society about the person of Christ? Is there false teaching about Christ in the church? If so, where and when have you been aware of it?

• Do you think most Christians understand why they are trinitarian? What authority should the Nicene and Chalcedonian creeds have?

• Can you think of present-day church groups that have Donatist-like attitudes? How would you describe the "true church?"

• Why do you think Pelagian ideas were so attractive? What about today?

Reflection on Scripture

Read: *Matthew 28:16-20*

• The disciples "worshipped" the risen Christ. What does this imply about their understanding of who he is? Why must Christian baptism be in the name of Father, Son and Holy Spirit?

Read: *Ephesians 4:1-16*

• If there is "one Lord, one faith, one baptism," why is there so much division in the body of Christ? How can believers promote unity throughout the Christian church?

Read: *Colossians 1:13-23*

• How is Paul's description of Christ's preeminence meaningful in your own experience? When did you first discover the authentic Jesus revealed in Scripture?

For Further Study

Bray, Gerald. *Councils, Creeds & Christ*. Downers Grove: InterVarsity Press, 1984.

Hall, Christopher A. *Learning Theology with the Church Fathers*. Downers Grove: InterVarsity Press, 2002.

Haykin, Michael A.G. *Rediscovering the Church Fathers*. Wheaton: Crossway, 2011.

Leith, John. *Creeds of the Churches*. Atlanta: John Knox Press, 1977.

Litfin, Bryan M. *Getting to Know the Church Fathers: An Evangelical Introduction*. Grand Rapids: Brazos Press, 2007.

Oates, Whitney J. Editor. *Basic Writings of Augustine*. 2 Vols, Baker Book House,1980.

Oden, Thomas. *How Africa Shaped the Christian Mind: Rediscovering the African Seedbed of Western Christianity*. Downers Grove: InterVarsity Press, 2007.

Pelikan, Jaroslav. *The Christian Tradition*. 5 Vols. Chicago: Univ. of Chicago Press, 1971-89.

Schaff, Philip. *Creeds of Christendom*. 3 Vols. reprint ed., Grand Rapids: Baker Book House, 1993.

Wright, David F. ed. *Baptism: Three Views*. Downers Grove: InterVarsity Press, 2009. [note chapter by Anthony N.S. Lane on church history]

CHAPTER FOUR: THE MIDDLE YEARS

Questions to Consider

• What role should monastic ideals have in the contemporary church? (i.e., separation from the world, a life of renunciation, celibacy, the giving away of one's possessions, fasting, a life of prayer).

• Why do you think some Protestants have lost a sense of awe and wonder in worship? What can we learn from the Eastern Orthodox churches?

• How is the church in America responding to the challenges of Islam? Do you have any suggestions?

• Describe your understanding of the relationship between faith and reason? In what ways do believers struggle with this issue today?

Reflection on Scripture

Read: *Matthew 16:24-28*

• How can contemporary believers practice self denial? Name ways in which you might deny yourself for the sake of Christ and his kingdom?

Read: *Hebrews 2:9-18*

• What is the connection of Christ's humanity to his suffering? What benefits do we receive from Christ's death? Why do people find the cross of Christ offensive?

Read: *Revelation 4:1-11*

• What's your reaction to the worship described in the book of Revelation? How could the experience of Sunday morning worship be enhanced by grasping the reality of participating in heavenly worship?

For Further Study

A'Kempis, Thomas. *The Imitation of Christ*. Grand Rapids: Zondervan Publishing House, 1983.

Allen, Diogenes. *Spiritual Theology: The Theology of Yesterday for Spiritual Help Today*. Boston: Cowley Publications, 1997.

Bede. *A History of the English Church and People*. Trans. Leo Sherley-Price. Reprint. NY: Barnes and Noble Books, 1993.

Churchhill, Leigh: *From Leif Erikson to Martin Luther (AD 1000-1517)*. UK:Authentic Media, 2004.

Evans, G.R. *Faith in the Medieval World*. Downers Grove: InterVarsity, 2002.

Fairbairn, Donald. *Eastern Orthodoxy Through Western Eyes*. Louisville: Westminster John Knox, 2002.

Kane, J. Herbert. A *Concise History of the Christian World Mission: A Panoramic View of Missions from Pentecost to the Present*. Grand Rapids: Baker Book House, 1982.

Ozment, Steven. *The Age of Reform 1250-1550: An Intellectual and Religious History of Late Medieval and Reformation Europe*. New Haven: Yale University Press, 1980.

Riley-Smith, Jonathan. *The Crusades*. Second ed. New Haven: Yale University Press, 2005.

CHAPTER FIVE: THE PROTESTANT MOVEMENTS

Questions to Consider

• What is the significance of Luther's understanding of justification by faith alone? What is the role of "good works" in the life of the believer?

• Is Calvin's teaching on predestination a comforting or disturbing doctrine to you? Why?

• Do Christians have a responsibility to transform their society? If so, how does one go about doing this in contemporary culture?

• Is the Reformation over? What barriers remain today between Protestants and Roman Catholics?

Reflection on Scripture

Read: *Psalm 119:1-16*

• Since we have God's Word in our own language, how does this increase our responsibility to obey its teachings? Why do you think so many professing Christians neglect reading the Bible on a regular basis? How about you?

Read: *John 6:41-59*

• Describe how participation in the Lord's Supper can be a blessing? How do you prepare your heart for this?

Read: *Romans 5:1-11*

• What is the relationship of the two phrases, "justified by faith" (vs.1) and "justified by his blood" (vs. 9) according to St. Paul?

For Further Study

Calvin, John. *Institutes of the Christian Religion.* ed. John T. McNeill. 2 Vols. Philadelphia: The Westminster Press, 1960.

Dillenberger, John. *John Calvin: Selections from His Writings.* American Academy of Religion, Scholars Press, 1975.

George, Timothy. *Theology of the Reformers.* Nashville: Broadman Press, 1998.

Graham, Fred W. *The Constructive Revolutionary: John Calvin and His Socio-Economic Impact.* Atlanta: John Knox Press, 1978.

Leith, John H. *An Introduction to the Reformed Tradition: A Way of Being the Christian Community.* Atlanta: John Knox Press, 1981.

McGrath, Alistair. *Reformation Thought: An Introduction.* Oxford: Blackwell Publishers, 1993.

McNeill, John T. *The History and Character of Calvinism.* New York: Oxford University Press, 1967.

Noll, Mark A. *Confessions and Catechisms of the Reformation.* Grand Rapids: Baker Book House, 1991.

Spitz, Lewis B. *The Protestant Reformation: 1517-1559.* New York: Harper and Row, 1985.

Wallace, Ronald S. *Calvin, Geneva and the Reformation: A Study of Calvin as Social Worker, Churchman, Pastor and Theologian.* Grand Rapids: Baker Book House, 1990.

CHAPTER SIX: REFORMATION IN THE BRITISH ISLES

Questions to Consider

• In what areas does the Protestant church need to be "purified" today? How can one encourage reform of the contemporary church?

• How important is it for Christian worship to conform to the norms of Scripture? Why?

• It was said of John Knox that he "feared no flesh." Why do some Christians fail to act with the courage of their convictions?

• Why is Christian education so important for the strength of the church? How can modern believers fortify this aspect of ministry?

Reflection on Scripture

Read: *Matthew 18:10-20*

• If discipline is one mark of the true church, why are local church leaders so hesitant to implement it? What are some misperceptions about church discipline? Is the process outlined in Matthew 18 practiced in your congregation?

Read: *Titus 1:1-16*

• Why must elders "be able to give instruction in sound doctrine"? Has an elder made an impact on your life? What was the nature of this influence?

Read: *James 1:19-27*

• Why is consistent listening to good preaching essential for the believer? Why does preaching sometimes produce so little life change? How can you be a "doer of the word" and not merely a "hearer of the word"?

For Further Study

Barker, William S. *Puritan Profiles: 54 Influential Puritans at the time when the Westminster Confession of Faith was written.* Scotland: Christian Focus, 1999.

Bray, Gerald. Editor. *Documents of the English Reformation.* Minneapolis: Fortress Press, 1994.

Collinson, Patrick. *The Elizabethan Puritan Movement.* Oxford: Clarendon Press, 1967.

Davies, Horton. *Worship and Theology in England: From Cranmer to Baxter and Fox, 1534-1690.* Grand Rapids: William B. Eerdmans Publishing Co., 1996.

Dickens, A.G. *The English Reformation.* University Park Pennsylvania: Penn State University Press, 1989.

Hall, David W. & Joseph H. Hall, ed. *Paradigms in Polity: Classic Readings in Reformed and Presbyterian Church Government.* Grand Rapids: William B. Eerdmans Publishing Co., 1994.

Knox, John. *The Reformation in Scotland.* Edinburgh: Banner of Truth Trust, Reprint, 1982.

Leith, John. *Assembly at Westminster: Reformed Theology in the Making.* Richmond: John Knox Press, 1973.

Packer, J.I. *A Quest for Godliness: The Puritan Vision of the Christian Life.* Wheaton: Crossway Books, 1990.

Ryken, Leland. *Worldly Saints: The Puritans as They Really Were.* Grand Rapids: Zondervan Publishing House, 1986.

CHAPTER SEVEN: NEW CHURCH AND NEW NATION

Questions to Consider

• If the U.S. experienced another "awakening" in the twenty-first century, what do you think it would look like?

• Why have some American believers lost their passion for holiness of life? Why is there sometimes little lifestyle difference between believers and unbelievers?

• Is ecclesiastical compromise a necessity for the peace of the church? Why or why not?

• How is separation of church and state understood in contemporary America? What are the challenges Christians face in a religiously pluralistic society?

• Why is connectionalism necessary for the spiritual health of the church?

Reflection on Scripture

Read: *Jeremiah 29:1-7*

• In what ways are believers exiles in America today? How can contemporary Christians "seek the welfare of the city" where they live? Name some practical ways you can do this?

Read: *Acts 15:1-35*

• When there is tension between members in your congregation, how have the elders intervened to restore peace? Why do some contemporary believers resist submission to the spiritual authority of church leaders?

Read: *1 Peter 1:13-25*

• How would your life change if you genuinely sought to "be holy in all your conduct"?

For Further Study

Alexander, Archibald. *The Log College: Biographical Sketches of William Tennent and Principal Alumni of the Log College. Together with an Account of the Revivals of Religion under their Ministry in the 18th Century.* Reprint. Birmingham, AL: Solid Ground Christian Books.

Barker, William S. and Samuel T. Logan Jr. *Sermons That Shaped America: Reformed Preaching from 1630 to 2001.* Phillipsburg, New Jersey: P&R Publishing, 2003.

Fortson, S. Donald, III ed. *Colonial Presbyterianism: Old Faith in a New Land.* Princeton Theological Monograph Series. Eugene, Oregon: Wipf and Stock, 2007.

Klett, Guy S. *Minutes of the Presbyterian Church in America, 1706-1788.* Philadelphia: Presbyterian Historical Society, 1976.

Noll, Mark A. *The Rise of Evangelicalism: The Age of Edwards, Whitefield and the Wesleys.* Downers Grove: InterVarsity Press, 2003.

Smith, Elwyn A. *The Presbyterian Ministry in America: A Study in Changing Concepts, 1700-1900.* Philadelphia: The Westminster Press, 1962.

Thompson, Ernest Trice. *Presbyterians in the South,* 3 vols. Richmond: John Knox Press, 1963.

Trinterud, Leonard. *The Forming of an American Tradition.* Philadelphia: Westminster Press, 1949.

Waldman, Steven. *Founding Faith: Providence, Politics, and the Birth of Religious Freedom in America.* New York: Random House, 2008.

Dictionary of the Presbyterian & Reformed Tradition in America. eds. D.G. Hart and Mark A.Noll. Downers Grove: InterVarsity Press, 1999.

CHAPTER EIGHT: OLD SCHOOL AND NEW SCHOOL

Questions to Consider

• Are there issues currently producing divisions in your denomination? If so, what do you think may resolve the situation?

• In your congregation, when there are strong differences of opinion, do members leave the church or are they committed to working things out? How can Christians cultivate a charitable spirit towards fellow believers?

• Is the church today sufficiently focused on evangelizing the world for Christ? How can we make this a priority in the local church?

• How would you evaluate race relations in the U.S.? Why is Sunday still the most segregated day of the week?

Reflection on Scripture

Read: *Deuteronomy 6:1-15*

• In your congregation, how are the parents taking initiative to train their children in the faith? In what ways does the body of believers assist the parents? To what extent should local church resources be committed to children's ministry and youth ministry?

Read: *Acts 13:1-5*

• Is your church challenged to respond to the Great Commission on a worldwide scale? Have you ever participated in a short-term mission trip? If so, how did it change your perspective on the church and the world?

Read: *Acts 15:36-41*

• Where have you witnessed a "sharp disagreement" that caused Christian brothers and sisters to separate? Is it legitimate for Christians to do this or is it always a hardness of heart that produces schism?

For Further Study

Calhoun, David. *Princeton Seminary*, 2 vols. Edinburgh: Banner of Truth, 1996.

Fortson, S. Donald, III. *The Presbyterian Creed: A Confessional Tradition in America, 1729-1870*. UK: Paternoster Press, 2008.

Hoffecker, W. Andrew. *Piety and the Princeton Theologians*. Phillipsburg, NJ: Presbyterian and Reformed Publishing Co., 1982.

Marsden, George. *The Evangelical Mind and New School Presbyterian Experience*. New Haven: Yale University Press, 1970.

Melton, Julius. *Presbyterian Worship in America: Changing Patterns Since 1787*. Richmond: John Knox Press, 1967.

Pope, Earl A. *New England Calvinism and the Disruption of the Presbyterian Church*, New York: Garland, 1987.

Noll, Mark A. *The Civil War as a Theological Crisis*. Chapel Hill: The University of North Carolina Press, 2006.

Hatch, Nathan. *The Democratization of American Christianity*. New Haven: Yale University Press, 1991.

Wells, David, ed. *Southern Reformed Theology*. Grand Rapids: Baker Book House, 1989.

CHAPTER NINE: FACING NEW CHALLENGES

Questions to Consider

- How would you answer a non-Christian who asked you why you believe the Bible is unique compared to any other religious book? Is there still a battle for the Bible going on inside the church?

- What beliefs would you put in the category of "essentials" of the Christian faith?

- What are some current attempts to revise historic Christianity to accommodate culture? At what point do revisionist theologies become apostate and no longer Christian?

- How should God's people respond to the challenges of modern science? Why do Christians respond to this issue in such dissimilar ways?

Reflection on Scripture

Read: *Romans 1:18-24*

- How would the phrase, "claiming to be wise, they became fools" apply to present-day American society? In what ways could it apply to parts of the church?

Read: *2 Corinthians 11:1-15*

- Where have you heard the preaching of a "different gospel" by one claiming to be a follower of Christ? Name some contemporary "false apostles"?

Read: *1 John 4:1-6*

- If the "spirit of the antichrist" is in the world already, in what ways should Christians respond to this reality? How can we discern "the Spirit of truth and the spirit of error"?

For Further Study

Armstrong, Maurice W., Lefferts A. Loetscher and Charles Anderson, eds. *The Presbyterian Enterprise: Sources of American Presbyterian History.* Philadephia: The Westminster Press, 1956.

Grentz, Stanley J. and Roger C. Olson, *Twentieth-Century Theology: God & the World in a Transitional Age.* Downers Grove: InterVarsity Press, 1992.

Hart, D.G. and John Muether, *Fighting the Good Fight: A Brief History of the Orthodox Presbyterian Church.* Philadelphia: The Committee for Christian Education and Committee for the Historian of the Orthodox Presbyterian Church, 1995.

Hill, Jonathan. *Faith in the Age of Reason: The Enlightenment From Galileo to Kant.* Downers Grove: InterVarsity Press, 2004.

Loetscher, Lefferts A. *The Broadening Church: A Study of Theological Issues in the Presbyterian Church Since 1869.* Philadelphia: University of Pennsylvania Press, 1957.

Longfield, Bradley J. *The Presbyterian Controversy: Fundamentalists, Modernists, & Moderates.* New York: Oxford University Press, 1991.

Marsden, George. *Fundamentalism and American Culture.* second ed. New York: Oxford, 2006.

Machen, J. Gresham. *Christianity and Liberalism.* reprint ed. Grand Rapids: Wm. B. Eerdmans Publishing Co., 1977.

Noll, Mark A. *The Princeton Theology, 1812-1921: Scripture, Science and Theological Method from Archibald Alexander to Benjamin Warfield.* Grand Rapids: Baker, 1983.

CHAPTER TEN: A HOUSE DIVIDED

Questions for Consideration

• What constitutes legitimate criteria for leaving one's denomination? Why do evangelicals have such diverse perspectives on this question?

• How can reclaiming the historic Reformed tradition add strength to the Presbyterian churches?

• Have you ever been part of a new church plant? Why are new church plants one of the most effective approaches to reaching people for Christ?

• What priority should ministry to the poor have in the local church? Why do you think some followers of Christ focus on mercy ministry while others give it very little attention?

Reflection on Scripture

Read: *Matthew 5:13-16*

• In what ways can your congregation be the "salt of the earth" in your community? As a Christian, how can you "let your light shine before others" in your neighborhood and workplace?

Read: *Luke 16:13-31*

• How can you apply Jesus' words, "you cannot serve God and money" in your life? Why do many professing Christians ignore Jesus' teaching in Luke 16:18? What does this say about the contemporary church?

Read: *Romans 1:26-32 and 1 Corinthians 6:9-11*

• Paul describes all homosexual practice as "dishonorable passions" and "shameful acts." Why have some in the church discarded this clear apostolic teaching? What does 1 Corinthians 6 say about being washed and sanctified from sexual sin? Do you need to ask God's forgiveness for any secret sin in your life?

For Further Study

Balmer, Randal and John R. Fitzmier. *The Presbyterians.* Westport, CT: Praeger, 1994.

Coalter, Milton, John M. Mulder and Louis B. Weeks. eds. *The Presbyterian Presence: The Twentieth-Century Experience.* 6 vols. Louisville: Westminster John Knox, 1992.

Hart, D.G. and John R. Muether. *Seeking a Better Country: 300 Years of American Presbyterianism.* Phillipsburg, New Jersey: P&R Publishing, 2007.

Lucas, Sean Michael. *On Being Presbyterian.* Phillipsburg, NJ: P&R Publishing, 2006.

Marsden, George. *Reforming Fundamentalism: Fuller Seminary and the New Evangelicalism.* Grand Rapids: Eerdmans Publishing Company, 1987.

Rosell, Garth. *The Surprising Work of God: Harold Ockenga, Billy Graham and the Rebirth of Evangelicalism.* Grand Rapids: Baker, 2008.

Smartt, Kennedy. *I Am Reminded: An Autobiographical, Anecdotal History of the Presbyterian Church in America.* 25th Anniversary Edition.

Smith, Morton H. *How is the Gold Become Dim: The Decline of the Presbyterian Church, U.S. as Reflected in its Assembly Actions.* Jackson, MS: Premier Printing Co., 1973.

Stewart, Kenneth J. *Ten Myths of Calvinism: Recovering the Breadth of the Reformed Tradition.* Downers Grove: InterVarsity Press, 2011

Williamson, Parker T. *Broken Covenant: Signs of a Shattered Communion.* Lenoir, NC: Reformation Press, 2007.

NOTES

Chapter One: Church History Matters

[1] All Scripture quotations will be from the *English Standard Version*.

[2] Jaroslav Pelikan, *The Vindication of Tradition* (New Haven: Yale University Press, 1984), 65.

[3] Mark Noll, ed. *Confessions and Catechisms of the Reformation* (Grand Rapids: Baker Book House, 1991), 170; Heiko Oberman, *The Harvest of Medieval Theology* (Durham, NC: Labyrinth Press, 1983), 370.

[4] Gilbert K. Chesterton, *Orthodoxy* (San Francisco: Ignatius Press, 1908), 53.

[5] Jaroslav Pelikan, *Obedient Rebels* (New York: Harper and Row Publishers, 1964), 13.

[6] "Augsburg Confession, Article XX," *in The Book of Concord*, trans. and ed., Theodore G. Tappert (Philadelphia: Fortress Press, 1959), 42, 43.

[7] Ralph Waldo Emerson, "The Sovereignty of Ethics" in *The Complete Works of Ralph Waldo Emerson*, vol. 10 (Boston and New York: Houghton Miffin and Company, 1903-1904), 204.

[8] John Calvin, *John Calvin, Selections from his Writings*, ed. John Dillenberger, "Reply of Letter by Cardinal Sadolet to the Senate and People of Geneva" (Scholars Press, 1975), 92.

[9] There were legitimate "unwritten traditions" that had been handed down by the apostles to the next generation of bishops. These oral traditions could be distorted and should not be afforded the same honor as Scripture, but, the early church had to depend on these instructions passed on by word of mouth. During the early periods, when few had access to all the canonical books, these "traditions" were necessary to direct the infant church.

[10] "Constitutions of the Holy Apostles," *The Ante-Nicene Fathers*, ed. Alexander Roberts and James Donaldson, vol. 7, reprint (William B. Eerdmans Publishing Co., 1993), 456.

[11] Augustine, "On Baptism, Against the Donatists," *The Nicene and Post-Nicene Fathers*, ed. Philip Schaff, vol.4, reprint (Grand Rapids: William B. Eerdmans, 1991), 454, 455.

[12] See Martin Luther, "Concerning Rebaptism" trans. Conrad Bergendoff, *Luther's Works*, vol. 40 (Philadelphia: Fortress Press, 1958); Ulrich Zwingli, "On Baptism," *Zwingli and Bullinger*, ed. G.W. Bromiley, Library of Christian Classics (Philadelphia: Westminster Press, 1953); John Calvin, *Institutes of the Christian Religion*, trans. Ford Lewis Battles (Philadelphia: The Westminster Press, 1960), 4.15.14 -18.

[13] John Calvin, *Institutes of the Christian Religion*, 4.15.1.

[14] *The Westminster Confession of Faith and Catechisms in Modern English* (The Summertown Company, 2004), Chapter 28, paragraphs 6, 7.

[15] J. Gresham Machen, *Christianity and Liberalism* (Grand Rapids: Wm. B Eerdmans Publishing Co., 1923, reprint. 1977), 52.

[16] Jaroslav Pelikan, *Luther's Works*, Companion Volume: *Luther the Expositor: Introduction to the Reformer's Exegetical Writings* (St. Louis: Concordia Publishing House, 19), 75.

Chapter Two: Early Christianity

[1] Tertullian, "Apology," *The Ante-Nicene Fathers*, ed. Alexander Roberts and James Donaldson, vol. 3, reprint (William B. Eerdmans Publishing Co., 1993), 55.

[2] Emperor Julian quoted in Hans Lietzmann, *From Constantine to Julian*, trans. Bertram Lee Woolf (New York: Charles Scribner's Sons, 1950), 278.

[3] J.B. Lightfoot, *The Apostolic Fathers*, "The Letter of the Smyrnaeans on the Martyrdom of St. Polycarp" (London: Macmillan and Company, 1891; reprint, Grand Rapids: Baker Book House, 1976), 112.

[4] Henry Bettenson & Chris Maunder, *Documents of the Christian Church*, third edition (Oxford: Oxford University Press, 1999), 3, 5.

[5] Eusebius, *Ecclesiastical History* (Grand Rapids: Baker Book House, 1988), 170.

[6] Tertullian quoted in Joseph Cullen Ayer, *A Source Book for Ancient Church History* (New York: Charles Scribner's Sons, 1930), 53.

[7] Origen, "That the Scriptures are Divinely Inspired," *The Ante-Nicene Fathers*, ed. Alexander Roberts and James Donaldson, vol. 4, reprint (William B. Eerdmans Publishing Co., 1994), 355.

[8] Eusebius, 109.

[9] Bettensen, 31.

[10] Eusebius, 111.

[11] Augustine, "Augustine Epistle 82" in *The Correspondence (394-419) Between Jerome and Augustine of Hippo* ed. Caroline White, Studies in Bible and Early Christianity, vol. 23 (Lewiston, NY: The Edwin Mellon Press, 1990), 146, 147.

[12] "Epistle of Ignatius to the Smyrnaeans" in Lightfoot, 84.

[13] "St. Clement of Rome to the Corinthians" in Lightfoot, 32.

[14] Cyprian, "Epistle 33" in Bettensen, 81.

[15] Eusebius, 439.

[16] Bettensen, 24.

[17] Ignatius, "To the Magnesians," *Early Christian Fathers*, trans. Cyril C. Richardson (New York: Macmillan Publishing Company, 1970), 96.

[18] Bettensen, 70.

[19] Ibid., 83, 84.

[20] Ibid., 70.

[21] Irenaeus, "Against Heresies," *The Ante*-Nicene *Fathers*, 1: 391; Origen, "Commentary on Romans" quoted in Joachim Jeremias, *Infant Baptism in the First Four Centuries*," trans. David Cairns (London: SCM Press, Ltd, 1960), 65; Cyprian, "Epistle 58," *The Ante-Nicene Fathers*, 5:353,354.

[22] Paul F. Bradshaw, Maxwell E. Johnson and L. Edward Phillips, *The Apostolic Tradition*: A Commentary, ed. Harold W. Attridge (Minneapolis: Fortress Press, 2002), 112; "Constitutions of the Holy Apostles," *Ante Nicene Fathers*, 7.457.

[23] *The Book of Church Order*, Presbyterian Church in the United States, 1982/1983. Office of the Stated Clerk of the General Assembly, PCUS (Atlanta: John Knox Press, 1982), 119.

Chapter Three: Church Fathers

[1] St. Augustine, *The Trinity*, XIII.3.12, trans. Edmund Hill, O.P.(Brooklyn, NY: New City Press, 1994), 353.

[2] Tertullian, "Against Praxeus," *The Ante-Nicene Fathers*, ed. Alexander Roberts and James Donaldson, vol. 3, reprint (William B. Eerdmans Publishing Co., 1993), 3.608.

[3] Henry Bettenson & Chris Maunder, *Documents of the Christian Church*, third edition (Oxford: Oxford University Press, 1999), 27.

[4] Athanasius, "On the Incarnation" 7, 8, *Christology of the Later Fathers*, ed. Edward R. Hardy, The Library of Christian Classics (Philadelphia: The Westminster Press, 1954), 62, 63.

[5] Philip Schaff, ed. *Creeds of Christendom*, vol. 2, reprint (Grand Rapids: Baker Book House, 1993), 59.

[6] Ibid., 62.

[7] Bettensen, 91, 92.

[8] John Leith, *Creeds of the Churches* (Atlanta: John Knox Press, 1977), 11.

[9] Schaff, vol. 2, 59.

[10] Irenaeus, "Against Heresies," *The Ante-Nicene Fathers*, 1:415.

[11] Gregory, *Letters*, 5:20 quoted in Williston Walker, *A History of the Christian Church* (New York: Charles Scribner's Sons, 1970), 173.

[12] Whitney J. Oates, ed. *The Basic Writings of St. Augustine*, vol. 1, reprint (Grand Rapids: Baker Book House, 1980), 128.

[13] Ibid., 2.39.

[14] Ibid., 274

[15] Augustine, "Homilies on the Epistle of St. John," *The Nicene and Post-Nicene Fathers*, ed. Philip Schaff, vol. 7, reprint (Grand Rapids: William B. Eerdmans Publishing Co., 1991), 524.

[16] *Enchiridion* 26,27 in Oates, 673.

[17] Augustine, "On the Spirit and the Letter," *Nicene and Post-Nicene Fathers*, 5:89.

[18] Leith, 43.

[19] St. Augustine quoted in Donald Bloesch, *Essentials of Evangelical Theology*, vol. 1 (San Francisco: Harper & Row, Publishers, 1978), 181.

[20] Benjamin Breckinridge Warfield, *Calvin and Augustine*, reprint (The Presbyterian and Reformed Publishing Company, 1974), 322.

Chapter Four: The Middle Years

[1] Anselm, "Why God Became Man" in *A Scholastic Miscellany: Anselm to Ockham*, ed. Eugene R. Fairweather, *The Library of Christian Classics* (Philadelphia: The Westminster Press, 1956), 165.

[2] *The Koran: Commonly Called the Alkoran of Mohammed*, trans. George Sale (London: Frederick Warne and Co., 1800), 4.62.

[3] Quoted in E.T. Thompson, *Through the Ages* (Richmond, VA: CLC Press, 1965), 112.

[4] Serge Trifkovic, *The Sword of the Prophet* (Boston: Regina Orthodox Press, 2002), 97. Trifkovic adds: "The postmodern myth, promoted by Islamic propagandists and supported by some self-hating Westerners – notably in the academy – claims that peaceful Muslims, native to the Holy Land, were forced to take up arms in defense against European-Christian aggression. The myth takes A.D. 1095 as its starting point, but it ignores the preceding centuries, starting with the early caliphs, when Muslim armies swept through the Byzantine Empire, conquering about two-thirds of the Christian world at the time."

[5] John Leith, *Creeds of the Churches*, reprint (Atlanta: John Knox Press, 1977), 55,56.

[6] *A Sourcebook of Medieval History*, ed. Frederic Austin Ogg, (NY: American Book Co., 1935), 262, 263.

[7] *Documents of the Christian Church*, ed. by Henry Bettenson & Chris Maunder, 3rd ed. (London: Oxford University Press, 1999), 114.

[8] Ibid., 127.

[9] Ibid., 149.

[10] Ibid., 148.

[11] Harold Fair, *Early Reformers: Winds of Change* (Nashville: Graded Press, 1988), 33.

Chapter Five: The Protestant Movements

[1] John Calvin, *Institutes of the Christian Religion*, trans. Ford Lewis Battles, vol. 1 (Philadelphia: The Westminster Press, 1960), 3.11.2.

[2] John Dillenberger, *Martin Luther: Selections From His Writings*, (Garden City, NY: Doubleday & Co., Inc, 1961), 11.

3 Ibid., 493, 499.

4 Ibid., 53.

5 Quoted in Roland Bainton, *The Reformation of the Sixteenth Century* (Boston: Beacon Press, 1952), 60, 61.

6 *Luther Works*, ed. Jaroslav Pelikan, vol. 32 (Minneapolis: Fortress Press), 11.

7 John Leith, *Creeds of the Churches*, reprint (Atlanta: John Knox Press, 1977), 79.

8 Martin Luther, *The Bondage of the Will*, trans. Henry Cole (Grand Rapids: Baker Book House, 1976), 267-269.

9 Martin Luther, *Commentary on Galations*, trans. Erasmus Middleton (Grand Rapids: Kregel, 1979).

10 *Luther's Works*, vol. 49, 19.

11 Quoted in Carter Lindberg, *Martin Luther: Justified By Grace* (Nashville: Graded Press, 1988), 32.

12 J. I. Packer, "The Faith of the Protestants," *Introduction to the History of Christianity*, ed. Tim Dowley (Minneapolis: Fortress Press, 1995), 374.

13 John Calvin, *Commentary on the Psalms*, Preface, trans. Henry Beveridge, *Calvin's Commentaries*, vol. 4, reprint (Grand Rapids: Baker Book, 1979), xl, xli.

14 Ibid., vol.19, *Commentary on Acts of the Apostles*, Acts 15:6.

15 John Calvin, *Institutes of the Christian Religion*, 4.17.10.

16 Ibid., 2.7.1.

17 Ibid., 4.12.1.

18 Quoted in Fred W. Graham, *The Constructive Revolutionary* (Atlanta: John Knox Press, 1978), 85.

19 Ibid., 80.

20 Bainton, 117.

21 The "five points" summarize the theological conclusions of Dordt: Total Depravity, Unconditional Election, Limited Atonement, Irresistible Grace, and Perseverance of the Saints. The exclusive identification of Calvinism with TULIP is historically inaccurate. The "Five points of Calvinism" were a response to specific historical questions fifty years after John Calvin had died, however, the doctrinal points were generally consistent with Calvin's teaching and thus became identified with his theology.

22 The entire document is accessible at www.lutheranworld.org.

Chapter Six: Reformation in the British Isles

1 *Scots Confession*, chp. 18 "The Notes by Which the True Kirk Shall be Determined From the False, and Who Shall Be Judge of Doctrine" in *Book of Confessions* (Louisville: Office of the General Assembly, Presbyterian Church (U.S.A.), 1991), 3.8. John Knox, assisted by five other ministers, produced the *Scots Confession* of 1560 with 25 articles in only four days.

2   *Documents of the English Reformation*, ed. Gerald Bray (Minneapolis: Fortress Press, 1994),113, 114.

3   *Book of Common Prayer*, Protestant Episcopal Church U.S.A.

4   Lewis W. Spitz, *The Protestant Reformation 1517-1559* (New York: Harper & Row, 1987), 270.

5   *The New Encyclopedia of Christian Martyrs*, ed. Mark Water (Grand Rapids: Baker Books, 2001), 715.

6   Ibid., 718.

7   John Knox, *The History of the Reformation of Religion within the Realm of Scotland*, ed. C.J. Guthrie, reprint (Edinburgh: Bannner of Truth Trust, 1982), 305.

Chapter Seven: New Church and New Nation

1   John Witherspoon, "Lectures on Divinity," *The Works of the Rev. John Witherspoon*, vol. 4 (Philadelphia: William W. Woodward, 1801), 10, 11.

2   Quoted in George F. Willison, *Saints and Strangers* (New York: Time Incorporated, 1964), 152.

3   William S. Barker and Samuel T. Logan, Jr. eds. *Sermons that Shaped America: Reformed Preaching from 1650 to 2001* (Phillipsburg, NJ: P&R Publishing, 2003), 35, 36.

4   Guy S. Klett, ed. *Minutes of the Presbyterian Church in America*, 1706-1788 (Philadelphia: Presbyterian Historical Society, 1976), 1. Quotations from this source retain the original spelling and capitalization.

5   Charles Hodge, *The Constitutional History of the Presbyterian Church in the United States of America*, Part I, 1705-1741 (Philadelphia: Presbyterian Board of Publication, 1851), 137-139.

6   Klett, 103, 104.

7   Ibid., 104.

8   Ibid.

9   Ibid.

10   Quoted in Leonard Trinterud, *The Forming of an American Tradition* (Philadelphia: Westminster Press, 1949), 148.

11   Varnum Lansing Collins, *President Witherspoon* (New York: Arno Press, 1969), 53.

12   "Thanksgiving Day Proclamation of the Confederation Congress" October 11, 1782 quoted in Matthew F. Rose, *John Witherspoon: An American Leader* (Washington, D.C.: Family Research Council, 1999), 85.

13   Quoted in Trinterud, 297, 298. The preface to the *Plan of Government* listed eight principles upon which Presbyterian ecclesiology would be established. These citations are from points I and VII.

14   See David Bebbington, *Evangelicalism in Modern Britain: A History from the 1730s to the 1980s* (London: Unwin Hyman, 1989).

Chapter Eight: Old School and New School

[1] Charles Hodge, "General Assembly of 1836," *Biblical Repertory and Theological Review* VIII (July 1836): 461, 475.

[2] Letter of Lyman to Beecher to Asahel Nettleton quoted in George Marsden, *The Evangelical Mind and the New School Presbyterian Experience* (New Haven: Yale University Press, 1970), 77, 78.

[3] Samuel Miller, *Letters to Presbyterians on the Present Crisis in the Presbyterian Church in the United States* (Philadelphia: Anthony Finley, 1833), 165.

[4] *Minutes of the General Assembly of the Presbyterian Church in the United States of America*, 1829, 374.

[5] Samuel Miller, Jr. *Life of Samuel Miller* vol.1 (Philadelphia: Claxton, Remsen and Haffelfinger, 1869), 357.

[6] Miller, *Letters to Presbyterians*, 165.

[7] *Minutes of the Presbyterian Church in the United States of America*. (New School) New York: Published by Stated Clerks, 1838-1858. reprint. Philadelphia: (Presbyterian Board of Publication and Sabbath-School Work,1894), 35-42.

[8] "The Mission of the Presbyterian Church," *Presbyterian Quarterly Review* I (June 1852): 21.

[9] *Presbyterian Historical Alamanac and Annual Remembrancer of the Church for 1865*, vol. 7 (Philadelphia: Joseph M. Wilson, 1865), 317.

[10] Ibid.

[11] Robert L. Dabney, "Dr. Dabney on the Plan of Union" *Southern Presbyterian*, Nov. 19, 1863.

[12] Henry B. Smith, "Presbyterian Reunion" in *American Presbyterian and Theological Review* V (October 1867): 643.

Chapter Nine: Facing New Challenges

[1] Clarence Edward Macartney, "Shall Unbelief Win? An Answer to Dr. Fosdick" in William S. Barker and Samuel T. Logan Jr. eds., *Sermons that Shaped America: Reformed Preaching from 1630 to 2001* (Phillipsburg, NJ: P & R Publishing, 2003), 343.

[2] "Creation, Evolution, and Mediate Creation" in *Evolution, Scripture, and Science: Selected Writings* of B.B. *Warfield* ed. by Mark A. Noll and David N. Livingstone (Grand Rapids: Baker Books, 2000), 209, 210.

[3] Cited by A.H. Freundt, "James Woodrow" in D.G. Hart and Mark A. Noll. eds. *Dictionary of the Presbyterian & Reformed Tradition in America* (Downers Grove: InterVarsity Press, 1999), 280.

[4] C.A. Briggs, "The Inaugural Address," quoted in Loefferts Loetscher, *The Broadening Church: A Study of Theological Issues in the Presbyterian Church since 1869.* (Philadelphia: University of Pennsylvania Press, 1957), 50.

[5] "Portland Deliverance" in Maurice Armstrong, Lefferts Loetscher and Charles Anderson, eds., *The Presbyterian Enterprise: Sources of American Presbyterian History* ed. (Philadelphia: The Westminster Press, 1956), 249.

[6] Loetscher, 46.

[7] "Auburn Affirmation" in *The Presbyterian Enterprise*, 284-288.

[8] J. Gresham Machen, *Christianity and Liberalism*, reprint (Grand Rapids: Wm. B. Eerdmans, 1977), 52.

[9] For OPC history see D.G. Hart and John Muether, *Fighting the Good Fight: A Brief History of the Orthodox Presbyterian Church* (Philadelphia: The Committee for Christian Education and Committee for the Historian of the Orthodox Presbyterian Church, 1995). Edwin Rian tells Machen's story from an OPC perspective in *The Presbyterian Conflict* (Grand Rapids: Wm. B. Eerdmans Co., 1940); for another perspective see Bradley J. Longfield, *The Presbyterian Controversy: Fundamentalists, Modernists, & Moderates* (New York: Oxford University Press, 1991).

[10] For an overview of twentieth-century theology see Stanley J. Grentz and Roger C. Olson, *Twentieth-Century Theology: God & the World in a Transitional Age* (Downers Grove: InterVarsity Press, 1992).

Chapter Ten: A House Divided

[1] Francis Schaffer, *The Great Evangelical Disaster* (Westchester, IL: Crossway Books,1984), 97

[2] Garth M. Rosell, *The Surprising Work of God: Harold John Ockenga, Billy Graham, and the Rebirth of Evangelicalism* (Grand Rapids: Baker Academic, 2008), 73-106.

[3] Milton Coalter, John M. Mulder and Louis B. Weeks, *The Re-Forming Tradition: Presbyterians and Mainstream Protestantism* (Louisville: Westminster/John Knox, 1992), 131-133.

[4] See James H. Moorhead "Redefining Confessionalism: American Presbyterians in the Twentieth Century" in Milton Coalter, John M. Mulder and Louis B. Weeks eds. *The Confessional Mosaic: Presbyterians and Twentieth-Century Theology* (Louisville: Westminster/John Knox, 1990), 59-83.

[5] For PCA history see: Kennedy Smartt. *I Am Reminded: An Autobiographical, Anecdotal History of the Presbyterian Church in America.* 25th Anniversary Edition; Frank Joseph Smith, *A History of the Presbyterian Church in America: The Continuing Church Movement* (Manassas, Virginia: Reformation Educational Foundation, 1985) and Don K. Clements, *Historical Roots of the Presbyterian Church in America* (Narrows, Virginia: Metakos Press, 2006). For a mainline perspective on the PCA see Rick Nutt, "The Tie That No Longer Binds" in Coalter, *The Confessional Mosaic*, 236-256.

[6] *The Plan of Reunion of the Presbyterian Church in the United States and the United Presbyterian Church in the United States of America*, 13.3.e, Prepared by the Joint Committee on Presbyterian Reunion, Final Edition, Second Printing (Stated Clerk of the General Assembly of the Presbyterian Church in the United States, 1981), 29.

[7] "Presbyterians and Human Sexuality" Report to the General Assembly (Louisville: Office of the General Assembly, PC(USA), 1991), 51.

[8] For a brief history of Presbyterian women's ordination see Barbara Brown Zikmund, "Ministry of Word and Sacrament: Women and Changing Understandings of Ordination" in Milton Coalter, John M. Mulder and Louis B. Weeks, eds. *The Presbyterian Predicament: Six Perspectives* (Louisville: Westminster/John Knox), 143-148.

[9] "Position Paper on the Holy Spirit," Office of the General Assembly of the Evangelical Presbyterian Church, 1992.

[10] Paul Heidebrecht, "Evangelical Presbyterian Church" in D.G. Hart and Mark A. Noll. eds. *Dictionary of the Presbyterian & Reformed Tradition in America* (Downers Grove: InterVarsity Press, 1999), 93, 94.

[10] For more information on ECO see http://www.fellowship-pres.org/eco.

Epilogue

[1] *Westminster Confession and Catechisms in Modern English*, The Summertown Company, 2004.

[2] Chuck Colson and Harold Fickett, *The Faith Given Once For All: What Christians Believe, Why They Believe It, and Why It Matters* (Grand Rapids: Zondervan, 2008).

[3] *Minutes of the Synod of New York and Philadelphia*, 29 May 1758, in Guy S. Klett, ed. *Minutes of the Presbyterian Church in America*, 1706-1788 (Philadelphia: Presbyterian Historical Society, 1976), 103, 104.

INDEX

Made in United States
North Haven, CT
17 April 2024

51443773R00147